PROFESSIONAL LIABILITY/RISK MANAGEMENT

A MANUAL FOR SURGEONS

Second Edition

Edited by Paul F. Nora, MD, FACS

Developed by
The Professional Liability Committee
American College of Surgeons

*The opinions expressed in this manual represent the views of profes-
sional experts and, as such, do not constitute policy of the American
College of Surgeons. The Table of Contents and subject material were
determined by the members of the College's Professional Liability Committee.*

© 1991, 1997 American College of Surgeons
55 East Erie Street
Chicago, IL 60611-2797

Library of Congress Cataloging-in-Publication Data

Professional liability-risk management: a manual for surgeons / edited by Paul F.
Nora; developed by the Professional Liability Committee, American College of
Surgeons. —2nd ed.
     p.   cm.
    Includes bibliographical references and index.
    ISBN 1-880696-08-8 (pbk.)
    1. Surgeons—Malpractice—United States. 2. Insurance, Physicians' liability—
United States. 3. Surgeons—Legal status, laws, etc.—United States. 4. Risk
management—United States. I. Nora, Paul F., date. II. American College of Surgeons. Professional Liability Committee.
KF2905.3.P76 1997
346.7303'32—dc20
[347.306332]   96-35880

TABLE OF CONTENTS

PROFESSIONAL LIABILITY COMMITTEE

This manual has been developed through the efforts of the Professional Liability Committee of the American College of Surgeons.

Chairman

Frank C. Spencer, MD, FACS, New York, NY

Committee Members

Susan H. Adelman, MD, FACS, Detroit, MI
Bruce L. Allen, MD, FACS, San Mateo, CA
Martin B. Camins, MD, FACS, New York, NY
Alfred J. Clementi, MD, FACS, Arlington Heights, IL
Josef E. Fischer, MD, FACS, Cincinnati, OH
William W. Kridelbaugh, MD, FACS, Albuquerque, NM
George D. Malkasian, Jr., MD, FACOG, FACS, Rochester, MN
Barry M. Manuel, MD, FACS, Boston, MA
Michael S. McArthur, MD, FACS, Tyler, TX
Ian Nisonson, MD, FACS, Miami, FL
Donald J. Palmisano, MD, JD, FACS, Metairie, LA
Andrew H. Patterson, MD, FACS, New York, NY

ACS Staff

Paul F. Nora, MD, FACS, Chicago, IL

LIST OF CONTRIBUTORS

SUSAN H. ADELMAN, MD, FACS
Private Practice
Clinical Assistant Professor
Wayne State University School of Medicine
Detroit, MI
II/Liability Under Managed Care
IV/Office and Outpatient Settings

BRUCE L. ALLEN, MD, FACS
Private Practice
Chairman, Department of Surgery
San Mateo County General Hospital
San Mateo, CA
IV/Departments of Surgery

W. EUGENE BASANTA, JD, LLM
Associate Dean and Associate Professor
Southern Illinois University School of Law
Carbondale, IL
II/Current Tort Law Overview

MARTIN B. CAMINS, MD, FACS
Associate Clinical Professor of Neurosurgery
Mount Sinai Hospital and Medical Center
New York, NY
IV/The Resident

SARA C. CHARLES, MD
Professor of Psychiatry
Department of Clinical Psychiatry
University of Illinois at Chicago
Chicago, IL
*VI/The Psychological Trauma of a Medical Malpractice Suit: A
Practical Guide*

ALFRED J. CLEMENTI, MD, FACS
Private Practice
Northwest Surgical Associates
Arlington Heights, IL
Director
Illinois State Inter-Insurance Service
Chicago, IL
III/Risk Financing

JOSEF E. FISCHER, MD, FACS
Christian R. Holmes Professor
Chairman, Department of Surgery
University of Cincinnati Medical Center
Cincinnati, OH
II/Reporting Requirements of the National Practitioner Data Bank and State Agencies
IV/Departments of Surgery

M. MARTIN HALLEY, MD, JD, FACS
Private Practice
Thoracic and Cardiovascular Surgery
Executive Director
Midwest Institute for Health Care and Law
Associate Clinical Professor
University of Kansas Health Science Center
Topeka, KS
II/Efforts to Reform and Change
V/Surgeon-Attorney Relationship; The Deposition; The Trial; Settlement; Protecting One's Assets

KENNETH V. HELAND, JD
Associate Director
Department of Professional Liability
American College of Obstetricians and Gynecologists
Washington, DC
IV/The Resident

WILLIAM W. KRIDELBAUGH, MD, FACS
Private Practice
Clinical Professor of Surgery
University of New Mexico College of Medicine
Albuquerque, NM
IV/Surgeon-Patient Relationship; Departments of Surgery

THEODORE R. LE BLANG, JD
Legal Counsel
Professor of Medical Jurisprudence
Department of Medical Humanities
Southern Illinois University School of Medicine
Springfield, IL
II/Current Tort Law Overview

GEORGE D. MALKASIAN, JR., MD, FACOG, FACS
Senior Consultant
Department of Obstetrics and Gynecology
Mayo Clinic
Professor
Mayo Medical School
Rochester, MN
IV/The Resident

BARRY M. MANUEL, MD, FACS
Associate Dean
Professor of Surgery
Boston University School of Medicine
Boston, MA
II/Liability Under Managed Care; Efforts to Reform and Change

MICHAEL S. McARTHUR, MD, FACS
Private Practice
Thoracic Surgery
Tyler, TX
IV/Surgeon-Patient Relationship

IAN NISONSON, MD, FACS
Active Staff - Urology
Baptist Hospital of Miami
South Miami Hospital
Clinical Assistant Professor
University of Miami School of Medicine
Department of Urology
Miami, FL
IV/Proper Documentation—The Medical Record; Office and Outpatient Settings

PAUL F. NORA, MD, FACS
Director
Professional Liability Program
American College of Surgeons
Professor of Clinical Surgery
Northwestern University Medical School
Chicago, IL
Editor; I/Introduction

DONALD J. PALMISANO, MD, JD, FACS
Clinical Professor of Surgery
Clinical Professor of Medical Jurisprudence
Tulane University School of Medicine
New Orleans, LA
President
The Medical Risk Manager Company/INTREPID, INC.
Metairie, LA
IV/Consent and the Process of Informed Consent

ANDREW H. PATTERSON, MD, FACS
Director of Orthopaedic Surgery
St. Luke's-Roosevelt Hospital Center
President
Medical Liability Mutual Insurance Company
New York, NY
III/Risk Financing

FRANK C. SPENCER, MD, FACS
Professor and Chairman
Department of Surgery
New York University Medical Center
New York, NY
Chairman
Professional Liability Committee
American College of Surgeons
Chicago, IL
V/Surgeon-Attorney Relationship; The Deposition; The Trial

ACKNOWLEDGMENTS

Sincere appreciation is extended to all of the people who helped with the content and production of the Second Edition of this manual.

Special mention is in order to the Fellows who generously assisted in the critique of the first edition of this manual, as well as to the following individuals who helped with the Second Edition.

Chapter II—Marsha Ryan, MD, JD, FACS, Adjunct Professor of Law, Southern Illinois University, and general surgeon in private practice, Carbondale, IL; and Relma J. Miller, law student, Southern Illinois University School of Law, Carbondale.

Glossary—Karla L. Kinderman, JD, LLM, American Medical Association; Staff Liaison, AMA/Specialty Society Medical Liability Project (AMA\SSMLP)

Overview—Paul G. Gebhard, JD, Senior Partner, Jenner & Block.

Recognition should also be given to the following members of the staff of the American College of Surgeons for their efforts in coordinating the project and producing this manual: Ruth Shea, administrative assistant, Professional Liability Program; Donna Gibson, general publications administrator, James Tansley, graphic design and desktop publishing manager, Tanisse Bezin, general publications manager, and Linn Meyer, director, Communications Department.

Also, my very special thanks to my wife, Valerie, for her courage during the preparation of the Second Edition.

Paul F. Nora, MD, FACS

FOREWORD

This book was developed by the Professional Liability Committee of the American College of Surgeons. It has been written as a *practical* manual for all surgeons; it is not a theoretical exposition of legal concepts. The manual is especially targeted toward practicing surgeons who are seeking guidelines for managing legal risks in the everyday practice of surgery.

The first edition of this manual, which was published in 1991, received many compliments. A Supreme Court Justice read the book while convalescing in a hospital and subsequently wrote me that it was one of the best publications the Justice had ever seen and asked for additional copies.

The importance of the book can be highlighted by making two observations. First, there is a high probability—almost a certainty— that a practicing surgeon will be sued at least once, perhaps even more, during a surgical lifetime. Patients can file suits for a variety of reasons. The frequency of suits varies both by the type of surgical practice and with the jurisdiction in which a surgeon practices. Historically, the highest frequency of suits have been in neurosurgical, orthopaedic, and obstetrical specialties. As the United States has grown increasingly litigious, the number of suits has increased annually for the past two decades.

The second observation is that surgeons must be able to maintain the highest quality patient care despite the inherent antagonism, complexity, and confusion that characterize the litigation process. It is important for surgeons to be fully versed with regard to the litigation process, the roles of the various participants—plaintiffs, defendants, and attorneys—and the reasons and potential bases for patients' claims.

Frank C. Spencer, MD, FACS

I / INTRODUCTION

Introduction

This second edition of *Professional Liability/Risk Management, A Manual for Surgeons* is an attempt to provide an update on subjects in the area of professional liability and risk management that have changed since our first edition was published. The Professional Liability Committee of the Board of Regents believes that although many aspects of risk management have remained constant, professional liability problems that have arisen with the growth of managed care make appropriate information and discussion a requirement for all health care providers—particularly surgeons.

This manual was written for the purpose of providing the practicing surgeon with an up-to-date reference that has as its main thrust to present in a clear, concise manner the nature of the law as it applies today in the area of medical torts. *Repetition* in certain areas that call for special emphasis is purposeful.

First, there is a review of the current tort law and pertinent legal principles on medical malpractice. The expansion of managed care, with its attendant liabilities, is discussed in detail. A section on the National Practitioner Data Bank (NPDB) and state reporting requirements has been included because of privilege modification and closed claims indemnification reporting. The final portion of this chapter deals with tort reform legislation that has been enacted and discusses possible future direction.

Attention is then turned to the topic of risk management as it applies to surgeons. As currently defined, risk management is a systematic approach to identifying, evaluating, reducing, or eliminating risk due to an undesirable deviation from an anticipated outcome, thereby preventing the loss of financial assets resulting from injury to patients. Thus, in this manual, the topic is divided into three functions: (1) risk financing (insurance), (2) risk prevention, and (3) loss control. It should be noted that these three aspects of risk management may take place concurrently.

In the discussion of risk financing, the reader is provided with data that can be used in making reasonable decisions about appropriate types of insurance coverage.

The cornerstone of risk prevention is the *competence* of the surgeon, both intellectually and technically. This competence is based on education, training, and experience. The importance of competence is implied in any discussion of risk prevention. Because surgical competence is the focus of so many of the College's programs and activities, it is not included as a part of the subject matter that is discussed in the section on risk prevention.

The discussion of risk prevention clarifies for the surgeon the many areas in which appropriate strategies may negate or lessen the likelihood of adverse legal action, whether factual or unfounded. Although the importance of maintaining solid and amiable physician-patient relationships is emphasized, the need to have adequate documentation is stressed. The section on risk prevention covers special situations, such as those that occur in the office, ambulatory surgery setting, or department of surgery. In addition, special problems faced by residents are addressed, and the process of informed consent is thoroughly explored.

Loss control is that function that attempts to minimize liability following an adverse occurrence to a patient. Loss control can be divided chronologically into incident management and claims management. Incident management relies heavily on two areas that are discussed in the risk prevention chapter—namely, the importance of good surgeon-patient communications and the need to have adequate documentation. These two areas become even more important if an adverse event occurs.

Because the appropriate approach to incident management is well described in the *Litigation Assistant*, a pamphlet that was published by the American College of Obstetricians and Gynecologists in 1986 and reprinted by the American College of Surgeons in May 1987, it is not included in this manual. However, the manual brings the claims management function into focus. This function relies heavily on the surgeon-attorney relationship and occurs if the patient files a claim at a later date.

Claims management refers to the appropriate activities that should be undertaken after a legal claim has been filed by a patient following an adverse event, whether real or perceived. Thus, as a major part of loss control, claims management is described in detail in this book. A review of interrogatories, depositions, and preparation for and behavior during trial are provided. The role of the plaintiff expert witness and methods for dealing with inappropriate testimony at a trial are included. The options of settlement and appeal are described, and protection of the defendant's assets is also addressed.

Finally, the psychological trauma of the litigation process for surgeons and their families—and patients—is elaborated upon in a realistic, but humane, fashion. The Glossary has been expanded to include new terminology commonplace in our changing health care environment.

The members of the Professional Liability Committee of the American College of Surgeons hope that this manual will provide significant guidance for surgeons in an era when so many adverse factors have come together to obstruct their primary goal of providing optimal patient care.

II / SUBSTANTIVE TORT LAW

Editor's Note

The major legal elements that are necessary to prove medical malpractice are described in detail. Appropriate examples of what is required for each of the specific elements are named, and citations reported from various jurisdictions are described.

The various types of damages and how they are assessed are detailed, and appropriate case examples are provided. A description of contract law as it applies to medical torts is given.

An understanding of the agency relationship as it relates to the surgeons who incur liability for the acts of others is thoroughly discussed with descriptive examples. The concepts of the Borrowed Servant and the Captain of the Ship doctrine as they apply to surgeons are presented. The importance of certain statutory immunities to encourage physician involvement in patient care and peer review without incurring liability are emphasized.

Several types of legal defenses in cases of medical malpractice are listed. Specifically, compliance of surgeons to adherence to a reasonable standard of care, appropriate determination of statutes of limitations, and the possibility of patient negligence as useful defenses are described.

The increasing presence of managed care, the National Practitioner Data Bank (NPDB), and other state regulatory agencies in the liability arena requires more familiarity by the practicing surgeon. The expansion of managed care with its attendant liabilities is the subject of a new section. Reporting requirements of the NPDB and state agencies concerning privilege modification and closed claims indemnification are described in detail.

In the final section, various types of tort reform that have been attempted or enacted are presented. The importance of caps on awards (particularly for noneconomic damages), modification of collateral source rule, and shortening of statutes of limitations are mentioned as the most effective reforms to reduce frequency and severity of claims. The negative effects on the physician-patient relationship of our existing tort system mandate a major change.

An overhaul of the present tort system is strongly recommended. Several methods of alternative dispute resolution (ADR) are mentioned. Specifically, the fault-based administrative alternative revising tort, the contractual approach, the early offer and recovery system, the no-fault patient compensation model, and the administrative system replacing tort are presented with both advantages and disadvantages.

Current Tort Law Overview

The medical malpractice climate in the United States today makes it imperative that surgeons be aware of the medical-legal environment within which the adjudication of malpractice liability occurs and of their rights and responsibilities in the surgeon-patient relationship.

The Surgeon-Patient Relationship

Under the law, a surgeon has no obligation to accept or treat every patient who seeks surgical care and treatment. Rather, the surgeon-patient relationship is consensual in nature, coming into being only when a patient requests treatment and a surgeon agrees to provide it or when a surgeon agrees to treat a patient on the basis of a referral. Once the relationship exists, however, the surgeon is obligated to employ skill, care, and knowledge in the performance of his or her professional duties. Whether or not the surgeon-patient relationship exists can itself become a legal issue.

For example, in the Illinois case of *Davis v. Weiskopf*, the court was asked to consider whether a physician-patient relationship existed under facts alleged by the patient in his complaint. According to the allegations in *Davis*, the patient's knee had been X-rayed in a hospital emergency room, showing a giant cell lesion. Without advising the patient of his observations, the treating physician consulted with a specialist, the defendant in the case, and referred the patient to him for treatment. The patient's initial appointment was rescheduled by the specialist before he saw the patient. When the patient called about the rescheduled appointment, he allegedly was told that the defendant would not treat him. The patient later claimed he was neither told of the lesion by the specialist nor referred to another physician. Because the lesion was cancerous, the patient's leg eventually was amputated, giving rise to a lawsuit.

The trial court dismissed the patient's complaint against the specialist, finding that, as a matter of law, no physician-patient relationship existed under the circumstances. However, an appellate court reversed that decision, holding that under the facts presented in the complaint, the defendant had a duty to the patient. The court observed that the defendant had allegedly accepted referral of the case and knew that the patient might have a malignancy of the knee, and that the patient's subsequent medical problems were reasonably foreseeable under those circumstances. The defendant easily could have discharged his duties, the court suggested, by advising the patient of his condition and of the need to consult with another physician promptly.

Terminating the Relationship

As a general principle of law, once the surgeon-patient relationship has been established, the surgeon is obligated to provide all appropriate care to the patient as long as the patient's condition requires it. Thus, courts typically have concluded that the relationship cannot be terminated at will by the surgeon, but must continue throughout the period during which treatment is necessary or until the relationship is concluded either by mutual consent of the parties or for another legally acceptable reason. A surgeon's failure to adequately provide for a patient's continuing welfare while medical or surgical attention is required may result in a malpractice claim based on a breach of professional standards or abandonment.

In *Allison v. Patel,* the defendant, the only vascular surgeon in Griffin, Georgia, ordered an arteriogram for his patient. Shortly after the procedure was performed, the defendant received a telephone call notifying him that his mother-in-law was very ill. In response, the defendant left the area and was unavailable when the patient complained of severe leg pain. The covering physician diagnosed a thrombosis, which he was unable to treat.

The defendant and the covering physician had previously discussed a transfer plan in the event an emergency arose while the vascular surgeon was away. After some effort, a cardiovascular surgeon was located in Atlanta, and this surgeon agreed to take the patient. The patient was transported to Atlanta by helicopter and underwent the first of several thrombectomies two hours later. The patient's right leg was amputated above the knee a month later. Further complications resulted in cardiac failure and ultimately death.

The jury found in favor of the defendant, and the plaintiff appealed. While the Court of Appeals of Georgia reversed on other grounds, it held that evidence as to the reason for the defendant's absence was admissible. The court cited other Georgia cases that held that "[a]bandonment of a patient is a tortious act. Before a physician can abandon or withdraw from a case without liability therefor, he must either give notice or provide a competent physician in his place." Physicians are liable, the court said, for "unwarranted" abandonment, or for abandoning the patient "without reason." Under these criteria, the court in *Allison* ruled that it was proper for the jury to hear testimony of the defendant's justification for his absence following the arteriogram.

A surgeon has a duty to provide treatment to a patient for as long as the patient's condition requires it. However, despite the clear obligations of a surgeon to provide for the ongoing care of a patient in accordance with established professional standards, there are circumstances in which a surgeon-patient relationship may be legally terminated. For example, the relationship may be terminated when the patient's care is fully transferred to another surgeon, when the patient no longer requires surgical or related follow-up care, when the contract or understanding between the surgeon and the patient specifically limits the treatment that the surgeon is obligated to provide (for example, when the surgeon's only responsibility to the patient is to perform a disability evaluation), or when the surgeon is discharged at the specific direction of the patient.

The relationship may also be legally terminated when the surgeon withdraws from it after providing adequate written notification. In that event, however, it is essential to provide the patient with a written notice that includes a statement of the reasons for terminating the relationship, as well as enough time to enable the patient to obtain future care elsewhere.

Medical Malpractice Tort Claims

Today, most medical malpractice actions in the United States that involve surgical treatment are based on the legal principles of tort law or negligence. A tort is defined as a civil wrong, other than a breach of contract, for which the law provides a remedy in the form of monetary damages. The primary basis for tort liability in medical malpractice is negligence, which may be described as an act or omission that deviates from what a reasonably prudent person would or would not do in a similar situation.

In assessing a medical malpractice tort claim, the courts measure a physician's conduct against what a "reasonably prudent" medical practitioner would have done in the same or similar circumstances. Thus, surgical malpractice may be characterized as an act or omission that constitutes a breach of the surgeon's obligation to employ reasonable skill and care in the treatment of a patient.

To recover damages from a surgeon on the basis of malpractice, a patient must prove four things: (1) that the surgeon owed the patient a particular duty to act in conformity with certain patient care norms or standards established by the profession, (2) that an act or omission on the part of the surgeon violated those norms or standards of care, (3) that there was a causal connection between the surgeon's act or omission and a resulting injury to the patient, and (4) that the patient suffered actual loss or damage as a result of the injury.

In litigating a medical malpractice claim, the patient bears the burden of proving each of these elements by a preponderance of the evidence. In other words, the patient must prove that it is more probably true than not true that the surgeon owed a duty to the patient and that this duty was breached, proximately causing injury that resulted in loss or damage to the patient.

The Standard of Care

As a general principle of law, a surgeon must possess and apply the knowledge, skill, and care ordinarily used by reasonably well-qualified surgeons practicing in similar cases and circumstances. These obligations are referred to as adhering to the standard of care. In some states, and under some circumstances, courts may measure the practice of reasonably well-qualified surgeons against the practices that are applicable in the same or similar localities. This measure of conduct is referred to as the locality rule.

The locality rule evolved in the United States in the 1800s to protect rural practitioners, who were then viewed as having less access to educational resources, equipment, and facilities than were available to their colleagues practicing in urban areas. Since then, as communications, transportation, and access to technologic advances have improved, many states have abandoned the rule, especially in relation to cases involving physicians who hold themselves out to the public as specialists in their field. Thus, it is not unusual for courts to conclude that specialists should be held to a nationally articulated standard of care, based on the fact that geographic conditions typically have less impact on specialty practice and that specialists are often members of organizations that publish nationally applicable criteria for training and certification.

While courts are thus inclined to rule that a specialist's practice locality or community is national in scope, this view may be less appropriate in cases that raise the issue of whether a rural specialist had access to medical technology that is available only in

15

urban centers. However, in reviewing cases that focus on such considerations as the method of treatment or kind of surgical technique used, the courts are most likely to conclude that nationally articulated standards constitute the most appropriate measure of due care, wherever it is provided. In this regard, it is reasonable to anticipate that practice guidelines or parameters, which have been developed or approved by surgical specialty or subspecialty groups, will have increasing influence in shaping the standard of care.

The nature of a particular patient's medical problem and the circumstances in which it is encountered will, of course, have a significant bearing on the standard of care that the courts are likely to apply in considering a given treatment situation. While it is obviously beyond the scope of this discussion to detail all the treatment procedures and disease entities that may be involved in malpractice actions, it is useful to discuss several situations to illustrate how the standard-of-care concept may be applied. It should be emphasized that the issues of consent and informed consent to treatment are discussed elsewhere in this text and, thus, are not addressed here.

Diagnosis

Surgeons are obligated to follow established standards of practice in diagnosing the causes of illness. Among other things, these standards include taking a proper medical history, conducting an adequate physical examination, properly utilizing laboratory and ancillary procedures, and reasonably evaluating available information in making a diagnosis.

As a general rule, surgeons are not held liable for diagnostic mistakes made when a patient's symptoms are unusual or obscure, or when the patient's condition is susceptible to varied or multiple interpretations. However, a surgeon could be held liable for mistakes made as a result of failure to conduct an adequate examination, and the surgeon's utilization of available scientific information and diagnostic tools is likely to be considered in determining the adequacy of such an examination.

The failure to diagnose Graves' disease prior to performing a blepharoplasty resulted in a finding of liability by the Louisiana court in *Gust v. Brint.* In *Gust,* the patient, a 56-year-old woman, had a 15-year history of thyroid problems and had undergone a partial thyroidectomy. She saw the defendant, an ophthalmologist, complaining of excessive tearing, sensitivity to light, difficulty with reading, and enlarged bags under her eyes. Although the patient informed the defendant of her thyroid problems and that she was currently under the care of an internist, the defendant only examined the patient's eyes, did no additional tests, and did not contact the internist prior to performing the blepharoplasty.

Within a month after the operation, problems began to develop. The patient had a "scratchy" sensation in her eyes when she awoke. Furthermore, she had pain in her eyes, excessive tearing, redness, and swelling of the eye sockets. At this time, the defendant also noted edema of the caruncle tissue, as well as ectropion. The defendant believed that these problems were the result of dryness of the cornea caused by the patient sleeping with her eyes open.

When these conditions persisted, the defendant referred the patient to another ophthalmologist who stated that given the patient's symptoms when she was first seen by the defendant, a diagnosis of Graves' disease was indicated. The second ophthalmologist further indicated that he would not have performed a blepharoplasty without monitoring the patient's condition to determine the amount of exophthalmos, which is a characteristic of Graves' disease. Following the blepharoplasty, the patient was treated by a number of physicians and underwent a variety of additional surgical procedures, including two decompressions, scleral grafts, and four skin grafts to correct the adverse effects of the blepharoplasty and to enable the patient to close her eyes.

The trial court concluded that the defendant's treatment of the patient did not meet the applicable standard of care, but that the defendant's actions were not the cause of the patient's injuries. On appeal, the Court of Appeals of Louisiana reversed the trial court and awarded the patient more than $230,000. The appellate court explained that the defendant's argument that he had not caused the patient's Graves' disease was misguided. As the appellate court stated, "The evidence and testimony is overwhelming that [the defendant] breached the standard of care...by failing to detect the onset of Graves' disease." As a result of this failure, the defendant performed a blepharoplasty that should not have been done. The court ruled that "[w]hile the blepharoplasty did not cause the Graves' disease, it clearly exacerbated its effects."

As *Gust* indicates, the importance of making an accurate diagnosis based upon available data and utilization of proper diagnostic tools cannot be overemphasized. Nevertheless, a surgeon is not obligated to render a flawless performance.

In *Holder v. Caselton*, an Illinois case, the appellate court upheld a jury verdict, finding no negligence on the part of a surgeon and another physician who failed to diagnose the patient's appendicitis. The patient in *Holder* came to the hospital emergency room in June 1991 after experiencing epigastric pain. One of the defendant physicians examined the patient and administered pain medication for what he diagnosed as acute gastritis. He instructed the patient to return if the pain persisted. Two days later, the patient again presented at the emergency room complaining of abdominal pain in the right lower quadrant, as well as nausea and a diminished appetite. The physician admitted the patient to the hospital. Laboratory tests, including a blood count and urinalysis, were ordered at this time. These tests showed an elevated white blood cell count, as well as blood in the patient's urine. In fact, the patient had previously experienced urinary tract problems, such as dilated ureters, uric acid stones, passing of stones, and blood in his urine. Given these previous problems and the test results, the treating physician concluded it was likely that the patient had urate calculi and uropathy. The physician directed the nursing staff to strain the patient's urine for both blood and uric acid stones. He also asked that the other defendant in this action, a general surgeon, examine the patient. The examination by the general surgeon revealed that the patient had normal bowel sounds, but was experiencing pain in both lower quadrants. After reviewing the results of an intravenous pyelogram, which showed no indications of a complete ureter obstruction, the surgeon concluded that an immediate exploratory operation was not needed.

Over the next several days, the patient's condition appeared to improve. He showed no tenderness or rigidity in his abdomen, and his white blood count was within normal limits. During this time, a "black prickly stone" was found in the patient's urine. After his apparent improvement, however, the patient's condition began to worsen. He again complained of abdominal pain in the lower right quadrant. Additionally, his blood pressure fell, and his urine became dark brown. The patient's treating physician concluded that he had "renal colic and a decompressing belly that was 'throwing off' pulmonary emboli." The treating physician then decided to transfer the patient to another facility for specialty care. During the transfer, the patient died. The subsequent autopsy showed that the patient's appendix had ruptured, causing his death from peritonitis.

The patient's estate filed suit against the treating physician and the general surgeon. At trial, the jury found in favor of both of the defendants, and the plaintiff appealed. Among other things, the plaintiff claimed that the jury's verdict was against the manifest weight of the evidence. The estate contended that the expert testimony presented at trial showed conclusively that the defendants violated the standard of care by failing to take the appropriate steps in ruling out acute appendicitis. However, in reviewing the evidence, the appellate court noted that the defendants had presented expert testimony that their care and treatment for the patient had conformed to the appropriate standard of care. Specifically, an expert appearing on behalf of the general surgeon testified that he had conformed to the proper standard of care in treating the patient. The expert explained that, in his view, when the general surgeon examined the patient, an operation did not appear to be appropriate. He also testified that under applicable standards, the surgeon was not obligated to further examine the patient unless requested to do so by the treating physician. In light of this and other testimony, the appellate court affirmed the decision of the trial court.

In view of these case illustrations, a surgeon is expected to possess and apply the knowledge and use the skill and care that ordinarily would be used by reasonably well-qualified surgeons in diagnosing a patient's condition. This standard of care does not require the surgeon to render a perfect performance or to be a guarantor of a diagnosis.

Recently, it has become evident that delay in diagnosis of breast cancer is one of the most common situations giving rise to medical malpractice claims. In 1995, the Physician Insurers Association of America (PIAA) released a comprehensive breast cancer study, which indicated that breast cancer malpractice claims tend to be the most prevalent and second most costly claims for malpractice insurers. The report further indicated that women under the age of 50 represented more than 60 percent of all claimants and that their claims were responsible for more than 71 percent of the total amount of indemnity payments. Furthermore, women under the age of 40 represented more than 30 percent of claimants, resulting in 37 percent of the total reported amount of indemnity payments.

Ranked by specialty, surgeons had the fourth highest frequency of claims, after radiologists, obstetricians/gynecologists, and family practice physicians. In terms of the average indemnity payment per claim, however, surgeons ranked second, at $256,933, after obstetricians/gynecologists, at $277,512.

As an additional consideration, the PIAA observed that in approximately 60 percent of all claims resulting from misdiagnosis of breast cancer, the patient first discovered the breast lesion and called it to the attention of the physician. This statistic represents compelling evidence to suggest that surgeons must be impressed by such findings and are well advised to order appropriate studies, following through until the possibility of malignancy is ruled out.

It is also important to note that in approximately 80 percent of cases in the PIAA study, mammogram results were reported as negative or equivocal, despite the fact that a lesion was present. Equivocal results, as well as false negatives, appeared to occur more frequently in females under the age of 40. In view of these considerations, the PIAA has emphasized that a high index of suspicion is indicated in diagnosing breast cancer, particularly in younger women.

The Supreme Court of Louisiana considered a case involving a surgeon's failure to diagnose breast cancer in *Turner v. Massiah*. In this case, the patient, a young married woman, had a breast augmentation operation performed by one of the two defendants, a plastic surgeon. The patient experienced hardening in her right breast following the operation and was examined by the surgeon regarding this problem several times over the next two years. In connection with each of these visits and examinations, the surgeon concluded that the hardening was the result of surgical scar tissue. He ordered no diagnostic tests. At or about the same time, the patient also was being seen by her personal physician, an obstetrician/gynecologist. His breast examinations of the patient revealed the hardening in her right breast. However, like the plastic surgeon, he did not order any diagnostic tests regarding this condition.

Three years after her breast augmentation operation, the patient was seen by other physicians who ordered mammograms and a biopsy. These diagnostic tests revealed that the patient had breast cancer that had progressed to stage II. As a result, a right mastectomy was performed. Evidence in the case indicated that had a proper diagnosis of the patient's condition been made by either the plastic surgeon or the obstetrician/gynecologist, the patient's chances of survival would have been in the range of 80 to 90 percent. However, given the delay in diagnosis and the progression of her cancer, by the time treatment was initiated, the patient's chances of survival were only 25 percent.

The patient and her husband filed suit against both the plastic surgeon and the obstetrician/gynecologist. The jury returned a verdict in favor of the plaintiffs, finding both physicians negligent. In connection with its verdict, the jury was asked to apportion fault between the defendants. In doing so, the jury attributed 60 percent of the fault to the plastic surgeon and 40 percent to the obstetrician/gynecologist. The trial judge then entered a judgment in accordance with the jury's verdict. On appeal, the Supreme Court of Louisiana reversed the lower court's judgment with respect to the amount of damages awarded. However, in all other respects, including determination of the surgeon's malpractice liability, the Louisiana Supreme Court affirmed.

Because of the frequency and severity of claims involving failure to diagnose breast cancer, the PIAA has offered a variety of risk management recommendations. For surgeons, these recommendations include the following: (1) when a patient is referred, always perform an adequate examination, carefully documenting all findings, especially when the findings of the referring physician were unimpressive; (2) when performing a biopsy, be certain the correct lesion is being removed, in both needle and open procedures, and always obtain a specimen X ray of the biopsy; and (3) promptly report biopsy results and consultative input to the referring physician.

Care and Treatment

The surgeon also has the responsibility of possessing and applying the knowledge and using the skill and care that ordinarily would be used by reasonably well-qualified surgeons in the care and treatment of patients.

In *McCarty v. Mladineo,* the Supreme Court of Mississippi considered the proper articulation of the standard of care expected of surgeons. In *McCarty,* the 30-year-old patient was diagnosed with cervical cancer and referred to the defendant for surgical treatment. As a preoperative measure to prevent blood clotting, the defendant ordered the administration of heparin, which the patient received for two days prior to her operation as well as postoperatively. As noted by the court, heparin is effective against blood clotting, but it carries with it the risk of causing a significant decrease in a patient's blood platelet count. In fact, this was the situation in *McCarty,* where the defendant continued to direct the administration of heparin after the patient's operation, although her blood platelet count had dropped dramatically.

Shortly after her operation, the patient experienced headaches and became very sensitive to light and noise. Thereafter, she suffered either a stroke or cerebral hemorrhage followed by a heart attack. As a result, the patient was permanently disabled. A lawsuit against the defendant followed.

At trial, the patient introduced testimony of an expert witness who stated that the defendant's failure to monitor administration of heparin to the patient was the cause of her stroke and heart attack. The expert further stated that the failure to monitor the drastic drop in the patient's platelet count was a violation of the standard of care. On appeal from a jury verdict in favor of the defendant, the Mississippi Supreme Court articulated the criteria by which the jury was to evaluate the defendant's care and treatment of the patient. Specifically, the court stated that the defendant could be found liable if he "failed to provide [the patient] with that degree of care, skill, and diligence which would have been provided by a reasonably prudent, minimally competent physician administering mini-dose heparin treatment when faced with same or similar circumstances...." Because the trial court had improperly instructed the jury with respect to this standard of care, the Mississippi Supreme Court reversed and directed that the matter be retried.

In 1994, the PIAA published a detailed study of medical malpractice claims arising out of laparoscopic procedures. Among other things, this study indicated that laparoscopic cholecystectomy presents serious malpractice liability risks for surgeons performing the procedure. The most common injury involves puncture, laceration, or transection of the common bile duct. Injuries to the hepatic ducts or other abdominal organs, including small intestines and liver, also have given rise to a large number of claims. Because these injuries involve considerable morbidity, the importance of adequate training and credentialing of surgeons regarding this procedure has been emphasized.

Injury to the duodenum during performance of a laparoscopic cholecystectomy was noted in the case of *King v. United States,* a federal case applying Virginia law. In *King,* after the surgeon began the laparoscopic cholecystectomy, he discovered extensive adhesions of the omentum layer to the gallbladder, which obscured the gallbladder. The surgeon was thus required to "take down" or cut away these adhesions. During this process, one of the surgeon's instruments "nicked" the patient's duodenum, causing a half-centimeter perforation. Neither the surgeon nor the surgical assistant discovered or repaired this perforation. Upon completion of the laparoscopic procedure, the patient was sent to postoperative care with the perforation of the duodenum remaining unrepaired. Subsequently, the patient began to experience great difficulty in breathing, as well as extensive abdominal pain and discomfort for which she was given pain medication. After seeing the patient early in the morning on the day after the operation, the surgeon did not again examine the patient. Further, no blood count was performed on the patient after the morning of the first postoperative day. Late that evening, members of the nursing staff found the patient pale with no pulse or respiration. Efforts to resuscitate the patient failed. Autopsy results showed that the patient died of peritonitis with sepsis secondary to the perforated duodenum.

In the litigation that followed, the trial court found that perforation of the duodenum is a known and recognized risk of a laparoscopic cholecystectomy. Additionally, the court observed that such a perforation is not, in itself, a violation of the appropriate standard of care, so long as the perforation is recognized and repaired either during the operation or early during postoperative recovery. In the court's view, however, perforating the duodenum during the laparoscopic procedure and then failing to recognize and repair the perforation is a violation of the applicable standard of care with respect to this surgical procedure. Therefore, the court concluded that the surgeon committed malpractice.

In view of the serious potential for malpractice liability arising out of performance of laparoscopic procedures, the PIAA has offered several risk management recommendations. Included among these recommendations are the following: (1) in evaluating patients for surgery, document all indications in support of performance of a laparoscopic procedure; (2) obtain and document informed consent, which should include any potential complications of the procedure; (3) document all reasons for performing or not performing cholangiography as part of any laparoscopic cholecystectomy; (4) evaluate each patient for injuries or complications prior to the conclusion of the procedure; (5) carefully monitor the patient during recovery for any previously unrecognized complications; and (6) promptly treat any complications as soon as they arise, carefully documenting all actions.

As noted, credentialing of physicians to perform laparoscopic procedures has spawned litigation. For example, in *Chandler General Hospital v. Persaud*, the Court of Appeals of Georgia found that a hospital could be held liable in a malpractice and wrongful death action for improperly granting privileges to a surgeon to perform a laparoscopic cholecystectomy.

Follow-up Care

The obligation to conform to the standard of care in performing an operation or surgical procedure is complemented by the surgeon's duty to provide adequate follow-up care. Among other things, the surgeon is obligated to appropriately monitor a patient's condition and respond in a timely fashion to evident complications. Problems in this regard are reflected in the Louisiana case of *Todd v. Sauls*. In that case, a Louisiana appellate court set aside a jury verdict in favor of the defendant and found him liable for malpractice. The defendant, a cardiovascular surgeon, breached the duty of care owed by a specialist and committed malpractice when he failed to diagnose and treat postoperative infections in a 55-year-old patient.

The patient, who had previous bypass surgery in 1984, underwent a repeat coronary artery bypass performed by the defendant in October 1988. During the operation, an intraaortic balloon pump was inserted to assist in weaning the patient from the cardiopulmonary bypass pump. Postoperatively, while in intensive care, the patient suffered a heart attack, which left his heart weakened. The intraaortic pump was removed on the first postoperative day, and fasciotomies were made on either side of the left calf to relieve swelling caused by decreased blood supply resulting from use of the pump. After leaving the intensive care unit, the patient ate little and had a fever. Over the next two and a half weeks, he lost 19½ pounds. Also during this period, attending nurses observed signs of infection surrounding all of the patient's surgical wounds. His white blood cell count was also elevated. Despite the patient's status, the defendant did not initiate treatment of these conditions.

Thereafter, a heart function test (multigated blood-pool imaging; MUGA) showed the patient's heart function at only 8 percent. The patient was then returned to intensive care, and administration of methicillin was initiated to treat staphylococcal infection. Within two days, at the request of the patient's family, he was transferred to another hospital. Physicians treating the patient following the transfer found staphylococcal infection at the site of all of his surgical wounds. Further, they found that the patient was severely malnourished. Tube feeding was initiated at once. Despite these treatment efforts, the patient died of cardiac arrhythmias a week after the transfer.

The appellate court found that the defendant had breached his duty of care to the patient. Following the operation, the defendant failed to aggressively treat the surgical wound infections, failed to respond appropriately to the nurses' observations of infection, and allowed the patient's body weight to rapidly waste away.

Referrals

Surgeons are ethically and legally obligated to refrain from practicing beyond their area of specialized competence. Therefore, surgeons are obligated to refer patients to appropriate subspecialists when their condition warrants it. The clinical indications demanding consultation or referral will, of course, vary from case to case. When a surgeon realizes, or reasonably should realize, that the nature of a patient's illness or condition requires the services of a subspecialist, the courts are likely to view the standard of care as requiring that the surgeon advise the patient accordingly.

Failure to refer a patient resulted in liability for several physicians in the Oklahoma case of *Haley v. United States*. There, the patient had been diagnosed as having Crohn's disease and had her colon removed and an ileostomy created. Four years later, when she experienced vomiting and abdominal cramps, a biopsy revealed inflammation in the rectal stump. The biopsy specimen was analyzed by one of the several defendant physicians, who, allegedly without reviewing the patient's prior treatment records, concluded that the patient might have either ulcerative colitis or Crohn's disease and that the rectal stump might be cancerous. Two reports of pathologic findings stated that a possible, but uncertain, diagnosis was chronic ulcerative colitis. Thereafter, another of the defendants, the hospital chief of surgery, took the patient's history and performed a physical examination, but did not consult the patient's medical records or reports from her prior operations. The patient was informed that the rectal stump might be cancerous and that its removal, although elective, was recommended.

Following an operation to remove the rectal stump, which was performed by a third defendant surgeon, the patient developed abdominal and perineal wound infections. The patient filed a lawsuit, claiming that the physicians' treatment was deficient in several respects. In particular, given their uncertain diagnosis of her condition as ulcerative colitis or Crohn's disease, she alleged that the proper course of treatment would have been to advise her to see a gastroenterologist to obtain a more accurate diagnosis.

The importance of obtaining a proper diagnosis under these circumstances was demonstrated at trial by testimony of the patient's expert witnesses. They stated that while an operation was appropriate for ulcerative colitis, it was generally to be avoided in cases of Crohn's disease because of the risk of postsurgical infection. Referral to a gastroenterologist for a proper diagnosis, they argued, would have confirmed Crohn's disease, and the patient could thus have avoided undergoing an inappropriate operation.

The trial court entered a judgment in favor of the patient. The appellate court affirmed the judgment, concluding that in order to obtain the patient's informed consent prior to the operation, the defendants had "a duty to advise her that the specialized knowledge of a gastroenterologist could aid in obtaining a more accurate diagnosis." Given the defendants' apparent confusion regarding the patient's condition, the court found that due care required such a referral.

As a general rule of law, a physician who refers a patient to a subspecialist for care and treatment is not liable for malpractice on the part of the subspecialist. There may be exceptions to this rule if, for example, the referring physician continues to provide treatment to the patient in close coordination or cooperation with the subspecialist. However, if the referring physician is only remotely or indirectly involved in the subspecialist's treatment, liability is not likely.

Once a referral has been made, subspecialists are responsible for responding in a timely and appropriate fashion. The subspecialist is therefore required to assess the patient's condition and render the necessary care and follow-up treatment. Failure to do so may result in liability based on principles of abandonment or a violation of the applicable standard of care.

Unnecessary Operation

In accordance with the standard of care, a surgeon is obligated to refrain from subjecting a patient to an unnecessary operation. Whether or not an operation is necessary must be determined by the exercise of reasonable clinical judgment in accordance with the facts of each case. Nevertheless, certain legal and economic considerations have enhanced the scrutiny to which such clinical decision making is subjected, especially when it involves a decision to perform a hysterectomy, cesarean section, prostatectomy, pallidotomy, cataract surgery, or carotid endarterectomy.

Lawsuits involving unnecessary operations typically are filed when a patient suffers postoperative complications that would not have occurred if the surgical procedure had not been performed. Such was the situation in *Zipes v. Abraham*, a case decided by the federal district court in Pennsylvania.

In *Zipes,* a female patient consulted with the defendant, a general surgeon, who also performed gynecologic and colorectal surgery. The patient complained of abdominal pains, as well as nausea, constipation, and related problems. The defendant initially recommended discontinuation of hormonal medications, which resulted in no improvement of the patient's condition. Upon further examination, the defendant diagnosed dysmenorrhea, uterine fibroids, and dyspareunia. This diagnosis led the defendant to recommend, and the patient to undergo, a total hysterectomy with bilateral salpingoophorectomy.

Following the hysterectomy, the patient's problems continued. Another physician who examined the patient determined that her symptoms were the result of a prolapse of the colon, enterocele, ostipation with secondary megacolon, redundant colon, and pelvic descensus. The patient thereafter underwent several additional operations, which resulted in the eventual correction of her problems.

The patient filed suit against the defendant, alleging that performance of the hysterectomy was unnecessary and inappropriate, thereby causing her pain and suffering, as well as unnecessary medical expense and work loss. The patient alleged that had the defendant properly diagnosed her problems as gastrointestinal rather than gynecologic, appropriate treatment would have been undertaken, and she would have avoided an unnecessary surgical procedure.

The case was tried to a jury, which returned a verdict in favor of the surgeon. The patient then sought a new trial. Among the points made by the court in denying the patient's motion for a new trial was that there was evidence in the record that would allow the jury to conclude that physicians could reasonably differ about the appropriate course of treatment for the patient given her symptoms prior to the operation. Based upon its review of the record, the federal court found that the patient had received a full and fair trial and that the motion for a new trial should be denied.

In determining whether a particular operation is necessary, the courts rely on criteria set forth by experts who are familiar with the standard of care in similar circumstances. As the *Zipes* case indicates, a surgeon is not likely to be deemed to have violated the standard of care simply because a subsequent diagnosis does not correlate with the original indications for the operation. Finding a physician liable would require demonstrating that his or her decision to operate was contrary to the decision that would have been made by a reasonably well-qualified surgeon practicing under the same or similar circumstances and in light of available diagnostic information. Clinical decision making is not, after all, a precise science. Accordingly, the legal system does not require a surgeon to conform to a standard of care enhanced by the clarity of hindsight.

Breach of Duty

As we have seen, proving medical malpractice requires a patient to establish that a specific standard of care was applicable and to provide evidence that a surgeon deviated from that standard, thus causing the patient's injuries. As a general rule, proof of a violation of the standard of care is established through expert testimony.

Expert testimony is required in medical malpractice litigation because lay jurors are not presumed to be capable of evaluating whether a surgeon has adhered to the proper standard of surgical care and treatment. Accordingly, to determine whether a violation of the standard of care has occurred, jurors must rely on evidence by surgeons who testify as expert witnesses.

The plaintiff in a medical malpractice action is required to present the jury with expert testimony setting forth the standard of care that applies to the defendant surgeon's conduct, as well as expert testimony indicating that the surgeon breached that standard. In most cases, the expert witness must have qualifications similar to those of the defendant surgeon and be familiar with the applicable standard of care. Whether an expert witness is qualified to testify in a medical malpractice case is a matter generally left to the trial judge.

In an Illinois case, *Gorman v. ShuFang Chen, MD, Ltd.*, the trial court allowed a plastic surgeon to testify as to the standard of care applicable to an orthopaedic surgeon. The patient had a bicycle accident and was taken to the emergency room. Following initial examination by the emergency room physician, the defendant, an orthopaedic surgeon, was called. His examination disclosed fractured ribs, a punctured lung, a dislocated hip, and a laceration to the chin. The surgeon also examined the patient's head and palpated her jaw. He did not detect any significant tenderness at the temporomandibular joint (TMJ) or mandible. The evidence showed, however, that the patient's jaw was severely swollen and her speech impaired.

When the patient visited her dentist 18 days later, the dentist diagnosed a fracture of the patient's right jaw. When more conservative treatments failed, an oral surgeon performed a total joint implant on the plaintiff's right jaw. In her suit, the patient argued that the defendant was negligent in failing to examine or have a specialist examine her TMJ, with the result that he did not properly diagnose her condition. The patient alleged this caused her to have to undergo the TMJ reconstruction and condylectomy.

Following a jury verdict for the patient, the surgeon appealed. Among his claims on appeal was that the lower court abused its discretion in allowing a plastic surgeon to testify as the patient's expert witness. The defendant argued that the patient's witness "as a plastic surgeon serving as an attending physician in a multiple-trauma case...was unqualified to render an opinion as to whether [the defendant], serving as an attending orthopaedic surgeon, deviated from acceptable medical practice." The appellate court rejected this argument. The court noted that the patient's expert was board-certified in general, thoracic, cardiovascular, and plastic surgery. Further, he was familiar with the treatment of fractured jaws. Given this witness's "educational and employment background," the lower court did not err in finding him qualified to testify regarding the medical issues presented.

While the courts usually determine whether an expert witness is qualified to testify, it is the responsibility of the jury to evaluate an expert's testimony. In that sense, the jurors become the sole judges of the credibility of an expert witness, focusing on such things as his or her demeanor, memory, manner of testifying, and apparent bias, as well as the reasonableness of the expert's testimony when evaluated in relation to other evidence presented in the case. Weighing the usually contradictory opinions offered by expert witnesses who testify for the two sides in a malpractice trial, the jurors must determine who are the more credible and persuasive, and this determination will have a significant bearing on their verdict.

Malpractice trials that involve the doctrine of *res ipsa loquitur* (literally translated, "the thing speaks for itself") may not require expert witnesses, however. When the doctrine is applied in a medical malpractice case, the court will permit the jury to draw an inference of negligence from circumstantial evidence. In such cases, the patient must prove (1) that the injury is of the kind that ordinarily does not occur in the absence of negligence, (2) that the injury was caused by an agency or instrumentality within the exclusive control of the defendant, and (3) that the injury was not due to any voluntary act or neglect on the part of the patient.

If the patient meets the burden of demonstrating those three things, then the burden shifts to the defendant to prove that the event may occur even in the absence of negligence or that there are other reasonable causes for the event. In such a situation, expert testimony is not required to prove a violation of the standard of care.

Typically, the *res ipsa loquitur* doctrine is applied in cases such as those in which a sponge or other foreign object has been left inside a patient's body, when the patient has suffered severe x-ray burns, or in other similar situations. In applying the doctrine, the courts are essentially taking the position that the alleged negligence is so obviously or grossly apparent that a lay juror would have no difficulty in evaluating it, even in the absence of expert testimony.

The North Carolina case of *Schaffner v. Cumberland County Hospital System, Inc.*, offers an excellent example of how the court applied the *res ipsa loquitur* doctrine, thereby eliminating the plaintiff's obligation to introduce expert testimony to establish a violation of the standard of care. In *Schaffner*, a surgeon scheduled an operation to remove the adenoids and insert drainage tubes in the ears of a child who experienced persistent ear infections. Following the operation, the patient's mother and grandmother observed a burn on the patient's right hand that had not previously been there. To treat the burn, the patient was hospitalized for a skin graft. Following this procedure, a scar remained.

The patient filed suit against the surgeon and the hospital. The trial court granted summary judgment in favor of the defendants on the grounds that no expert evidence had been presented at trial to allow the jury to conclude that the defendants had been negligent. Appealing that decision, the patient argued that no expert evidence was necessary because the *res ipsa loquitur* doctrine would apply to the case. The court agreed. It observed that although the patient had produced no expert testimony as to the cause of her injury, the surgeon's deposition had suggested that a malfunctioning hyfrecator used during the operation could have been a possible cause for the burn. "[W]hen, as here, the facts can be evaluated based on common experience and knowledge, expert testimony is not required," the court stated, further holding that while any patient receiving medical treatment faces certain inherent risks, it is reasonable for a jury to conclude that being burned is not among them. Moreover, because the patient's burn would not ordinarily have occurred unless someone in control of the instrumentality that caused the injury was negligent, the court concluded that summary judgment in favor of the defendants was improper.

Causation

The legal connection between a surgeon's negligent act or omission and the injury that results therefrom is referred to as proximate causation. Proximate cause is usually defined as any cause that, in natural or probable sequence, results in an injury. The link between cause and result must be reasonably certain and cannot simply be speculative. Unless the causal linkage between injuries sustained by a patient and negligent acts or omissions is reasonably clear, the patient cannot recover damages in a medical malpractice lawsuit.

Russell v. Kanaga, a Delaware case involving injury to the bladder during an operation, illustrates a situation where the plaintiff's evidence failed to establish proximate causation. In *Russell*, the female patient experienced urinary incontinence. After an initial diagnosis of urinary disorder, the defendant surgeon performed a cystoscopy and concluded that the patient had a rectocele, a cystocele, stress incontinence, and a prolapsed uterus. Based on this diagnosis, the defendant recommended the surgical repair of the rectocele and the cystocele, as well as a vaginal hysterectomy. During the course of the operation, the defendant inadvertently lacerated the lower left side of the patient's bladder. This laceration, which measured approximately one-half centimeter, was immediately stitched by the defendant with chromic suture material and the operation was completed. After the operation, the defendant informed the patient of the bladder laceration and undertook steps to determine that the laceration had been successfully repaired. Subsequently, the patient was discharged from the hospital.

Four days later, the patient was readmitted complaining of severe abdominal pain and high fever. This pain, which persisted, could not be relieved by any medical treatment. Another physician performed an exploratory laparotomy and found that the patient's bladder, fallopian tube, and sigmoid colon were adhering together. When tissue removed during this procedure was analyzed by a pathologist, suture material was found in the tissue connecting the sigmoid colon to the bladder.

The plaintiff and her husband thereafter filed suit against the defendant alleging various acts of negligence. After review by a malpractice review panel, the patient proceeded with only a single claim of negligence—namely, that the defendant had sutured her sigmoid colon to the dome of her bladder during the operation. The patient asserted that the suture material found by the pathologist established that such improper suturing had occurred.

The defendant advanced a number of theories to explain the presence of the suture material and to suggest that she had not negligently sutured the colon and the bladder. Initially, the defendant submitted that the suture material was a remnant from an operation performed on the patient in 1952. The patient disputed this, however, arguing that chromic suturing material would be absorbed into the body in a relatively short period of time and certainly would not be present so many years after an operation.

Alternatively, the defendant suggested that the presence of the suture material could be explained by examining the surgical procedures she had followed with respect to the patient. As described by the defendant, during the surgical procedure performed on the patient, after the uterus is outside the body, the surgeon clamps the fallopian tubes near the point where they join the uterus, cuts them from the uterus, and places a lasso stitch around the end of the fallopian tube. Thereafter, when the clamp is released, the fallopian tube retracts into the body carrying with it the lasso suture. From this perspective, the defendant reasoned that the small amount of suture material discovered by the pathologist was a remnant of this lasso stitch.

The patient presented the expert testimony of two physicians at trial. While these experts testified that the patient's subsequent problems were the result of the adhesions, both testified that the presence of the adhesions did not establish malpractice. Consistent with the defendant's own testimony, the patient's experts testified that such adhesions can result from any surgical procedure as part of the healing process. Further, one of the patient's experts testified that he could find no link between the patient's problems and the operation performed by the defendant.

At the close of the presentation of the evidence, the defendant moved for a directed verdict, asserting that the patient had failed to establish that her injuries had been proximately caused by the defendant's alleged malpractice. The trial judge denied this motion. Subsequently, following a jury verdict for the defendant, the plaintiff appealed. The defendant cross-appealed, asserting that the trial judge had erred in denying the motion for a directed verdict.

The Supreme Court of Delaware concluded, based on the evidence presented, that the defendant was entitled to a directed verdict. The court noted that the theory advanced by the patient in her claim was that in repairing the bladder laceration, the defendant had negligently sutured her colon and her bladder. The patient claimed that the presence of the suture material found by the pathologist was sufficient to allow the jury to make such a determination. The court rejected this analysis. The patient had presented no expert testimony that the defendant either had deviated from the appropriate standard of care or that any negligent acts on the part of the defendant were the cause of the patient's problems. Therefore, the defendant was entitled to a directed verdict.

In contrast to the result in *Russell*, the Illinois court in *Bombagetti v. Amine* ruled that the evidence presented in connection with the patient's injury during back surgery was sufficient to establish that the surgeon's negligence was the proximate cause of the injury. This case arose in connection with a laminectomy performed by the defendant on the patient following a diagnosis that the patient had a herniated disk at the L4–L5 space, as well as a narrowing of his spine at the L5–S1 space. The operation was apparently uneventful. Two days after the operation, however, while reviewing X rays, the defendant discovered that he had mistakenly removed the disk at the L3–L4 space. The defendant at once informed the patient of this error, and shortly thereafter the proper operation was performed.

Following the initial operation, the patient's back pains increased. Additionally, he felt a burning sensation down both his legs and across his back. These problems, as well as difficulty in walking, were corrected by the second operation. Subsequently, six months after the operation, while lifting materials at work, the patient experienced a "snap" in his back. Within a few days his back became "kinked" and he began to have severe lower back pain. The defendant examined the patient and concluded that the symptoms reflected a "facet dislocation."

The evidence presented showed that the patient, who had been a pipe fitter prior to the operation, had been forced to change jobs because of his inability to lift items. The evidence also showed that following the operation, the patient's ability to participate in family and recreational activities was significantly reduced.

In his lawsuit, the patient presented expert testimony that the defendant's removal of the wrong disk had caused retrolisthesis and subluxation. These conditions, the patient's expert testified, were permanent in nature and were the probable source of the patient's continuing pain. The defendant's own expert testified at trial that, in his view, the patient's pain had its source either at the L3–L4 or the L4–L5 space and that the mistaken removal of the wrong disk had made the patient more susceptible to injury in the future.

The trial court found that the evidence clearly established that the defendant was negligent and that his negligence had proximately caused at least some injury to the patient. Thus, it directed a verdict in the patient's favor. The jury was then instructed to decide to what extent the patient's injuries were proximately caused by the defendant's negligence and the appropriate money damages. The jury awarded $750,000, and the defendant appealed. Among the various contentions of the defendant upon appeal was that the patient's evidence was insufficient to prove that his negligence had proximately caused the patient's injury and his pain and suffering.

The appellate court examined the proximate causation question with respect to several facets of the case. Initially, the court found that the evidence clearly established that the pain experienced between the first and second operations was the result of the removal of the wrong disk. "The testimony of the experts, as well as defendant himself, sufficiently support a finding of proximate cause between defendant's negligent removal of the wrong disk and the exacerbated pain of plaintiff between the two operations."

Next, the court considered whether the evidence was sufficient to establish that the "facet dislocation" experienced by the patient after the second operation was proximately caused by the defendant's negligence. This question was more difficult for the court, which began by outlining the appropriate standards by which to analyze this question. The court observed that in a suit against a physician for malpractice, "a plaintiff must produce evidence...that injuries exist and that they were the result of the occurrence at issue." Further, granting that "an action may not be based upon conjecture or speculation," the court observed that "the patient is not required to prove his case beyond a reasonable doubt." Except when the evidence clearly shows otherwise, the court said, it is for the jury "to weigh the facts, judge the credibility of the witnesses, and ultimately ascertain the truth."

With these criteria in mind, the court found the evidence sufficient to establish proximate cause. While none of the testifying experts could state with certainty that the "facet dislocation" was the result of the improper operation, each testified that this problem was probably caused by the removal of the wrong disk. The court therefore concluded that the jury properly could have found that the defendant's negligence not only caused the patient's increased pain between the two operations, but also the subsequent "facet dislocation."

Damages

Awarding monetary damages is the way in which a remedy is provided to individuals who sustain injury as the proximate result of negligent conduct by a physician. Typically, damages are intended to compensate for loss or injury sustained by the patient. In cases involving gross negligence, an injured party may also be entitled to an award of punitive damages, depending on the state in which the action is brought.

Compensatory Damages

Monetary damages awarded to compensate a wrongfully injured person are referred to as compensatory damages. A medical malpractice plaintiff may recover such damages for a variety of losses, including those related to the reasonable expense of medical care and treatment necessitated by the injury; the value of earnings, salaries, and profits lost and reasonably certain to be lost in the future as a result of the injury; aggravation of a preexisting ailment; and the patient's pain and suffering.

Another recognized basis for the award of compensatory damages in medical malpractice litigation is loss of consortium. Such awards typically reflect losses sustained by one spouse as the result of injury to the other. A jury may award compensatory damages for loss of consortium on the basis of the reasonable value of the companionship, society, and conjugal relationship of which a spouse has been deprived and is reasonably certain to be deprived in the future. Damages also may be awarded on the basis of loss of consortium between parents and children when, for example, parents are deprived of the society of a child who dies as the result of medical malpractice.

Damages also may be awarded to compensate a surviving spouse or the next of kin for pecuniary injuries suffered. Among the factors that may be considered by a jury in awarding such damages are the customary contributions of the decedent in the past; his or her former and likely future earnings; and the value of any instruction, training, and supervision of education that the decedent might reasonably have been expected to provide to the family had death not occurred. A surviving spouse also might recover such expenditures as hospital, medical, and funeral costs incurred in connection with the decedent's death.

In the West Virginia case of *Reager v. Anderson*, the court's discussion of the basis for the jury's damage award is instructive. *Reager* involved a claim by a 13-year-old boy and his father against a general surgeon and an orthopaedic surgeon for negligence that resulted in amputation of the boy's left leg. The orthopaedic surgeon allegedly had been negligent by failing to see the boy in a timely fashion, failing to diagnose an injury to the boy's popliteal artery, and failing to debride dead tissue in his leg upon discovery.

While the general surgeon agreed to settle the case after all the evidence had been presented at trial, the orthopaedic surgeon did not. Following a jury verdict of approximately $1.27 million in favor of the patient and his father, the orthopaedic surgeon appealed to the West Virginia Supreme Court. Among various arguments, he asserted that evidence regarding projected costs related to a novel prosthetic device for the boy and of the boy's loss of future earnings was speculative and, therefore, should not have been considered by the jury.

At trial, the patient's expert witness testified that the annual maintenance cost of the prosthetic device needed by the boy, when reduced to present value, was $260,000. This estimate was based on costs related to conventional prosthetic devices on the grounds that while the plaintiff's device was novel, it incorporated many of the same components of more conventional devices. The jury also heard estimates of the patient's lost future earnings from his economic expert and a vocational rehabilitation expert. The testimony was undisputed that these lost future earnings would range from $192,230 to $1,155,000, based on five possible vocational scenarios in which the potential earnings of a person with two legs was compared with those of a person with only one leg.

The appellate court rejected the defendant orthopaedic surgeon's argument that this evidence was too speculative, finding it adequate to support the jury's damage award. The court further stated that even if those particular damage claims were not considered, the evidence in the record would support an award of damages in the same amount for the patient's pain and suffering alone.

A jury's determination of the amount of damages to award a patient must reasonably be based on evidence presented during the course of a trial, and courts will place great weight on the jury's decision. Unless a damage award is clearly based on sympathy or prejudice, courts rarely overturn or alter the amount of damages awarded by juries.

As the New York case of *Merrill v. Albany Medical Center Hospital* demonstrates, however, a court may reduce a jury verdict that it finds to be excessive and the apparent product of sympathy or prejudice. *Merrill* involved a 22-month-old child, diagnosed as having a possible malignant tumor on her right lung, who experienced cardiac arrest during an operation to remove the tumor. Although the surgeon was able to restore the patient's heartbeat by manual massage, the child remained comatose for two months and was later determined to have suffered severe brain damage as a result of oxygen deprivation during the incident.

Suit was filed against the surgeon, various anesthesiologists involved with the operation, and the hospital. At the end of a six-week trial, but prior to closing arguments, a $2 million settlement was agreed to by all of the parties except the surgeon. The case then was submitted to the jury for a decision related to the surgeon's liability, without disclosure to them of the settlement amount.

The jury apportioned percentages of liability among the various defendants, assessing the surgeon's liability at 3 percent. The jury set the patient's total damages at almost $12.4 million and her mother's damages at $261,000. After reducing these amounts to $10.4 million and $177,000, respectively, based on evidentiary considerations, the trial court apportioned 3 percent of each amount to the surgeon.

The surgeon appealed, arguing that the jury's damage verdict was excessive, even as reduced by the trial judge. The appellate court reviewed the uncontested testimony regarding the patient's condition as a result of her injuries, noting that she was blind, could neither talk nor ambulate on her own, was spastic, and had cerebral palsy and, therefore, would need extensive assistance for the rest of her life. This evidence, the court noted, "would engender sympathy in abundance even from the most calloused sort." The jury was in an understandably difficult position "and may well have been overcome with sympathy." Accordingly, the court ordered a new trial on the issue of damages unless the plaintiff agreed to reduce the total damage award to $6.1 million.

Punitive Damages

In addition to compensatory damages, some states also permit punitive damages to be awarded when the evidence in a medical malpractice trial establishes that a surgeon has acted willfully or with negligence so gross as to indicate a wanton disregard for the patient's rights.

The objective of punitive damages is to punish a wrongdoer, thereby presumably deterring others from committing similar wrongs. Punitive damages often are awarded in product liability cases in which serious harm has been caused as a result of defects in the design, manufacture, testing, or marketing of a product. Juries also have awarded punitive damages in cases in which a manufacturer knew, or reasonably should have known, of dangers associated with use of a product, but failed to adequately warn consumers about the product's dangers or defects.

While awards of punitive damages are not uncommon in product liability litigation, awarding them in medical malpractice cases has never been favored by the law. The courts are therefore inclined to carefully evaluate the facts of any case in which punitive damages are at issue. The New Jersey case of *Tonelli v. Khanna*, illustrates this point. In *Tonelli,* the patient was referred to a radiologist for a sonogram because of pain and lumps in her left breast. The radiologist reported a "well-circumscribed, well-outlined" area in the patient's breast that was "probably cystic in origin." Believing the condition to be lobular hyperplasia, he recommended a biopsy. Based on this information, the patient's family physician suggested that she see a surgeon. The patient's prior medical reports were read over the telephone to the surgeon, who subsequently examined the patient. Feeling a lump in her breast, he recommended that it promptly be removed surgically.

The evidence presented at trial as to whether the surgeon discussed the consequences of the operation with the patient was conflicting, although the surgeon maintained that there had been such a discussion, and the patient had signed a consent form. When the operation was performed, the tissue removed showed fibrocystic breast disease. While later visiting friends in Florida, the patient experienced a postoperative infection and was given antibiotics. After returning home, she began to see another physician, who treated her condition with hormones, vitamins, and dietary changes.

The patient sued the surgeon, claiming, in part, that his performance of the unnecessary operation without her informed consent was an intentional wrong, entitling her to punitive damages. Following a jury verdict of $10,000 for the patient, she appealed, arguing that based on the evidence she had presented, the jury could have concluded that the defendant had performed the unnecessary operation for his own financial gain and that punitive damages were justified. However, a review of the evidence convinced the appellate court that the trial judge had properly rejected the patient's claim of an intentional wrong as wholly unsupported by the evidence. "To warrant a punitive damages award, defendant's conduct must have been an intentional wrong...or accompanied by wanton and willful disregard of the rights of others," the court concluded.

Contract Liability

Although most medical malpractice actions in the United States are based on the legal principles of tort law or negligence, some have been based on contract principles. For that reason, physicians should at least be aware of the circumstances under which such actions may arise.

As a general rule, two types of contracts are recognized under the law: express contracts and implied contracts. An express contract is entered into when the parties to it reach a specific agreement as a result of an exchange of written or spoken words. The terms and conditions of express contracts are usually set forth with specificity, clearly delineating the rights and responsibilities of the parties. In contrast, the obligations of the parties in implied contracts are not specifically delineated, but, rather, are imposed as a matter of law, usually on the basis of the particular relationship between the parties. For example, when a surgeon agrees to provide treatment to a patient, the law imposes an implicit obligation on the surgeon to use reasonable skill and care in providing that treatment.

Lawsuits against a surgeon based on a breach of an implied contract are rare, but litigation against physicians and surgeons involving express contracts is not unknown. Most medical malpractice lawsuits based on contract theory allege the breach of an express promise by a physician or surgeon, such as a promise to cure a particular illness or achieve a particular outcome. As a general rule, however, the courts have not been inclined to recognize that express promises exist in the surgeon-patient relationship. To the contrary, most courts understand that a surgeon's statements to a patient are most likely to be expressions of opinion that are intended to afford therapeutic reassurance. A surgeon may, however, inadvertently make an express promise to a patient that either constitutes more than therapeutic reassurance or guarantees the accomplishment of a specific result or results. When that situation occurs, the courts may permit a patient to sue on the basis of breach of a contractual promise or guarantee, even in situations in which the surgeon has utilized proper skill and care in providing treatment.

In the Washington, DC, case of *Scarzella v. Saxon*, for example, the patient was diagnosed as having diverticulum of the urethra. The defendant, a urologist, recommended an operation to re-move the diverticulum. The patient alleged that the urologist had assured her and her husband in a discussion prior to the operation that the procedure would be simple and without complications, that it would require only a very short hospital stay, and that it would interfere only temporarily with the patient's work and the couple's sexual relations. These assurances were allegedly reiterated at a subsequent meeting, after which the patient consented to the op-eration. Complications from the operation developed, necessitat-ing two additional operations and leaving the patient with chronic problems. As a result, the patient and her husband filed suit against the urologist based on a breach of express warranty theory.

The appellate court upheld a judgment of $75,000 for the patient based upon the trial court's instruction to the jury that to find a breach of warranty "the language or statement used or al-leged to have been used by the surgeon must be clearly and un-mistakably a positive assurance...to produce or to avoid a particular result...." While the court acknowledged that a physician does not typically warrant a specific result or cure, it observed that under the facts of this case, the jury could have properly concluded that the urologist's representations rose to the level of an express war-ranty.

It should be emphasized that despite this case example, a patient who brings suit against a surgeon based on the breach of contract theory bears the arduous legal burden of alleging and prov-ing that a specific guarantee or express promise has been made, as well as proving that the patient relied on that promise in deciding to undergo the treatment. Because of the difficulty of proving that those things have occurred, such cases typically result in a ruling or judgment in favor of the surgeon.

Thus, more typical than *Scarzella* is the South Dakota case of *Van Zee v. Witzke*, in which the appellate court upheld a judg-ment in favor of a reconstructive and plastic surgeon. Under the facts of *Van Zee*, the patient claimed that a surgeon had expressly agreed to cure a deformity of her finger that had occurred as a result of a childhood accident, a deformity that would cause her finger to "lock" when she typed, thereby impeding her work as a court reporter. The patient consulted the surgeon, who found metallic sutures in the flexor tendon and a hyperextension of the first joint of the finger. Three months later, after a second examination, an operation was performed. Subsequently, an infection occurred, which the surgeon treated. The surgeon also referred the patient to a physical therapist who, during one session, broke the patient's finger, which required additional treatment by the surgeon.

After healing, the patient's finger remained stiff, had a slight deformity of the distal tip, and was largely useless to her. She therefore sued the surgeon, basing her suit on several theories of law, including breach of an express contract.

On appeal, the South Dakota Supreme Court upheld the trial court's judgment in favor of the surgeon on the contract theory, observing that the defendant's office notes showed that he had thoroughly discussed the risks and problems of the operation with the patient. The court further noted that the patient had told her mother prior to the operation that no physician would guarantee results. The court found that the defendant's alleged statement that the patient's finger would be no worse following the operation than it had been prior to the operation was insufficient to constitute an express contract to heal her finger.

As previously indicated, courts are generally inclined to rule against patients who sue surgeons on the basis of contract theory. Nevertheless, the fact that such actions may be brought argues strongly for surgeons to carefully avoid making express promises that may be viewed as representing more than therapeutic reassurance or entering into written or verbal agreements guaranteeing the accomplishment of a specific result.

Liability for the Acts of Others

When one individual is authorized to act for or on behalf of another, a so-called agency relationship is established under the law. The parties to such a relationship may be referred to as the principal and agent or as the master and servant.

Under principles of agency law, the principal is legally responsible for the negligent conduct of an agent. This accountability, which is referred to as vicarious liability, constitutes the mechanism by which the law has endeavored to maximize the likelihood that a person who is harmed as a result of the conduct of another person will be fully compensated. The law allows for imposition of this liability on the basis of the "deep pocket" theory, under which the principal in an agency relationship is viewed as being more capable of absorbing the costs of liability and is thus held responsible for the negligent acts or omissions of an agent. The doctrine of vicarious liability most commonly applies to the employer-employee relationship, making employers legally responsible for the negligent conduct of their employees.

Respondeat Superior

The application of vicarious liability principles also is referred to by the Latin phrase, *respondeat superior*, "let the master respond." This legal doctrine holds employers responsible for the negligent conduct of employees that occurs during the course of their employment. Under this doctrine, the employer may be held liable whether or not the employer approved the employee's action or, for that matter, even knew about or observed the negligent conduct. A surgeon thus may be held vicariously liable for the negligent conduct of an employee nurse, receptionist, or office worker. Similarly, a medical or service corporation may be liable for the negligent conduct of its employees.

In part, the basis for a lawsuit in the Connecticut case of *Howat v. Passaretti* was a claim that receptionists employed by the defendant, an orthopaedic medical group, had negligently provided information to the patient, thereby causing a delay in treatment and eventual death. The patient in *Howat* fractured his left ankle while playing softball. An orthopaedic surgeon employed by the medical group treated the patient at the hospital, applying a short cast to his leg. Later, the surgeon examined the patient at the defendant's offices and scheduled an appointment four weeks later to remove the cast. Shortly thereafter, the patient's father telephoned the surgeon, because the patient was experiencing pain in his leg. The surgeon instructed the father that his son should elevate his leg and contact him if the pain continued. A week later, the patient died from a massive pulmonary embolus.

In the lawsuit filed against the medical group after the patient's death, it was alleged that the patient had called the group's offices twice in the period immediately before his death because of pain in his leg. Further, it was alleged that each time he called, he was told by one of the defendant's receptionists to keep his leg elevated, take aspirin, and keep his appointment for removal of the cast. The basis of the lawsuit was that these responses were improper, that the receptionists should have instructed the patient to come in at once for an examination, and that if the patient had been appropriately examined, the thrombophlebitis would have been detected. Further, the plaintiff asserted that the medical group, as the employer of the receptionists, was liable for their negligent conduct. The defendant denied receiving these calls and that any of its receptionists had advised the patient as was alleged.

At the close of the trial, the jury returned a verdict for the defendant. The plaintiff moved that the trial judge set aside this verdict. Following denial of this motion, the plaintiff appealed.

The plaintiff argued on appeal that the trial court had improperly instructed the jury in terms of which employees could be considered by the jury in making its determination of possible liability in the case. The appellate court found no error in the jury instructions. Additionally, the court ruled that even if there was an error, it was harmless. The court observed that the jury had heard the testimony of each of the defendant's receptionists, all of whom denied receiving any calls from the patient or advising the patient in any way regarding the care and treatment of his injuries. Therefore, although it was clear in the court's mind that the defendant could be held liable if its employees were found to have made these statements to the patient, the jury had concluded that no such statements had been made by any of the medical group's receptionists.

Most cases discussing the doctrine of vicarious liability focus on liability of hospitals and other health care institutions that arises out of the negligence of their employees, holding such institutions liable when personnel, such as staff nurses, laboratory personnel, and x-ray technicians, negligently cause injury to a patient. The North Carolina court considered a hospital's liability for the alleged negligence of its nursing staff in *Horton v. Carolina Medicorp, Inc.*

The female patient in *Horton* was admitted to the defendant hospital for a total abdominal hysterectomy. A Foley catheter was inserted during the surgery. Following removal of the catheter, the patient had difficulty urinating, causing her bladder to become distended. Further, the patient's inability to urinate for a 24-hour period caused a vesicoperitoneal fistula in her bladder. Thereafter, the patient underwent a cystourethroscopy and pelvic examination, as well as an exploratory laparotomy. Eventually, after being treated in the intensive care unit, the patient was discharged from the hospital.

In a lawsuit against the hospital, the patient asserted that the hospital's nursing staff had failed to monitor her bladder following the operation, thereby causing her complications. Given the time of filing of the lawsuit, the hospital successfully argued before the trial court that the patient's claim was time barred. On appeal, however, the Court of Appeals of North Carolina rejected this conclusion. In doing so, the court stated that under clearly established law, "hospitals may be liable in a medical malpractice action for damages for personal injuries or death arising out of the hospital's furnishing or failure to furnish professional services." Here, the patient alleged that the hospital could properly be held liable because its nurses had failed to monitor the voiding of her bladder for a 24-hour period, thereby injuring the patient and necessitating further surgical procedures.

Even in situations where an employment relationship is found to exist, not all wrongful conduct of an employee will result in vicarious liability for an employer, unless the conduct occurred within the scope of the employment relationship. Therefore, if the employee had committed an intentionally wrongful act that was not within the scope of his or her employment, vicarious liability principles usually would not apply.

For example, in the New York case of *Noto v. St. Vincent's Hospital & Medical Center*, a hospital was not found to be vicariously liable for an employee's wrongful conduct. The patient in *Noto* had sought care at the hospital for depression, drug and alcohol abuse, and "seductive behavior." The patient claimed that she and a psychiatrist in the hospital's residency program who provided her care had developed a "close relationship," which continued after the psychiatrist rotated off her case. Following the patient's discharge, she and the psychiatrist entered into a sexual relationship, which also allegedly involved the use of drugs and alcohol. After terminating the relationship, the patient filed suit against the psychiatrist and the hospital, basing her claim against the hospital on its status as the psychiatrist's employer under the *respondeat superior* doctrine.

The court noted that the employer's liability under the doctrine depends upon whether "the tortious conduct of the employee [was] in furtherance of the employer's business and within the scope of the employer's authority" and concluded that the hospital was not liable for the psychiatrist's acts. In the court's view, the psychiatrist's conduct clearly was not in furtherance of the hospital's business, but, rather, of his own personal affairs. Further, the court said the psychiatrist's actions exceeded his authority and certainly were not a "natural incident of his employment or duties."

The Borrowed Servant and Captain of the Ship Doctrines

The borrowed servant doctrine, in which the employee or servant of one master is temporarily borrowed by another who exercises specific control over that person to accomplish a particular purpose, represents another application of vicarious liability principles. When a third party temporarily "borrows" the "servant" of another "master" and exercises supervision and control over the servant's conduct, vicarious liability principles may apply to the temporary master. For example, when a surgeon directly controls the conduct of a hospital employee as an aspect of a particular course of treatment, the employee becomes a borrowed servant of the surgeon. Should negligent conduct of the borrowed servant result in injury to a patient, the surgeon may be vicariously liable for the injury.

The most common application of this doctrine in medical malpractice litigation arises when patient injury is caused by negligence that occurs in a hospital operating room. Ruling in this context, courts have held the chief surgeon vicariously liable for negligence of members of the surgical team whose conduct the surgeon clearly has the right to control. Historically, some courts referred to the chief surgeon in the operating room as the "captain of the ship." These courts expanded the borrowed servant doctrine to hold the chief surgeon responsible for negligence of other personnel in the operating room, whether or not the surgeon has the right to exercise control over their actions.

More recently, however, courts have come to recognize that some members of the operating room team perform highly specialized and independent functions that may not come under the direct control and supervision of the surgeon. Accordingly, rather than automatically impose the borrowed servant doctrine in the operating room scenario, courts will evaluate whether or not the surgeon had direct control and supervision over a hospital employee whose conduct was negligent. In making that determination, courts will focus on the specific responsibilities of the hospital employee relative to the applicable clinical facts and circumstances, also taking into account pertinent custom and practice.

In an older Ohio case, *Baird v. Sickler*, the court held that the evidence was clear that the surgeon defendant had in fact assumed direct control of the conduct of a hospital employee. Under the facts of the case, the surgeon had performed a laminectomy to treat Klippel-Feil syndrome in a patient who also suffered from spondylosis. Rendered a C-6 paraplegic during the operation, the patient sued the surgeon. Evidence was introduced at trial to suggest that the patient's paralysis resulted either from faulty positioning and intubation or from aggravation of a minor intubation injury through sustained hypotension during the laminectomy.

Anesthesia for the operation had been provided by a nurse-anesthetist employed by an agency under contract with the hospital. The surgeon, who had helped the nurse-anesthetist position the patient's head and torso for intubation, testified that he had instructed the anesthetist regarding the preferred intubation technique and position, watched the intubation, and would have halted the procedure had he observed any misfeasance. He had not, however, performed the actual insertion of the endotracheal tube.

The trial court directed a verdict in favor of the surgeon, finding that no reasonable juror could conclude that the surgeon was responsible for the nurse-anesthetist's negligence. The appeals court noted, however, that a master-servant relationship exists when a party possesses and exercises a right to control another's actions, and those actions are in furtherance of the master's objectives. Further, the court held that if a master lends a servant to another, then the servant is deemed to be the servant of the borrower, even though the servant continues to be paid by the master. Under this analogy, the court held that although an operating physician is not responsible for overseeing each detail that occurs in the highly technical environment of an operating room, a surgeon who controls or has the right to control a procedure may be liable for the negligence of a nonemployee who performs the procedure. The patient therefore prevailed on appeal.

Despite this particular ruling, courts are increasingly reluctant to utilize the captain of the ship doctrine and impose liability on a surgeon unless there is convincing evidence that a hospital employee was functioning under the surgeon's direct control and supervision. Arthur Southwick, a noted commentator on hospital law, has observed that when medical care is provided by a sophisticated and highly specialized team of professionals working in the institutional setting, it is difficult to determine who is exercising direct control over whom at any given point in time. Thus, he has emphasized as reasonable the tendency of the courts to hold hospitals rather than private physicians liable for the conduct of hospital employees.

This trend is reflected in the Maryland case of *Franklin v. Gupta*, in which the court demonstrated its unwillingness to apply the captain of the ship doctrine and find a surgeon vicariously liable for the negligence of hospital employees without evidence that the surgeon had in fact exercised control over the conduct of those employees. In *Franklin*, a lawsuit was brought by a patient who had undergone an operation for carpal tunnel syndrome. The patient, who was a "high-risk patient for anesthesia," developed complications during the operation, becoming cyanotic, bradycardic, and asystolic, allegedly as a result of the negligence of the anesthesiologist and the nurse-anesthetist. Although the patient's heartbeat was restored, and he was revived, the operation had to be canceled.

The patient thereafter filed an action against the anesthesiologist, the nurse-anesthetist, the hospital, and the surgeon. Because there was no evidence that the surgeon had in any way supervised or controlled the anesthesiologist or the nurse-anesthetist during the operation, the trial court declined to instruct the jury on the captain of the ship doctrine, and the jury rendered a verdict in favor of the surgeon. The patient appealed, arguing that the trial judge had failed to properly instruct the jury on the law it was to apply to the surgeon's possible liability. The appellate court upheld the trial court's decision not to apply the doctrine. Observing the trend to reject the captain of the ship doctrine as being an inappropriate expansion of the traditional borrowed servant rule, the court absolved the surgeon of legal responsibility for the acts of hospital employees, unless it could be shown that the surgeon had in fact exercised control over them during the operation.

Defenses

The frequency and severity of medical malpractice litigation in the United States is a matter of record. Nonetheless, a substantial number of claims are successfully concluded without payment of a settlement or damage award, thanks, in large part, to the availability of a number of substantive, procedural, and statutory defenses.

Adherence to the Standard of Care

Introduction of evidence establishing that the surgeon complied with the applicable standard of care is the most important defense in a medical malpractice lawsuit. It should be emphasized that in applying this defense, it is not necessary to measure the surgeon's conduct against the highest degree of skill possible. Indeed, it is sufficient to demonstrate only that the surgeon possessed and applied the knowledge, skill, and care ordinarily used by reasonably well-qualified surgeons practicing in similar cases and circumstances.

Nor is a surgeon obligated to be a guarantor of satisfactory results, and the fact that a surgical procedure or course of treatment is unsuccessful does not in itself constitute evidence of negligence. Unless the surgeon's conduct deviated from the standard of care, an honest mistake will not result in liability. Moreover, when alternate acceptable treatment methodologies are available, selection by a surgeon of one method over another is not alone likely to form a basis for liability.

The court underscored these considerations in the Washington, DC, case of *MacGuineas v. United States*. In a lawsuit brought after a patient had died from shock due to intraoperative hemorrhage resulting from laceration of her left innominate vein by a subclavian vein catheter, *MacGuineas* alleged negligence on the part of the surgeon. The surgical procedure had been performed to place a Port-A-Cath in the patient to provide venous access for treatment of her Hodgkin's disease.

At the time of the operation, the patient's cancer had progressed to stage III, and she had recently been treated with both chemotherapy and radiation therapy, which necessitated repeated invasive procedures. After she volunteered to participate in a National Cancer Institute study, comparing the site infection rates of two commonly used catheter systems, the risks of the operation were explained to the patient, and she agreed to the procedure.

Insertion of the catheter was attempted on the left side. During the operation, difficulties were encountered in attempting to pass the catheter into the vein. After a second attempt to place the catheter, the patient's blood pressure dropped precipitously, and emergency procedures were initiated. A 5-mm tear in the patient's left innominate vein was repaired, but the patient went into a coma and died two days later.

In filing suit, the patient's estate argued that the operation had been done on the wrong side of the patient's body, that the surgeons had failed to use radiopaque confirmation of the placement of the guide wire for the catheter, that the wrong size dilator had been used, that excessive force had been employed in trying to insert the catheter, and that the procedure should have been discontinued when resistance to insertion of the catheter was encountered. Eight physicians testified at the trial. Except for one who testified that the surgeons should have moved to her right side when difficulties in inserting the catheter on the left were encountered, all agreed that the defendants had met the proper standard of care.

Rendering a judgment for the defendants, the court noted that a physician is not required to use "the highest degree of care known to the profession," but, rather, "that reasonable degree of care and skill which physicians and surgeons ordinarily exercise in the treatment of their patients." While "it was obvious to everyone that something went wrong" during the operation, the court stated it was equally "clear that the existence of the laceration does not automatically mean that the standard of care was violated." Given the inexact nature of medicine, and keeping in mind the severity of the patient's medical problems and the complexity of the procedure, the court concluded that the surgeons had exercised a reasonable degree of skill and care and were not liable for the unfortunate outcome.

As the court acknowledged in *MacGuineas*, medicine is not an exact science. Differences of professional opinion do exist, and an expert's testimony that he or she might have performed a surgical procedure differently is not adequate to prove negligence. Instead, evidence must establish, more probably than not, that a surgeon's conduct violated the applicable standard of care and that the conduct proximately caused injury to the patient. Even when such evidence is introduced by a patient, a surgeon can meaningfully defend against it by providing credible expert evidence demonstrating that the surgeon's conduct did not violate the applicable standard of care.

Statutes of Limitations

Statutes of limitations are intended to establish a particular time frame within which medical malpractice litigation must be initiated. Intended to foster timely prosecution of litigation, these statutes are designed to ensure that a defendant's ability to muster an adequate defense is not compromised because witnesses or other evidence are no longer available.

Although the specific statutory period within which medical malpractice litigation must be commenced varies from state to state, the period in most states is approximately two years following the date on which a claimant knew, or through the use of reasonable diligence should have known, about the injury or death for which damages are sought. In some states, the statute of limitations may specify an absolute date beyond which litigation may not be commenced. Should a patient file a lawsuit after the applicable statutory period has concluded, the surgeon may interpose the defense of the statute of limitations. Such a defense is characterized as procedural, because it essentially blocks the patient from prosecuting a claim, without regard for the merits of the claim.

As historically applied by the courts, the statutory limitations period begins on the date of the last act of negligence that gave rise to the patient's claim. Thus, it was possible that the statutory period could lapse before a patient even learned of a negligently caused injury. This situation might occur when a foreign object that was difficult to detect had been left in the patient's body during an operation. In an effort to minimize the impact of strict application of statutes of limitations, the courts have adopted a rule known as the discovery rule. In accordance with the discovery rule, the period of limitations begins when a patient knows, or reasonably should know, of an injury and also is aware, or reasonably should be aware, that the injury was wrongfully caused.

The discovery rule was in issue before the United States Court of Appeals for the Fifth Circuit in *Buford v. Howe*, a suit brought more than seven years after performance in 1983 of an allegedly unnecessary hysterectomy. The patient, who at the time of the operation was in her early fifties, saw the defendant when she began experiencing abdominal pains. Evidence conflicted as to the nature of the patient's complaint and the defendant's diagnosis. The defendant stated that he diagnosed the patient as suffering from "pelvic relaxation" or "uterine descensus" because the patient complained of a "pelvic falling-out sensation." The patient stated that she never experienced or complained of such a sensation. Both the patient and the defendant agreed that part of the patient's difficulty included pain while standing, as well as pressure sensations on her tail bone. The defendant informed the patient that her uterus was twice the normal size and that its removal was necessary in order to relieve the pain that she was experiencing. The patient was admitted to the hospital, where the defendant's admitting notes indicated that his diagnosis of the patient's condition included chronic pain, fibroid tumors, and an enlarged uterus. A diagnosis of uterine descensus was not reflected in any of the hospital records for the patient.

A week after the defendant saw the patient, he performed a hysterectomy. The postsurgical pathology report indicated that the patient's uterus, rather than being enlarged, was about one-half the normal size and showed no signs of fibroid tumors. The defendant did not discuss the pathology report with the patient. Following the operation, the patient continued to experience the problems, including abdominal pain, that allegedly necessitated her operation in the first instance.

The patient's daughter also was being treated by the defendant. Shortly after her mother's operation, she also underwent a total hysterectomy, allegedly because of chronic pelvic pain, uterine bleeding, and fibroid tumors. Again, the pathology report indicated that the patient's daughter did not have fibroid tumors. In October 1989, the daughter filed suit against the defendant alleging medical malpractice. In June 1990, the patient obtained copies of her medical record from the defendant for review by another physician. It was allegedly at this time that the patient first became aware that the defendant's diagnosis did not reflect the problems that she had experienced and that the defendant's diagnosis was basically the same as his diagnosis of her daughter. In February 1991, the patient filed suit against the defendant claiming that the hysterectomy performed on her in 1983 had been unnecessary.

At trial, following presentation of the patient's case to the jury, the defendant moved for judgment as a matter of law, in part on the grounds that the applicable two-year statute of limitations barred the claim. The trial court granted this motion, reasoning that because the patient had continued to experience problems following the operation in 1983, she should have known at that time that she had a cause of action against the defendant. The patient appealed.

On appeal, the court noted that under the controlling Mississippi law, a "cause of action accrues and the limitations period begins to run when the patient can reasonably be held to have knowledge of the injury or disease." Applying this standard, the appellate court disagreed with the trial court's analysis. As the court stated, the fact that following the 1983 operation the patient "continued to have chronic abdominal pain only demonstrates that she knew or should have known that her surgery was unsuccessful." However, given that the basis of the patient's claim against the defendant was for the performance of an unnecessary hysterectomy and not an unsuccessful one, the court found the fact that the patient should have been aware of the unsuccessful operation in 1983 irrelevant. Instead, it was for the jury to decide when the patient knew or should have known that she had undergone an allegedly unnecessary surgical procedure.

As already noted, some states have established a maximum period within which a malpractice lawsuit must be filed, regardless of the applicability of the discovery rule. For example, a statute may establish a two-year limitations period and a maximum four-year period of repose. In such a situation, a patient would be able to bring a lawsuit at any time up to two years following the date when he or she knew, or reasonably should have known, of an injury and also knew, or reasonably should have known, that it was caused by negligence. If, however, more than four years had elapsed since the negligent conduct occurred, then the patient would be precluded from commencing litigation because of the maximum four-year period of repose. In such a situation, when a patient does not discover medical malpractice until one year after the negligent act in question, the patient has two years from the discovery date within which to file the litigation—that is, three years from the date of the last negligent conduct. If, however, a patient discovered the medical malpractice three and a half years following the last date of negligent conduct, then the patient would have to initiate litigation within six months of the discovery date in order to meet the four-year filing requirement. A patient who did not discover a negligently caused injury until four and a half years after the negligent conduct would be forever barred from initiating litigation. Under certain circumstances, often involving fraudulent misrepresentation, a repose period may be extended.

In *Hernandez v. Amisub (American Hospital), Inc.,* a Florida appellate court applied a seven-year statute of repose when the medical provider allegedly engaged in fraud, concealment, or intentional misrepresentation of fact that prevented the patient from discovering his injury. The patient underwent an emergency abdominal operation at the defendant hospital in April 1988. During the operation, a folded laparotomy towel was accidentally left inside the patient. In April 1990, the patient began to suffer acute abdominal pains and consulted his personal physician, who diagnosed viral gastroenteritis. Treatment temporarily relieved the pain.

By April 1993, the plaintiff was suffering frequent and severe abdominal pain, digestive problems, and overall physical weakness. He again consulted his personal physician, this time receiving a diagnosis of indigestion and ulcer flare-ups. The patient subsequently consulted another physician who, after X rays and other tests, discovered the laparotomy towel in the abdomen. The plaintiff underwent an operation in May 1993 to remove the towel.

In December 1993, the plaintiff filed a complaint for medical malpractice against the surgeon, the hospital, and his personal physician. The plaintiff alleged that the surgeon and the hospital were negligent in leaving the towel in his abdomen during the operation. The complaint also alleged that the hospital and its employees knowingly misrepresented the laparotomy pad count in their operating notes, thus preventing the plaintiff from discovering that the towel had been left in his abdomen.

The hospital claimed the complaint was barred by the four-year statute of repose, because it was filed more than four years after the date of the operation. The trial court agreed, dismissing the plaintiff's claim. The appellate court found the actions of the hospital, in the form of the operative notes, to be a misrepresentation of material fact, made knowingly, and therefore intentionally, which prevented the plaintiff from discovering his injury within the four-year repose period. The court therefore applied a Florida statute that extended the repose period to a maximum of seven years after the date of the alleged malpractice in situations involving fraudulent misrepresentation.

It should also be noted that most limitations statutes identify various disabilities on the part of a patient that will prevent the limitations period from beginning to run. Among others, protection is afforded to minors, persons imprisoned on criminal charges, and those who are mentally disabled or incompetent. In the case of a minor, limitations statutes either provide an extended period within which a malpractice lawsuit must be initiated or delay the start of the limitations period until the minor reaches adulthood. Such statutory protection ensures that minors will not necessarily be deprived of their rights to pursue a malpractice claim simply because their parents failed to file a timely lawsuit on their behalf.

Similarly, the law is unwilling to hold a person who is mentally disabled or incompetent accountable for failing to initiate a malpractice lawsuit in accordance with the applicable statute of limitations. Ordinarily, the limitations period for a mentally disabled or incompetent person does not begin to run until the disability is removed. Such protection also is afforded in various states to persons imprisoned on criminal charges, thus precluding the limitations period from beginning until the disability of imprisonment is removed.

When surgical care is provided to individuals who are under a legal disability that blocks the statute of limitations from running, a surgeon must be cognizant of the extended period of liability. In fact, because medical malpractice litigation in such cases may be initiated many years after the last date of treatment, despite statutes of limitations, surgeons are well advised to retain medical records for as long a time as possible.

Patient Negligence

Although a surgeon may be held liable for injuries proximately caused by his or her negligent conduct or the negligent conduct of third parties on the basis of vicarious liability, a surgeon may not be liable for injuries that result when a patient fails to follow the surgeon's specific instructions, delays obtaining surgical treatment, or otherwise is the cause of his or her own injuries.

In the Louisiana case of *LaCombe v. Dr. Walter Olin Moss Regional Hospital*, the court found that the patient did not contribute to her nerve injury when she failed to disclose a prior back injury. The patient was admitted to the hospital for a bladder suspension operation. Following the operation, she complained of severe pain in her right buttock. A specialist diagnosed sciatic nerve injury. The patient underwent a computed tomographic scan, a magnetic resonance imaging, and a myelogram, all of which showed normal results.

A lawsuit was filed against several physicians and the hospital. At trial, the court ruled that the evidence supported a finding of negligence. The defendant hospital argued, however, that the patient's failure to disclose her previous back injuries contributed to her nerve injury. The patient had been involved in two automobile accidents several years prior to her operation and sought chiropractic treatment as a result. The defendant argued that if the patient had informed the hospital and her physicians of these previous injuries prior to her operation, then steps could have been taken to prevent her injury. The appellate court, finding no evidence to show any connection between the patient's past injuries and the sciatic nerve damage suffered here, affirmed the trial court verdict in favor of the plaintiff.

There are, of course, instances in which both the patient and the surgeon are negligent. Depending upon the law of the individual state, the extent of a patient's negligence in such cases will bear upon the question of the surgeon's liability, as well as on the amount of damages that may be recovered.

Under the traditional negligence doctrine, a jury's conclusion that a patient's negligence contributed in any way to an injury would preclude the patient from recovering damages against the surgeon. Referred to as contributory negligence, this bar to recovery was viewed as harsh and unfair by many state courts and legislatures. Accordingly, most, if not all, states have replaced the doctrine of contributory negligence with the doctrine of comparative negligence. Under this latter doctrine, a patient's negligence has an important bearing on the amount of damages that may be recovered, although it is only in situations in which the negligence is substantial that recovery may be totally barred.

Under the pure form of comparative negligence, a jury is required to determine whether a patient's injury is proximately caused by a combination of the negligence of the patient and the negligence of one or more of the defendants. If so, the jury is then instructed to determine the damages to which the patient would have been entitled in the absence of his or her negligence and then to reduce the award by the percentage of negligence attributable to the patient, regardless of what this percentage may be. Thus, if a jury concluded that a patient was entitled to $500,000 in damages for an injury, but that negligent conduct on the part of the patient contributed to the injury by a factor of 60 percent, then the actual damage award would be reduced by $300,000, or 60 percent of the amount to which the patient would otherwise have been entitled.

Under a modified form of the comparative negligence doctrine, when a patient's negligent conduct is more than 50 percent responsible for the injury in question, the patient is barred from recovering any damages. A patient whose negligence is viewed as being less than 50 percent responsible for his or her injury is awarded damages in an amount that is reduced in accordance with the same rules that apply to the pure form of comparative negligence.

The modified comparative negligence doctrine seeks to strike a balance between the rigors of the contributory negligence doctrine and the liberality of the more patient-oriented pure comparative negligence doctrine. Determining the degree to which a patient is negligent thus has a significant potential to reduce, if not bar, a damage award.

Statutory Immunities

Various state statutes have been developed with the intent of fostering certain conduct on the part of physicians and surgeons. These statutes usually are designed to encourage physician participation in activities that further the state's interest in protecting the public health. Typically, such statutes confer immunity from potential medical malpractice liability in connection with the provision of emergency medical care, participation in peer review, disclosure of confidential medical information when significant interests of third parties are affected, and in other situations in which the risk of malpractice liability could discourage surgeons from engaging in activities believed to contribute to the public good.

Although a comprehensive detailing of these state and federal statutes is beyond the scope of this discussion, a brief review should suggest how they are intended to operate.

Encouraging surgeons to provide emergency medical care at the scene of automobile accidents and other emergency situations probably has been the major impetus behind the enactment of state immunity legislation in the United States. Referred to as Good Samaritan statutes, these statutes specify that physicians and surgeons who act in good faith to provide emergency medical care, without charging a fee, are immune from liability for acts or omissions that might otherwise have resulted in a medical malpractice damage award. Typically, this protection is afforded to surgeons licensed in the state in question or in any other state and is applicable so long as the surgeon is not guilty of willful and wanton misconduct, such as acting with utter indifference to or conscious disregard for the safety of another.

The courts have been increasingly inclined to construe Good Samaritan statutes quite broadly, maximizing the protection they afford. For that reason, a surgeon may not only be protected in providing emergency medical care at the scene of an event, such as a highway emergency, but even in the provision of emergency medical care in a medical setting. For example, in *Kearns v. Superior Court*, a California court concluded that a physician who had provided emergency medical care in a hospital setting to a person who was not his patient was entitled to immunity from malpractice liability.

The *Kearns* case arose out of an incident that occurred during surgical removal of a malignant ovarian tumor. When the surgeon performing the procedure encountered difficulties and requested immediate assistance, another physician who was in the hospital at the time seeing his own patients responded. In the course of removing the tumor, its contents were spilled into the patient's abdomen, seeding it with cancer cells. The patient subsequently brought suit against both the surgeon and the physician who responded to the call for emergency assistance.

Relying on provisions of the California Good Samaritan law, the assisting physician moved for summary judgment. When the trial judge denied this motion, the physician successfully sought an order from the California Court of Appeals directing the judge to grant the motion. Noting that the situation had constituted an emergency, the appeals court observed that previous California court decisions had applied the Good Samaritan statute to hospital situations and affirmed the propriety of applying the statute in such a case. The court stated, "[I]t is in the best interests of the public that the Good Samaritan laws be applied in a manner which encourages a physician who happens to be in the hospital and available to provide intraoperative assistance when unexpected complications arise during surgery to provide the assistance requested." Such judicial reasoning has been followed in other states, especially when the surgeon in question acted in an emergency and without receiving a fee for the Good Samaritan services rendered.

Fostering the involvement of surgeons in medical peer review contributes to ensuring the quality of health care. Some physicians, however, have legitimate concerns about potential liability for libel, slander, defamation of character, and other liability that could arise from participation in the process. Such concerns have tended to have a chilling effect on the willingness of medical professionals to participate in peer review. In response, state legislatures have enacted statutes that encourage physicians and surgeons to serve on, or otherwise provide service to, peer review or other committees whose purpose is to improve or benefit patient care or otherwise reduce morbidity and mortality rates.

The mechanism used to encourage such involvement is statutory immunity from civil or criminal prosecution. Surgeons are thereby encouraged not only to participate in the peer review process, but to offer frank and candid discussion of the quality of medical care provided by their peers.

In the interest of protecting public health, statutory immunity has been provided to physicians in certain situations that involve disclosure of information acquired in the surgeon-patient relationship that might otherwise be deemed confidential. For example, a surgeon who, in good faith, reports a suspected incident of child abuse or neglect generally is immune from civil or criminal liability that might otherwise have resulted from disclosure of information acquired in the surgeon-patient relationship. Similarly, state statutes that require surgeons to disclose sexually transmitted disease or information relating to injury reasonably believed to have been caused by discharge of a firearm or other involvement in criminal activity also provide immunity from civil liability.

Reporting information that may protect an innocent third party from serious physical injury also may be encouraged by state statutes. For example, some state mental health laws provide immunity to physicians who disclose confidential health information in situations in which disclosure is necessary to protect a third party from a clear and imminent risk of serious physical injury.

In all, a diverse array of statutory provisions have been enacted to provide immunity to physicians and surgeons in connection with the kind of conduct deemed to advance public health objectives. These statutes often provide immunity from professional disciplinary action by the state medical licensing board as well. Surgeons whose alleged medical malpractice may involve conduct that is protected under a statute should examine whether the allegedly negligent conduct may be immune from liability, because such immunities can provide an excellent mechanism for disposing of medical malpractice litigation.

Liability Under Managed Care

Managed care has become a major part of the health care delivery system in the United States. Currently, a substantial portion of the nation's population is enrolled in health maintenance organizations (HMOs) and preferred provider organizations (PPOs), and this number continues to increase rapidly. In 1994, the American Managed Care and Review Association Foundation indicated that combined enrollment in HMOs and PPOs increased from 67 million in 1990 to more than 100 million in 1994.

The growth of these managed care organizations has had a sweeping impact on all aspects of the nation's health care system. The impact has been particularly severe for surgeons, who have experienced loss of professional autonomy, interference with the traditional surgeon-patient relationship, increased demands for non-patient care, administrative tasks, and reductions in income. Perhaps the most pernicious effect of managed care on the surgeon has been the expansion of legal liability. An overview of areas of potential liability under managed care follows.

Contract Liability

Contract provisions define the relationship between a managed care organization (MCO) and the surgeon, setting forth legal rights and responsibilities. A surgeon who contemplates signing a managed care contract should have the document reviewed by his or her professional liability insurer and by an attorney who not only specializes in health care law, but also has knowledge and experience with issues relating to managed health care delivery. In addition, the surgeon should be thoroughly familiar with the critical issues in the managed care contract, some of which will be discussed here. While the typical managed care contract usually contains a good deal of "boiler plate" language, the critical issues must be identified and thoroughly understood by the surgeon. The document is simply too important to leave solely to others.

Obligations and Responsibilities

The contract between the MCO and the surgeon should clearly spell out the obligations and responsibilities of each of the parties. Litigation has occurred when these obligations and responsibilities were absent or ambiguous. The potential exposure to contract liability must be kept in mind when a surgeon reviews the terms of a managed care contract, because failure to conform to the contract requirements may place the surgeon at risk, even when there is no negligence.

In the Massachusetts case of *St. Charles v. Kender*, a physician was sued for breach of contract and negligent infliction of emotional distress on the basis that he allegedly failed to return several telephone calls made to him over a period of two days by a pregnant patient. Under the contract between the physician and the HMO, the physician agreed "to provide health services for HMO members in a manner consistent with professional standards of medical care generally accepted in the medical community at the time." The patient alleged that the physician's failure to return her telephone calls in a timely manner represented a breach of this contractual provision. The trial court declined to find liability for breach of contract. However, on appeal, the court ruled that there was, in fact, a basis for a judge or jury to find that the physician had committed a breach of contract. In this regard, the court relied upon a provision in the HMO handbook that said, "Occasionally, a situation may arise in which your Personal Care Physician has not returned your call within a reasonable length of time (1–2 hours). If this occurs, call [the HMO]...and a plan administrator will be available on call to assist you in obtaining health care."

The appeals court concluded that this language constituted some evidence of an applicable professional standard with respect to a reasonable time within which the patient's telephone calls should have been returned. The physician's failure to respond to the patient's calls for two days, when the plan viewed the reasonable length of response time as one to two hours, was seen as violative of the physician's reasonable obligations to the patient. Thus, the court utilized certain provisions of the managed care contract to establish a legal duty between physician and patient. Nevertheless, because the patient did not appear to suffer actual injury as a result of the physician's failure of timely response to the patient's calls, the court concluded that, under these facts, a breach of contract claim could not succeed.

Surgeon-Patient Relationship and Duty of Care

It has long been held, and the courts have concurred, that in order to assess professional liability against a surgeon, a surgeon-patient relationship has to have been established, with both the surgeon agreeing to treat the patient and the patient agreeing to be treated. A Texas case looms important, as it may set a new standard for defining the nature and scope of the doctor-patient relationship and, in the process, significantly expand the potential for malpractice liability.

In the case of *Hand v. Tavera*, Lewis Hand presented at the emergency room of San Antonio's Humana Hospital-Village Oaks complaining of severe headaches of three days' duration. This 49-year-old man had a history of hypertension and had a father who died of an aneurysm. The emergency room physician, Dr. Daniel Boyle, treated the patient with medication, which only slightly lowered his pressure. After two or three hours of observation, Dr. Boyle, fearing a stroke, decided to admit the patient with a diagnosis of "hypertension urgency." Because the patient was a member of the Humana Health Care Plan, Dr. Boyle had to obtain authorization, and that evening, he called Dr. Robert Tavera, who was the Humana physician responsible for authorizing such admissions.

Dr. Tavera disagreed with hospitalization and told Dr. Boyle that the patient "should be controlled by outpatient medication and followed up in the office." He also "recommended something for pain." Dr. Boyle claims he argued vigorously with Dr. Tavera for admission but to no avail. Dr. Boyle's options were limited: he himself did not have admitting privileges, and because, according to Dr. Boyle, the available staff physicians were not Humana doctors, they were reluctant to admit Humana patients because of previous difficulties. Dr. Boyle documented his position in the hospital record and then explained the situation to the patient and his wife, reiterating his opinion that the patient should be hospitalized. Fearing that he might have to pay the hospital bill himself, the patient declined admission and went home. A few hours later, Mr. Hand suffered a stroke that required several weeks hospitalization and left him disabled. He was unable to work following the stroke and qualified for Social Security disability payments.

Mr. Hand sued the hospital, Dr. Boyle, and Dr. Tavera. He could not sue Humana Health Care Plan, because employer-sponsored health plans are exempt from liability under federal law. The hospital settled its portion of the claim, and Dr. Boyle was voluntarily dropped from the lawsuit by the plaintiff. Dr. Tavera, the sole remaining defendant, moved for summary judgment on the ground that he and Mr. Hand never established a physician-patient relationship, and, therefore, he owed Mr. Hand no duty. The trial court entered a summary judgment in favor of Dr. Tavera. The appeals court, however, reversed the decision.

In its ruling, the appeals court construed the contract between Humana and Southwest Medical Group, which employed Dr. Tavera. The court stated, "The contracts in the record show that the Humana Plan brought Hand and Tavera together just as surely as though they had met directly and entered the physician-patient relationship." The court concluded that "when the health care plan's doctor on call is consulted about treatment or admission, there is physician-patient relationship between the doctor and the insured." The court further concluded that once Dr. Tavera was consulted, the physician-patient relationship came into being, and the physician owed the patient a duty of care. The appellate court sent the matter back to the trial court for a jury finding regarding whether or not Dr. Tavera's conduct negligently caused injury to the patient.

Regardless of the outcome of the trial, the ruling in *Hand v. Tavera* merits careful consideration. The court's pronouncements significantly expand the potential for liability on the part of the managed care physician or surgeon, even when a traditional surgeon-patient relationship has not been established by the two parties. Furthermore, the *Hand* case demonstrates that a contractual relationship between an MCO, its physicians, and its subscribers may create a physician-patient relationship and a duty of care, even if the parties have never met. Thus, in practical terms, it would appear that when a surgeon signs a contract with an MCO, the surgeon may assume a surgeon-patient relationship with every enrollee in the plan and, when called upon, may owe each enrollee a contractually articulated duty of care. Also, when performing utilization review or on-call coverage, the MCO surgeon may be viewed as acting within the scope of a surgeon-patient relationship, even though the surgeon has never seen or spoken to the patient.

Length of Contract Agreement and Procedures for Renewal

Managed care contracts must contain information regarding the length of the agreement and procedures for renewal. Is renewal automatic unless otherwise terminated, or is notification of desire to renew required? How much advance notice of renewal is necessary?

Termination Policy

The termination policies of MCOs must be spelled out clearly. How much advance notice is given to the surgeon? Can termination be with or without cause? Is due process afforded a surgeon who is terminated, and what is the process?

How much advance notice is required if a surgeon wants to terminate? Most would suggest that a 90-day advance notification for termination would be satisfactory. Fewer than 90 days does not provide adequate time to arrange for the transfer of patient responsibility. Greater than 90 days places too heavy a burden on the surgeon who, for whatever reason, does not want to continue. In the past, surgeons have signed contracts with as long as a one-year termination clause, which essentially renders the surgeons indentured servants with no ability to resist substantial changes by the MCO.

Notification and Transfer of Patients

The mechanism for notification of patients and transfer of patient care responsibilities when a surgeon resigns or is terminated by an MCO must be addressed in the contract in order to avoid claims of abandonment.

Substantial Change

A surgeon's input in and notification of substantial change should be addressed in the managed care contract. A substantial change by an MCO must require not only adequate input from the surgeon, but a period of notification that should coincide exactly with the period of notification relative to termination. Should the MCO want to make major changes, such as the selection of hospitals, specialists, practice guidelines, fees, and so on, an unwilling surgeon should be able to resign prior to the implementation of substantial changes.

Insolvency Indenture

The insolvency indenture policy of the MCO must be included. If a managed care company becomes insolvent, the surgeon must continue the care of patients currently under treatment. The question is, however, how long is the surgeon contractually obligated to accept new patients or see current patients with new illnesses? This issue was highlighted when an indemnity insurer in the South became insolvent, and participating physicians were contractually obligated to continue to see all patients with little or no reimbursement for a protracted period of time.

Appeals

Appeal provisions for patient care decisions should be clearly spelled out, so that the surgeon and the patient can appeal denial or delay of care or location of service decisions.

Dispute Resolution

There should be unambiguous language as to how a dispute between an MCO and surgeon is to be settled (that is, arbitration, mediation, and so on).

Managed care contracts can place very strict limits on how and where surgeons practice medicine, and it is vitally important that surgeons understand the managed care contract thoroughly before agreeing to participate.

Assumed Third-Party Liability (Vicarious Liability)

Indemnification (hold harmless) clauses are increasingly finding their way into managed care contracts. Under these contracts, surgeons are required to indemnify MCOs for claims arising out of surgical negligence. The courts appear to be saying that an MCO has a responsibility to its subscribers to protect them from surgeons who may commit medical malpractice.

Because the MCO may be sued under vicarious liability principles when a surgeon member of the MCO is negligent, MCOs assert that they must be indemnified against potential liability under such circumstances. Managed care contracts often contain indemnification clauses that make the surgeon responsible to defend and/or indemnify the MCO for liability arising out of negligent conduct by the surgeon. In certain instances, these indemnification clauses require the surgeon to hold the MCO harmless, even when the injury may be caused by the MCO, as when medical care is delayed or denied.

Because professional liability insurers ordinarily cover only the negligent conduct of the insured surgeon, extreme care must be exercised before signing a managed care contract in which a surgeon contractually agrees to indemnify the MCO and hold it harmless from liability. Such "contractual" liability may not be covered under a professional liability insurance policy. Although there is some indication that professional liability insurers are beginning to offer coverage for assumed third-party liability, this practice is not yet widespread. Thus, if possible, the surgeon should resist signing managed care contracts that contain indemnification clauses. If no other option is available, the surgeon should not sign until coverage for the added liability risk has been obtained from a professional liability carrier. This additional coverage may be an expensive undertaking.

Gatekeeper Liability

Gatekeepers, especially those with financial incentives, have great pressure to reduce utilization of services and extend their own therapeutic boundaries. Carried to excess, this initiative can have serious patient care consequences, leading to liability for "failure to diagnose," "failure to perform," and "loss of opportunity for cure." In the past several years, the St. Paul Fire and Marine Insurance Companies and the Medical Underwriters of California have published studies indicating that the "failure to diagnose" category of claims has increased steadily to where it is now the number one cause of action in professional liability allegations against physicians. With MCOs having greater influence on medical practice, one can only speculate that this disturbing trend will continue, with resultant negative effects on patient care and professional liability costs.

Gatekeeper activity can also have a negative effect on the doctor-patient relationship. It is very difficult for a gatekeeper physician to remain a patient advocate and still fulfill his or her role as gatekeeper. Despite an explanation that restrictions are imposed by the patient's insurance company, the gatekeeper physician will find it challenging to maintain a good relationship while limiting the patient's access to specialists, comprehensive drug formularies, laboratories, and hospitals.

Before contractually agreeing to assume the role of gatekeeper for an MCO, the physician should be certain that the MCO has enough locally available specialists in every medical specialty and/or the ability to utilize out-of-plan specialists when the primary care physician feels it is necessary. In addition, MCO specialists must have privileges at hospitals in close proximity to the patient population. In states where the doctrine of joint and several liability applies, practitioners should be certain that all MCO physicians are required to carry sufficient professional liability insurance.

The physician contemplating gatekeeper responsibility should know whether he or she has to approve treatments or tests approved by specialists. The gatekeeper also should be aware of any plan limits on medications, diagnostic tests, inpatient and outpatient hospital utilization, and so on. The gatekeeper physician should be aware of any practice guidelines mandated by the MCO and whether there was adequate physician input in formulating these guidelines. Finally, gatekeeper physicians should insist that they be involved in utilization review and quality assurance in the context of MCO activities. Knowledge of these issues should be necessary before a physician agrees to accept gatekeeper responsibility.

Practice Liability

Denial of Care

Denial of care is a common allegation in our new health care environment. Although the MCO may deny a request for admission or consultation or insist on a premature discharge, it remains the responsibility of the surgeon to do what he or she feels is necessary for proper patient care, including resisting with all vigor any attempt by the MCO to limit care that may not be in the best interest of the patient.

In the well-publicized California case of *Wickline v. State*, Lois Wickline was hospitalized with an aortofemoral occlusion (Leriche's syndrome). She underwent aortofemoral bypass on January 1, 1977. Postoperatively, a clot formed in the graft, necessitating reoperation later that day. Subsequently, the patient experienced pain and spasm in the vessels of her lower leg, and on January 12, 1977, she underwent a lumbar sympathectomy. Because of postoperative complications, her physicians requested eight additional days of hospitalization beyond the scheduled discharge date.

The Medi-Cal consultant, a general surgeon who no longer performed surgery, approved only four additional days. The consultant did not discuss the case with the patient's surgeon, nor did he review the patient's hospital record prior to making his decision. The patient's physicians did not protest the Medi-Cal decision and discharged the patient after the four approved days. While at home, the patient developed gangrene and had to undergo an above-the-knee amputation. Wickline sued Medi-Cal, but not her physicians. Although Medi-Cal prevailed in the litigation, the California court offered meaningful guidance regarding potential medical malpractice liability in these types of situations. The court stated that "the physician who complies without protest with the limitations on treatment imposed by a third-party payor when his medical judgment dictates otherwise cannot avoid his ultimate responsibility for his patients' care." The court warned the MCO that "third-party payors of health care services can be held legally accountable when medically inappropriate decisions result from defects in the design or implementation of cost-containment mechanisms, such as when appeals made on a patient's behalf for medical or hospital care are arbitrarily ignored or unreasonably disregarded or overridden." The court concluded by declaring: "This court appreciates that what is at issue here is the effect of cost-containment programs upon the professional judgment of physicians to prescribe hospital treatment for patients requiring the same. While we recognize, realistically, that cost consciousness has become a permanent feature of the health care system, it is essential that cost limitation programs not be permitted to corrupt medical judgment."

The courts take a particularly dim view of negligence or denial of care that they perceive to have been motivated by perverse financial incentives. This fact is demonstrated in the California case of *Fox v. Health Net*. Nalene Fox was a 38-year-old woman with advanced breast cancer who was denied coverage for an autologous bone marrow transplant by Health Net, her HMO. Although the patient and her family raised sufficient funds to enable her to have the operation, she died seven months later. The patient's husband and three daughters sued Health Net for bad faith, breach of contract, and intentional infliction of emotional distress. During the trial, evidence suggested that Health Net awarded generous bonuses to executives who were successful in reducing overall plan costs, which could include denial of costly treatments. Although this fact was denied by Health Net, evidence of such financial incentives apparently had a telling effect on the jury, which awarded the plaintiff $89 million (this was later reduced on appeal). When questioned after the trial, the jurors expressed outrage that the decision by Health Net to deny coverage of a potentially life-saving treatment to a dying woman could have been financially motivated.

Delay of Care

Another common allegation in recent professional liability lawsuits is delay of care, which can cause harm to the patient and lead to "loss of opportunity for cure." Liability for the delay of care may be placed on the physician or surgeon, even when the policy of the MCO may require additional consultations, tests, and authorizations prior to approving expensive treatment and procedures. This situation was illustrated in the California case of *Pena v. Rouhe*.

A 13-year-old boy was referred to an orthopaedic surgeon complaining of progressive pain in the left hip. X rays revealed a 20 percent slippage of the left capital femoral epiphysis. The orthopaedic surgeon testified that he recognized the need for early surgical reduction, but did not regard this condition as an emergency. As required by the patient's HMO, the surgeon submitted a request in writing for authorization. The patient was given crutches, instructed to place no weight on the left leg, and allowed to return to school. While at school, the patient slipped and fell, resulting in a nearly complete separation of the epiphysis. The patient was immediately hospitalized and placed in traction. The following day, the patient underwent surgical repair with the placement of three pins. The patient developed avascular necrosis to the femoral head, and while undergoing arthrodesis, the left iliac vein was lacerated, requiring transfusions of more than 20 units of blood. Three subsequent operations were necessary prior to achieving a successful arthrodesis, which left the patient with a left leg six centimeters shorter than the right. At trial, the case centered around the urgency of the operation. The plaintiff alleged that the surgeon was negligent in not conveying the urgency of the operation in the request for authorization and failing to follow up when the HMO did not respond within a few days. The defense claimed that in the absence of an emergency, it was not unreasonable to delay the operation in order to obtain authorization as required by the patient's HMO. A unanimous jury verdict was returned in favor of the plaintiff for $750,000, which was later reduced to $400,000 under applicable California law.

Restriction of Services

Restrictive access to the use and selection of specialists, pharmaceuticals, treatment facilities, laboratories, and imaging centers can add to the difficulty in patient care and the potential for medical error. Physicians develop confidence in specialists and the way they handle clinical situations and communicate their findings. Similarly, confidence and familiarity with laboratories, imaging centers, reporting procedures, and methods of communicating abnormalities are important parts of good patient care. Dealing with multiple formularies, laboratories, and imaging centers can cause difficulty and introduce new sources of potential error and liability.

Restrictive access to specialists can cause additional problems, as illustrated by a California case that provides an example of how the individual and the public can respond to inappropriate denials and/or restriction of care. Carley Christie was a 9-year-old girl who was diagnosed with Wilms' tumor and referred by her family physician to a surgeon at Stanford University Hospital. The family learned that the assigned surgeon, who later admitted he had never treated a patient with this disease, was not part of Stanford's multidisciplinary team on Wilms' tumor and requested the involvement of Dr. Stephen Shochat, Chief of Pediatric Surgery at Stanford and Surgical Coordinator for the National Wilms' Tumor Study. The MCO, TakeCare Health Plan, denied the request. Nevertheless, the family went outside the network and consulted Dr. Shochat, who performed the operation. TakeCare refused to cover Dr. Shochat's fee and the hospital charges of $47,000. Due to a prior contractual agreement with TakeCare, the family went to arbitration where, after a hearing, the arbitrator ordered TakeCare to pay all of Carley's medical expenses, as well as arbitration costs. In addition, the California Department of Corporations, following its own investigation, fined TakeCare $500,000 for failing to provide appropriate access to quality medical care.

Practice Guidelines

Practice guidelines also can present a potential for liability in the managed care context. Although the state of Maine now allows guidelines to be used as an affirmative defense in professional liability actions, these guidelines have been developed and approved by recognized medical organizations. Guidelines that have been developed by an MCO without adequate expert physician input may be successfully challenged in court. Before agreeing to be bound by MCO guidelines, it is incumbent upon managed care surgeons to be knowledgeable about who created the guidelines and whether there was proper, independent medical input and approval. Several other states are contemplating the use of practice guidelines in professional liability litigation. A somewhat disquieting note, however, is that practice guidelines typically are being used by plaintiffs more often than by defendants to establish the standard of care in professional liability litigation.

Administrative Liability

Medical Peer Review

Medical peer review is usually defined by statute to protect committees engaged in the evaluation and/or improvement of the quality of health care, such as credentialing, quality assurance, and utilization review. Medical peer review may be performed for clinics, hospitals, MCOs, professional associations, and professional liability insurers.

The Federal Health Care Quality Improvement Act of 1986 was enacted in response to the rising number of cases of antitrust liability in peer review and credentialing activity. This act provides immunity to surgeons and others involved in peer review, providing certain requirements are met. In addition, this act establishes reporting requirements for the National Practitioner Data Bank. Surgeons should be familiar with the requirements for protection under this act. In addition, many states provide statutory immunity for those participating in peer review, but there are strict requirements that must be met, and the surgeon should not assume immunity without full knowledge of applicable state laws.

Peer review laws, at both the federal and state levels, provide two types of protection. The first is privilege or confidentiality of peer review records. This protection is currently under attack in many states by plaintiff attorneys. Second, peer review laws provide immunity or protection from legal prosecution for good faith activities.

Peer review is an integral part of any MCO. Participating physicians are often contractually required to participate in these activities. The importance and liability exposure that this type of activity entails cannot be overstated. Surgeons whose performance is found to be substandard and who are dropped from an MCO suffer not only economic effects, but also potential disciplinary action from state licensing boards, most of whom require reporting of disciplinary action by MCOs.

The usual method used by a disciplined surgeon against the practitioner who has participated in the peer review process is to initiate an antitrust action. Such a claim typically is based on anticompetitive conduct, restraint of trade, and/or group boycott. Antitrust liability can be severe, as it can involve not only civil penalties, but also treble damages and prevailing attorneys' fees. An example is the well-publicized United States Supreme Court case of *Patrick v. Burget*. The plaintiff, Dr. Timothy Patrick, was a general and vascular surgeon employed at the Astoria Clinic with surgical privileges at the Columbia Memorial Hospital, the only hospital in Astoria, Oregon, a city of about 10,000 people. After approximately one year, the plaintiff was invited to become a partner in the clinic, but declined and instead began an independent practice in competition with the clinic. Dr. Patrick alleged that thereafter he experienced difficulty in his professional dealings with the clinic physicians, which culminated in those physicians initiating and participating fully in a peer review process alleging that care provided by Dr. Patrick to his patients was below the professional standards of care generally accepted in the medical community at the time. The executive committee of Columbia Memorial Hospital medical staff heard the complaints and voted to refer the complaints to the State Board of Medical Examiners.

Following a hearing, the State Board of Medical Examiners issued a letter of reprimand, which they later retracted in its entirety after Dr. Patrick sought judicial review of the proceedings. Some two years later, the medical staff of Columbia Memorial Hospital initiated a review of Dr. Patrick's care of patients at the request of a clinic surgeon. This review resulted in the termination of Dr. Patrick's privileges on the grounds that his care of patients fell below hospital standards. Dr. Patrick filed suit in federal district court against several clinic physicians, alleging violation of the Sherman Act and interference with prospective economic advantage under Oregon law. He claimed that by initiating or participating in peer review proceedings, the defendants were attempting to reduce competition, rather than improve patient care. A jury returned a verdict against the defendant physicians and awarded Dr. Patrick damages of $650,000. The district court, as required by law, trebled the damages. The case was appealed, and a federal court of appeals reversed the decision, but the United States Supreme Court disagreed and reinstated the original judgment. Thus, under certain circumstances, involvement in the peer review process may give rise to litigation and potential liability under federal and state antitrust laws.

Utilization Review and Quality Assurance

Utilization review and quality assurance have been an integral part of our health care delivery system for many years. Because of the strong emphasis on cost containment by MCOs, additional areas of potential liability can occur for participating surgeons, such as when a utilization review decision is determined to be a substantial factor in causing a bad outcome.

Credentialing

Surgeons who are responsible for credentialing or recredentialing of peer professionals in the managed care context take on an additional risk of potential liability. It is the duty of the MCO and its designated peer reviewers to protect patients from what is referred to as foreseeable harm by assessing the credentials of new surgeons, as well as regularly monitoring the performance of participating surgeons.

Although few statutory requirements for credentialing exist, the courts may find managed care companies liable for failure to properly screen participating physicians. Some guidance in this area can be obtained from the National Committee for Quality Assurance accreditation program for MCOs. Its credentialing process requires the following: verification of current licensure; full disclosure of all complaints, investigations, and disciplinary actions by state licensing boards; verification of current hospital staff privileges and information regarding formal complaints, restrictions, and/ or denial of privileges; verification of board certification or eligibility, education, training, and competence; evidence of current professional liability insurance and history of prior professional liability claims; work history; and search of the National Practitioner Data Bank.

It is important for the surgeon who participates in medical peer review, utilization review, quality assurance, and credentialing activities to be sure that his or her professional liability insurance policy covers such activity. If not, the physician should insist that the organization for whom the surgeon is performing these services provide liability coverage for this activity.

Directors and Officers Insurance

When a surgeon serves as an officer, director, or employee of an MCO, it is important to be sure that the MCO has errors and omission insurance coverage, as well as directors and officers insurance coverage. It is unlikely that the physician's professional liability insurer will cover liability arising in the context of a physician serving as an officer or administrator of a managed care company (MCC).

ERISA

The concerns over the new areas of physician liability already discussed are magnified by the effects of ERISA (Employee Retirement Income Security Act) legislation. This federal legislation, enacted in 1974, allows self-insured groups to circumvent many state insurance laws and mandates. ERISA was originally promulgated primarily to protect employee pension plans, but in the final language of the legislation, the term "employee benefit plans" was used, and thus health and accident benefits were included as well. These benefits were not an issue prior to managed care, as the areas of dispute were limited to retrospective payment for services and thus not costly. Under managed care, we are dealing with denial of services and possibly other areas of plan and physician negligence.

The federal courts have been divided as to whether ERISA preempts coverage denials, malpractice, and negligence claims against HMOs or HMO physicians. In earlier cases involving coverage denials, legal experts advised and the courts confirmed that ERISA plans were exempt from negligence claims. In the Louisiana case of *Corcoran v. United Healthcare, Inc.*, a utilization review firm determined that hospital care was unnecessary for a high-risk pregnant woman nearing her due date, despite her physician's opinion to the contrary. Following discharge from the hospital, the fetus went into distress and died. In its 1992 decision, the Fifth US Court of Appeals, while acknowledging ERISA exemption, expressed regret that under ERISA it could not consider compensation for the emotional distress caused by the wrongful death of Corcoran's unborn child.

A similar position was taken by the US Court of Appeals for the Ninth Circuit in *Spain v. Aetna Life Insurance Co*. In this case, the plaintiffs claimed that the delay of approval by Aetna for the third part of an autologous bone marrow transplant resulted in the death of a patient with testicular cancer. The appellate court affirmed the US District Court's opinion that ERISA preempts a state law claim for wrongful death, and thus victims of ERISA plan negligence cannot be awarded damages from the plan.

In more recent cases, the courts seem to be taking the position that claims that involve the quality of care by an HMO physician should not be preempted by ERISA, as these claims do not involve a question of denial of health plan benefits.

In *Dukes v. U.S. Healthcare*, the Tenth Circuit joined the US Court of Appeals for the Third Circuit when it held that ERISA does not preempt malpractice and negligence claims against an HMO or HMO physicians. The Third Circuit reasoned that such claims do not seek to recover benefits or enforce rights under a benefit plan, and thus should not fall under ERISA exemption. A similar action was taken by the US Court of Appeals for the Tenth Circuit in the *PacifiCare of Oklahoma, Inc., v. Burrage*. In this case, the plaintiff brought a malpractice action against PacifiCare, alleging the HMO was vicariously liable for the negligent actions of one of its physicians, which resulted in the death of the patient. The district court found that the questions of physician negligence and agency relationship between the HMO and the physician could be determined without referring to the underlying benefit plan.

Finally, in *Whelan v. Keystone Health Plan East*, the US District Court of the Eastern District of Pennsylvania ruled that a medical malpractice claim against an HMO and its physicians should be decided in state court and not be preempted by ERISA, because the allegations involved the quality of benefits provided rather than the recovery of benefits denied.

This issue is of particular importance to physicians who have indemnified an MCC contractually. If MCCs are to be held accountable for the quality of benefits provided, as well as for the negligent acts of its affiliated physicians, then assuming MCO liability contractually could result in major consequences for the physician. This area is evolving case law, which bears close scrutiny and serves to further emphasize that physicians should, whenever possible, decline to assume third-party liability, but if assumed, should arrange for professional liability insurance coverage for these potential claims.

Conclusion

In this discussion, some of the professional and legal issues associated with surgical practice in the managed care context have been highlighted. Many of the topics discussed are relatively new, and the potential for liability is still evolving in the courts. Nevertheless, it is important to emphasize that surgeons who plan to join or align with MCOs must be thoroughly familiar with potential areas of physician liability in the managed care environment before undertaking a final contractual commitment. Although attorneys can offer valuable guidance, there is no substitute for personal knowledge and familiarity with these issues on the part of the surgeon.

Reporting Requirements of the National Practitioner Data Bank and State Agencies

The National Practitioner Data Bank

The purpose of the National Practitioner Data Bank (NPDB), which was established under Title IV, Part B, of the Health Care Quality Improvement Act of 1986 (HCQIA) PL 99-660 was to collect and disseminate to "authorized professional review authorities" information concerning "medical incompetence." The announced purpose of the NPDB was to prevent "incompetent practitioners" from transferring across counties, different parts of a state, and states without being detected by state licensing boards and American medical authorities. To ensure that such "incompetent practitioners" would be detected by the appropriate state medical boards and licensing and credentialing committees, state licensing boards, hospitals, and other health care entities, including professional societies, must report to the NPDB certain adverse licensing and disciplinary action taken against individual practitioners. Under the terms of the legislation, the NPDB makes the information available when it is queried by licensing boards and credentialing authorities; however, this information is not to be made available to a plaintiff's attorney.

A practitioner (not limited to physicians) is listed in the NPDB per the following criteria.

1. Adverse action* against a practitioner by any of the following:
   a. Hospital or an entity representative*
   b. Other health care entities* or an entity representative*
   c. Professional society*
   d. State licensing board*
2. Payment of a claim against a practitioner that is made by any of the following is to be reported:
   a. Insurance company
   b. Hospital or an entity representative*

A problem in item 2 is that if the insurance company reports payment, and the hospital also reports the payment, no mechanism currently exists in the NPDB for determination of whether two separate reports are actually duplications of the same filing. Also, pursuant to a recent court decision, a practitioner who pays his/her own claim out of personal funds is not listed in the NPDB.

There is an appeals process by which a practitioner may appeal his/her listing in the NPDB. However, if the appeal is lost, once the practitioner is in the NPDB, there is no mechanism by which the practitioner can be "delisted," no matter how many years of liability free practice the practitioner has.

Funding of the NPDB

Taxpayer funds were used to cover the development and start-up costs of the NPDB, but currently, the NPDB is funded entirely by user fees.

Law mandates that all hospitals query the NPDB about practitioners under the following circumstances:

1. Hospitals must query the NPDB upon a new application from a practitioner with whom they are unfamiliar.

---

* See Glossary. Definition applies to usage in conjunction with the NPDB and its policies and procedures.

2. When hospitals, HMOs, or PPOs grant credentials to practitioners every two years, they are strongly encouraged to query the NPDB first.

Most disturbing is that some HMOs and PPOs use the NPDB as a test of initial membership in their organization. A positive filing for a trivial complaint involving a relatively small amount of money may prevent a practitioner from having access to patients of the HMO or PPO.

According to the original legislation, attorneys (especially plaintiff attorneys) are barred from receiving this information. However, an increasing amount of the querying is being done electronically. It is uncertain what safeguards prevent attorneys from gaining access to this information.

The number of queries has increased dramatically. In its first four years of operation, the NPDB processed 4,586,262 queries.[2] Queries during 1994 totaled 1,504,842 (or about 6,000 queries per working day), a 31.4 percent increase over the previous year's 1,145,260 queries, and an 85.8 percent increase over the 809,900 queries during 1991, the NPDB's first full year of operation. This increase suggests that managed care companies are trying to determine whether practitioners are listed in the NPDB and are acting accordingly.

Relation of Payment to Medical Negligence

A note of caution has crept into some of the reports of the NPDB over the past several years. The argument is along the following lines: Less than 2 percent of injuries caused by "medical negligence" in a hospital setting lead to malpractice claims, let alone payments. Of claims entered, considerably less than 50 percent lead to payments.[2] On the other hand, claims are sometimes filed in situations in which there is no medical negligence. In a study of claims filed with one insurer, payments were made for only 43 percent of claims filed, and 21 percent of payments were made for claims that were clearly defensible by that insurer, but paid because the insurer estimated that it would be less costly to settle the claims than to defend against them.[2] Nor is it clear that all of the payments represent significant payments. The state of California has a threshold of $30,000, because an amount under $30,000 is believed to constitute a claim of nuisance value and does not reflect "medical incompetence."

Of the practitioners who are currently listed or reported in the NPDB, physicians of course are the most regularly reported and constitute 70 to 80 percent of the reports. The percentage of dentists is approximately 15 to 16 percent, and other practitioners make up the remaining percentage.

Questionable Accuracy of Data

There is a large discrepancy in the percentage of reports from various states, ranging from a low of 7.5 percent in Alabama to 40 to 45 percent in Montana, Michigan, and West Virginia. There are no data to explain such regional differences in reporting. Probably the single most disturbing aspect is duplicate reporting, for which no mechanism currently exists to determine whether separate entities are reporting the same incident. At the end of 1994, the mean number of disclosable reports per practitioner was 1.3. Although the NPDB has no idea if multiple reports are of the same incident or different incidents, only 16 percent of the practitioners listed in the NPDB with malpractice reports had more than one report; 12.4 percent had two malpractice payment reports; and 4.2 percent had three or more liability payment reports. Assuming that a good percentage of 12.4 percent with two malpractice reports are likely to be duplicate reporting of the same claim by both hospital and insurer, the number of physicians with multiple reports seems small indeed.

Does Past Experience Predict the Future?

This question is a critical issue for the NPDB and is the area around which the argument revolves. The number of reports has remained reasonably steady, going from 22,517 in 1991 to 24,621 in 1992; 24,334 reports were received in 1993, a slight decrease; and 25,262 reports were received in 1994, a 13 percent increase. Of course, as the number of incidents increased, so did the number of positive matches, which have progressively increased from 1.5 percent in 1991 to 4.9 percent in 1992, 6.0 percent in 1993, and 7.9 percent in 1994. The matches should always increase due to the cumulative method of reporting.

Whether or not the future will be predicted from the past, in the state of Florida, for example, only 3 percent of the practitioners have any claim payment of any size. The remainder of the claim payments are at an average of $12,000 and are nuisance claims (hardly consistent with serious injury or solid theories of practice below the standard). Only 140 practitioners (or less than 1 percent of the practitioner population) have any significant claims against them. We do not know if these practitioners are in high-litigation areas or specialties or if the payments have any merit.

Two reports[3,4] of the Office of the Inspector General from the United States Department of Health and Human Services indicate that the NPDB information was only influential in 1 percent of hospital decisions about physician credentialing. In a commentary to the Bovbjerg and Petronis[5] paper published in *The Journal of the American Medical Association*, Smarr[6] stated that it is "difficult to conclude that the exclusion of small-claim payment data will erode the already limited usefulness of the NPDB." The failure to have a threshold for payment and the inclusion of a majority of claims in the nuisance category seriously erode the accuracy of the NPDB and its usefulness.

State Agencies

Health providers, including surgeons, should be aware of the reporting requirements of their particular state relative to disciplinary actions. This is particularly important for chairpersons of departments of surgery. Although reporting requirements differ among states, all states require hospitals to report privilege revocation, suspension, and restriction. The degree of confidentialities in these matters is open to question.

Liability insurers in most states are required to notify appropriate state agencies concerning payment of medical malpractice claims. California has a threshold of $30,000, and New Jersey, $25,000. Any closed claim above this stated amount has to be reported. The vast majority of states have no threshold.

Summary

The NPDB has been in operation for more than six years, having been established by law in 1986. When the NPDB was originally proposed, the state licensing boards* were not linked and had no regular method of communication with the NPDB. This aspect of the NPDB no longer seems necessary, since all state licensing boards* are now computer-linked. Actions taken by a state licensing board* in one situation will probably be reported to all other 49 state licensing boards.* Thus, moving from state to state without the state licensing boards* being informed should not occur. Nonetheless, the NPDB dissemination and collection of information about disciplinary actions related to licensure is worthwhile if it prevents incompetent doctors from moving from state to state.

There are significant problems with the accuracy of the NPDB closed claim malpractice data, in particular the lack of a mechanism for detecting duplicate payments and/or reports. There is no threshold for payment, and in one state (Florida), only 3 percent of the practitioners who are listed in the NPDB were listed because of a significant claim. In addition, once a practitioner is listed in the NPDB, it is impossible to become "delisted," no matter how many years of professional liability free service a practitioner has.

The overall effect of the NPDB is pejorative and unfair. Were it not for the fact that HMOs and PPOs are ostensibly using some of this inaccurate data to decide which practitioners they will cre-

---

* See Glossary. Definition applies to usage in conjunction with the NPDB and its policies and procedures.

dential, the NPDB would be nothing more than a bad dream. Unfortunately, the lives of individuals are being affected by data that may be riddled with inaccuracies.

It would be prudent for surgeons, particularly chairpersons of surgery, to be familiar with reporting requirements in their own state.The physician should be familiar with state reporting requirements concerning privilege restrictions. These requirements may vary with each state (see Table[7] on page 94). In most states, hospitals are required to report modification of privileges. In several states, other health care entities such as HMOs are required to report restriction of physician privileges if it is based on substandard care as judged by a Professional Review Action.[*] Liability insurers must report closed paid malpractice claims to the state.

---

* See Glossary. Definition applies to usage in conjunction with the NPDB and its policies and procedures.

What hospitals must report

	Privilege Revocation	Privilege Suspension	Privilege Restriction	Voluntary Surrender of Privileges	Voluntary Restriction of Privileges
AL	X	X	X	X	X
AK	X	X	X	X	X
AZ-M	X	X	X	X	X (If to avoid formal action)
AZ-O	X	X	X	X	X (If to avoid formal action)
AR	X	X	X	X	X
CA-M	X	X	X	X	X
CA-O	X	X	X	X	X
CO	X	X	X	X	X
CT-M	X[1]	X[1]	X[1]	X[1]	X[1]
DE	X	X	X	X	X
DC	X	X	X	X	X (If to avoid formal action)
FL-M	X	X	X	X	X
FL-O	X	X	X	X	X
GA	X	X	X	X	X
GU	—	—	—	—	—
HI-M	X	X	X	X	X
ID	X	X	X	X	X
IL	X	X	X	X	X (If to avoid formal action)
IN	X	X	X	X	X

continued on page 96

[1] Hospitals must report to Board any physician deemed unable to practice with reasonable skill and safety.

What liability carriers must report

	All Claims	All Liability Payments Made by Carrier	Dollar Amount Above Which All Payments Must Be Reported	Self-Insureds Must Also Report
AL	X	X	—	X
AK		X	—	X
AZ-M	X	X		X
		(Claims reported by plaintiff attorney)		
AZ-O	X	X	—	
AR	—	—	—	—
CA-M	—	—	30,000	X
CA-O	—	—	30,000	X
CO		X	—	—
CT-M	X		—	X
DE	X	X		
		Reported through Delaware Insurance Commissioner		
DC		X	—	
FL-M	Only notice of policy cancellation/non-renewal required			
FL-O	Only notice of policy cancellation/non-renewal required			
GA		X	10,000	X
		(All payments over $10,000 or if two prior)		
GU	—	—	—	—
HI-M		X	—	X
ID		X	—	X
IL		X	—	X
IN	Indiana Department of Insurance reports "panel opinions"			

continued on page 97

What hospitals must report

	Privilege Revocation	Privilege Suspension	Privilege Restriction	Voluntary Surrender of Privileges	Voluntary Restriction of Privileges
IA	X	X	X	X	X
KS	X	X	X	X	X
KY	X	X	X	X	X
LA	X	X	X	X	X
ME-M	X	X	X	X	X
ME-O	X	X	X	X	X
MD	X	X	X	X	X
MA	X	X	X	X	X
MI-M	X	X	X	X	X
MI-O	X	X	X	X	X
MN	X	X	X	X	X
MS	X	X	X	X	X
MO	X	X	X	X	X
MT	X	X	X	X	X
NE	X	X	X	X	X
NV-M	X	X	X	X	X
NV-O	X	X			
NH	X	X	X	X	X
NJ	X	X	X	X	X
NM-M	X	X	X	X	X
NM-O	X	X	X	X	X
NY	X	X	X	X	X
NC	X	X	X	X	X
ND	X	X	X	X	X

continued on page 98

What liability carriers must report

	All Claims	All Liability Payments Made by Carrier	Dollar Amount Above Which All Payments Must Be Reported	Self-Insureds Must Also Report
IA	X		—	
KS	X	X	—	X
	Reported through Kansas Insurance Commissioner			
KY		X	—	
	Reported through Kentucky Department of Insurance			
LA		X	1,000	X
ME-M	X	X	—	
ME-O	X	X	—	
MD		X	—	X
MA	X	X	—	X
MI-M	X		—	
MI-O	X		—	
MN		X	—	X
MS	X	X	—	X
MO	X		—	X
MT	X		—	X
NE	X	X	—	X
NV-M	X	X	1.00	X
NV-O	X	X	—	
NH	X		—	X
NJ			25,000	X
NM-M	X	X	—	X
NM-O			—	
NY	X	X	—	X
NC	X	X	—	
ND	X	X	X	X

continued on page 99

What hospitals must report

	Privilege Revocation	Privilege Suspension	Privilege Restriction	Voluntary Surrender of Privileges	Voluntary Restriction of Privileges
OH	X	X	X		
OK-M	X	X	X	X	X
OK-O	X	X	X	X	X
OR	X	X	X		
PA-M	X	X	X	X	X
PA-O	X	X	X	X	X
PR	—	—	—	—	—
RI	X	X	X	X	X
SC	X	X	X	X	X
SD	X	X			
TN-M	X	X	X	X	X
TN-O	X	X	X	X	X
TX	X	X	X	X	X
UT-M	X	X	X	X	X
UT-O	X	X	X	X	X
VT-M	X	X	X		
VT-O					
VA	X	X	X	X	X
VI	—	—	—	—	—
WA-M	X	X	X	X	X
WA-O	X	X	X		X
WV-M	X	X	X	X	X
WV-O	X	X	X	X	X
WI	X^2	X^2	X^2	X^2	X^2
WY	X	X	X	X	X
	64	64	62	58	59

[2] Only if hospital actions resulted from peer review

What liability carriers must report

	All Claims	All Liability Payments Made by Carrier	Dollar Amount Above Which All Payments Must Be Reported	Self-Insureds Must Also Report
OH			X	X
OK-M	X	X	X	
OK-O	X	X	—	
OR	X	X	—	X
PA-M	X	X	—	X
PA-O	X	X	—	X
PR	—	—	—	
RI	X	X	NA	X
SC		X	—	
SD		X	—	
TN-M			5,000	
TN-O			5,000	
TX	X	X	—	X
UT-M			10,000	X
UT-O			10,000	X
VT-M		X	—	
VT-O		X		
VA		X	—	X
VI	—	—	—	
WA-M			20,000	
WA-O			20,000	
WV-M	X	X	—	X
WV-O	X	X	—	X
WI	X	X	—	
WY	X		—	
	34	42		36

Efforts to Reform and Change

Overview

The inadequacies of the present system for resolving malpractice claims through court-based adversarial litigation under the tort system have become apparent in recent years, as substantial increases in malpractice claim frequency, claim severity, and insurance costs have occurred. For health care, the result has been a deterioration of the physician-patient relationship and the development of widespread defensive practices, which have had a negative impact on health care delivery, access, and cost. Another result has been a proliferation of tort reform and the consideration of alternative dispute resolution (ADR) methodology, partially or totally removing claims resolution from the tort system.

Two major malpractice crises have occurred: the first was in the 1970s and was highlighted by both increases in insurance costs and decreasing availability of liability insurance; the second was in the 1980s, when costs again escalated while insurance remained available. As a result of these crises, which jeopardized health care delivery, most state legislatures passed some type of tort reform for medical malpractice controversies, frequently including tort actions in other fields. Two major waves of tort reforms resulted, changing "the legal rules of the tort system, establishing alterations in insurance practices, and formulating procedures for provider quality assurance."[8]

This chapter discusses specific types of changes in legal rules. Responses to the availability of insurance and its costs, which include the creation of new sources of insurance, such as state-operated compensation funds, joint underwriting associations, and physician-owned companies, and kinds of insurance policies are discussed in Chapter III. Provider practice patterns were addressed by programs for quality assurance and risk management, which have been widely implemented.

The "Bad Doctor" Myth and Causation

Although the actual effect of quality assurance and risk management programs on the malpractice problem is as yet unclear, one effect has been the further propagation of the "bad doctor" myth, which maintains that the principal cause of the malpractice problem is "bad doctors" (incompetent physicians).[9,10]

This paradox has occurred even though all detailed analyses and available data, as well as general experience, indicate that most claims involve competent practitioners and result from the specific nature of their practices (which is also reflected in the premium structure utilized by liability insurers), or from momentary lapses or poor decisions. Moreover, the origins of the malpractice problem are known to be multifactorial, caused by a combination of events—primarily the expansive application of tort law, an increasingly complex health care environment, and a litigious society.

The "bad doctor" theory, unsupported by data, has been perpetuated and enhanced by repetition, publication, unwarranted conclusions, and sometimes statements by prominent individuals. The concept appears in news media and in publications by public agencies and is seen in the increasing requirements for reporting malpractice claims to hospitals, other organizations, and licensing authorities. The result has been the illogical conclusions that "bad doctors" are the major cause of the malpractice problem, and that physicians involved in malpractice claims are presumptive "bad doctors."

The most visible example of this line of reasoning is the National Practitioner Data Bank, discussed elsewhere in this manual, which joins consideration of physicians involved in malpractice actions with incompetent physicians. The data bank was established to help ensure that unethical or incompetent practitioners do not compromise health care quality and to restrict the ability of incompetent practitioners to move from state to state. Although the bank was established to control incompetent physicians, the largest volume of information in the data bank relates to malpractice awards and settlements. Thus, the large group of practicing physicians involved in malpractice claims is lumped together with the very small number of physicians who manifest grossly aberrant behavior, who are convicted of crimes or violate licensing statutes, or who are incompetent for reasons such as mental illness or substance abuse. The dynamic expansion of tort law that has occurred is, therefore, now accompanied by a dynamic "bad doctor" stigma.

Reforms and Proposals for Change

Reform of Legal Rules of Tort

State legislatures have taken a piecemeal approach to the professional liability problem, enacting more than 20 specific types of legal rule changes as individual statutes or as part of tort reform packages. The reforms vary considerably from state to state, but as a general rule, fall into three categories: those that affect the initiation of claims, those that affect the standard of care and proof of its breach, and those that affect the amount recoverable in a malpractice suit. These reforms include recently legislated practice guidelines in the state of Maine[11] and a recent proposal for "enterprise liability."[10-14]

Elimination of the Ad Damnum *Clause*

The *ad damnum* clause refers to the statement of the amount of damages sought by a plaintiff in a claim. Publication of these amounts may generate unfavorable publicity, needlessly harm a defendant's reputation, and perhaps influence a jury. Many states have, therefore, prohibited inclusion of the clause in a pleading or permit only a statement that damages exceed a certain specified amount.

Requirement of Arbitration

Arbitration and other methods for ADR for resolving controversies have assumed increasing importance in recent years, both in freestanding formats and as part of court proceedings. Under reforms enacted in various states, this method of nonjudicial dispute resolution by a neutral third party may be elected by agreement (voluntary), may be imposed by law (mandatory), and may be binding or nonbinding.

Arbitration, probably the oldest and best known ADR procedure, has long been suggested as a substitute for litigation in malpractice cases and has been used by at least two major health care plans one of which, Kaiser Permanente, has utilized arbitration in conjunction with preexisting health care agreements. Advantages of arbitration are less formality, greater privacy for the parties, perhaps the availability of a higher level of technical expertise to evaluate a claim, faster claim resolution with lower costs, and less emotional trauma to the parties. Presently available data, however, indicate that malpractice claim resolution times, as well as costs, may only be slightly lower than with the litigation process. Although arbitration has been used with a great deal of success in commercial and labor disputes, its widespread use in resolving medical malpractice claims has, therefore, not been established.[14,15]

Regulation of Attorney Fees The contingent fee, the most common arrangement for payment of plaintiff attorneys in malpractice cases, allocates to the attorney a predetermined significant percentage of any final award or settlement, usually in addition to expenses of litigation. Additional charges may also be made for postverdict proceedings and appeals. If the plaintiff loses, the plaintiff attorney receives no fee, while defense attorney fees are ordinarily billed on an hourly basis and covered by the insurer. Regulation of plaintiff attorney fees, which has been legislated in some states, may consist of establishing a sliding scale to determine the percentage of the award that may be paid to the attorney, may limit the fee to a certain percentage of the total award, or may require court determination or approval of a reasonable fee. Proponents of attorney fee regulation argue that it would allocate more funds to the injured party, reduce nonmeritorious claims, and encourage earlier settlement. Opponents view the contingent fee as "the key to the courthouse" for claimants and as a screening mechanism that encourages attorneys to eliminate small claims, as well as claims unlikely to result in recovery of damages.

Modification of the Collateral Source Rule Traditionally, this rule has prevented a jury from considering evidence concerning payments to the injured party from other sources, including private health or disability insurance, workers' compensation, and governmental benefit payments. Proponents of reform advocate modification or abolishment of the rule, maintaining that such recovery from multiple sources provides an unwarranted windfall for claimants and contributes to the high cost of malpractice litigation. The rule has been modified in a number of states to reduce duplicate payments for medical malpractice, either by permitting the jury to be informed about such payments or by mandating that the amounts of some or all collateral benefits be deducted from the awards.

Data Collection and Processing The unavailability of reliable data has been a major impediment to objective evaluation and resolution of the medical professional liability problem. Some reform efforts have, therefore, provided for improved data reporting and processing programs that have, however, largely focused on provider disciplinary procedures and insurance factors. Responsibility for improved data collection has been vested largely in state licensing authorities, state insurance departments, or the federally mandated National Practitioner Data Bank.

Establishment of Expert Witness Qualifications   Expert witnesses play a crucial role in medical malpractice cases, a fact that raises important concerns about the qualification and regulation of paid experts, especially those who testify for the plaintiff. Guidelines have been published by the American College of Surgeons concerning the quality and behavior of the "Expert Witness" (see Chapter V, page 216). Legislation in several states has established minimum qualifications for expert witnesses, such as requiring an expert to have devoted at least half of his or her time within the preceding two-year period to actual clinical practice in the same profession as the defendant, to have a current license to practice in the same or related specialty as the defendant, or to have spent a substantial portion of time in actual clinical practice in the same or related specialty.

Passage of Frivolous Claim Provisions   Several states have passed legislation to discourage nonmeritorious malpractice claims. Such statutes may involve requiring an unsuccessful plaintiff to reimburse the defendant's attorney fees, witness fees, and other costs; requiring an expert affidavit or *certificate of merit* as a prerequisite to filing a claim; requiring a plaintiff to post a bond to initiate a claim; or permitting a defendant to file an affidavit of noninvolvement in the lawsuit, allowing expeditious dismissal from the case.

Clarification of Informed Consent Requirements   Disclosures required under the informed consent doctrine vary from state to state and frequently lack specificity, making compliance by health care providers difficult. Proponents of reform advocate legislation to clarify what and how much information providers must disclose to satisfy this requirement. This topic is further discussed in Chapter IV.

Itemization of Jury Verdicts   Common law verdicts are traditionally rendered in lump sums, although juries deliberate upon the individual components of a lawsuit, such as the plaintiff's past and future medical expenses, past and future income loss, past and future pain and suffering, or other nonpecuniary losses. Proponents of reform argue for itemization of amounts awarded in malpractice cases in the interest of encouraging realistic assessment of losses and more objective awards, as well as to permit more effective subsequent analysis of verdicts.

Limitations on Joint and Several Liability   Except where changed by state statute, the present law holds each defendant named in a lawsuit "jointly and severally liable," which means that each is responsible for paying the full cost of a plaintiff's award, regardless of the degree of participation or negligence. Under this system, the defendant with the most resources—or the one who in legal terminology is said to have the "deep pocket"—may bear the greatest share of the damage award, even though having had only a marginal role in causing the injury. This law has led to abusive litigation practices, such as "shotgun tactics," under which those with assets or insurance may be named as defendants in a lawsuit, although they have no readily apparent responsibility for the injury. The practice creates serious problems for insurers, who must project costs and determine the price of insurance. In addressing this problem, a number of states have passed comparative negligence legislation, which generally limits a defendant's responsibility to payment of that defendant's portion of the fault.

Limitations on Statutes of Limitations   Some states' statutes of limitations, or the closely related statutes of repose, permit a plaintiff significant time in which to initiate a suit, presenting major problems for insurers in establishing rates and reserves and for defendants in producing evidence and witnesses. These problems are compounded by the doctrines of discovery and continuing treatment, which may toll the statutes until injury is discovered, or reasonably should have been discovered, or until the patient is no longer under treatment. In some states, reforms of these statutes have been enacted, shortening the time in which a lawsuit must be filed after an injury occurs, is discovered, or should have been discovered. Analyses indicate that reducing statutes of limitations in this way effectively decreases the frequency of malpractice claims.

Limitations on Liability Placing caps on the amounts of awards, either by limiting the total amounts that may be recovered or, more commonly, *limiting awards for such noneconomic damages as pain and suffering* has been the most effective method in reducing the severity of claims, according to currently available data. A majority of states have passed legislation to limit the liability of health care providers and others. This legislation has been subjected to extensive constitutional challenge, and some statutes have been struck down. Others, however, have survived, including statutes presently in place in California, Indiana, and Louisiana.

Implementation of Periodic Payment Schedules Judgments and settlements in civil litigation, such as malpractice litigation, are traditionally awarded and paid in a lump sum. Proponents of reform advocate periodic or structured payments, which result in significant savings for defendants and insurers by reducing the total costs of awards, or by modifying an award if a plaintiff recovers from the injury or dies unexpectedly. From the claimant's point of view, the mechanism provides certainty of payment over a period of time and avoids the possibility of mismanagement of the initial lump sum.

Establishment of Practice Guidelines Legislation to establish the legal standard of care by statutory practice guidelines was initiated as a demonstration project by the state of Maine in 1991.[11,12,14] Statutory standards of care were established in four specialties: anesthesiology, emergency medicine, obstetrics and gynecology, and radiology. If a physician follows the standards, there may be little basis for litigation, since these practice parameters may be introduced as an affirmative defense in any malpractice litigation during the project period. The statute does not permit a plaintiff to introduce the parameters at any phase in the litigation process. An affirmative defense in this context means that when a physician follows the practice parameters, the physician has met the standard of care, and thus there can be no negligence and no damages recovered. It is expected that the legality of this approach will be challenged, and insurers are concerned that if the approach is found to be unconstitutional, they may be held liable retrospectively for claims arising from care provided by the physicians who used this defense. Initial results using practice guidelines for legal protection have been disappointing and have usually been inculpatory rather than exculpatory.[11,12,14]

Establishment of Pretrial Screening Panels Medical review panels for pretrial screening of claims are intended to discourage nonmeritorious claims and encourage the expeditious settlement of others. Proponents of screening hope that panel decisions will reduce the number of claims that go to trial. Opponents, however, argue that screening adds an additional and ineffective step to the already long scheduling delays and frequently provides only a dress rehearsal for the real trial. These opponents further contend that this step provides an opportunity for plaintiff attorneys to better educate themselves about the matters at issue and for plaintiffs to reap the benefit of inexpensive expert testimony. The opponents maintain that there is no evidence to date of the effectiveness of screening in reducing the frequency of claims, and that empirical evidence has not indicated that these panels produce additional or faster voluntary settlement of controversies.

Elimination of Punitive Damages Punitive or exemplary damages have been carried over from the criminal law into the law of torts. These damages may be awarded if a wrongdoer's acts have been deliberate, intentional, or otherwise outrageous. Such behavior is generally associated with crime and is seldom a component in the unintentional acts on which negligence actions are based. Proponents of reform contend that allegations of extreme behavior are frequently used inappropriately in liability cases as bargaining chips for settlement purposes and that review by institutions and provider licensing boards or resorting to the criminal justice system are more appropriate methods for resolving questions of gross professional misconduct. Opponents of reform emphasize the potential deterrent value of punitive damages and their role in reimbursing the actual expenses of litigation that are not otherwise recoverable by a plaintiff.

Prohibition or Clarification of the Res Ipsa Loquitur *Doctrine*

As previously noted in Chapter II, citation of this legal doctrine shifts the burden of proof from the plaintiff to the defendant, requiring the defendant to show that the injury did not result from the defendant's negligence. Although application of the doctrine was expanded in the early 1970s, it does not appear to be a major factor in malpractice litigation at the present time. The doctrine applies to injuries that ordinarily do not occur without negligence in situations where the defendant had exclusive control, and the plaintiff did not contribute to the injury. In malpractice claims, the doctrine is commonly used when a foreign object, such as an instrument or a sponge, has been left in a patient's body; for procedures on an inappropriate body part or on the wrong patient; for injuries, such as burns, to unaffected tissues; or for extreme deviations from routine procedures. Its application, however, places malpractice defendants at a disadvantage, inasmuch as medically caused injuries, sometimes difficult to account for, are not always the result of provider negligence. Reform legislation, passed by several states, may prohibit use of the doctrine, codify it, or otherwise clarify the circumstances under which it applies.

Establishment of Study Commissions for Professional Liability

The establishment of such bodies was a feature of tort reform efforts in a number of states. Study commissions were frequently appointed by the governor and typically are made up of insurance commissioners, legislators, providers, consumers, and others. As a general rule, study commissions were charged with reviewing and making recommendations on the professional liability situation in their states.

Other Reforms of Legal Rules   A number of other approaches to tort reform have at least been considered, including that a breach of contract must be documented by a written and properly executed document, that notice of the intent to sue be made a prerequisite to initiating litigation, and that expressions of humane concern by the defendant be inadmissible in the establishment of liability. Minimum rules for jury instructions regarding the standard of care also may be established or revised, and physicians' countersuits may be facilitated by eliminating the requirement that they must demonstrate that the physician was actually damaged as a result of the original suit.

One other recent proposal is "enterprise liability," or organizational liability, under which the individual hospital or other health care organization would be exclusively liable for all damages resulting from negligent treatment of patients by affiliated physicians.[13] Proponents of this concept emphasize the potential administrative simplicity in eliminating multiple defendants, the removal of physicians from the tort system, and the elimination to some extent of the need for individual insurance. On the other hand, critics point out that enterprises are expected to place surcharges on participating physicians in lieu of insurance premiums and that merely shifting the focus of liability while retaining court-based tort litigation leaves fundamental tort system problems uncorrected, replacing multiple defendants with the "deepest pocket." It is further feared that such an approach would subject physicians to increased regulation and enforcement measures by the responsible organizations and could have an unfavorable impact on claim frequency, claim severity, total malpractice costs, and the quality of care.

Tort Reform Results

Although in both the 1970s and 1980s, malpractice crises abated after each wave of reforms, the complex and cyclical nature of the malpractice problem, the variations in reform packages, and the lack of adequate data, make it difficult to evaluate the real effects of tort reforms. Nor are the specific effects of individual reforms easy to quantitate, a process further complicated by frequent challenges to the constitutionality of the various reforms, thus delaying their implementation or ultimately reversing them in a number of states. The results of available analyses are equivocal in indicating the effectiveness of various reforms or even suggest that many are ineffective in reducing the frequency and severity of claims. Additionally, specific reforms do not correlate with decreased insurance premiums.

Nevertheless, tort reforms do appear to have moderated and improved the malpractice climate, most visibly in California and Indiana, where legislative reforms have been implemented and subsequently upheld. That experience, the available analyses, and expert opinions all indicate that the three methods of reform appearing statistically to be most effective in reducing either the frequency or severity of claims are: *placing caps on awards, modifying the collateral source rule to reduce awards by amounts payable by collateral sources, and shortening statutes of limitations.* Although arbitration did appear in some studies to reduce the severity of claims, that fact may be due to an increase in frequency of small claims. The periodic payment of awards and elimination of joint and several liability are generally expected to decrease insurance costs and are otherwise beneficial and fair.

Although tort reform has mitigated the past malpractice crises, it is widely believed that a permanent solution of the medical malpractice problem will not occur within the tort system. The proponents of this view emphasize that application of tort law, even with reforms, is a lottery providing uneven compensation—overcompensation for a few and undercompensation or no compensation for a larger number. These proponents further maintain that the deterrent effect of tort law on unintentional negligent behavior is hypothetical and unconfirmed by data. They emphasize that the tort system is marked by slowness and delay, inefficiency, high litigation costs, as well as by hardship and emotional trauma to the parties involved in the adversarial process. On the other hand, advocates of the tort system, including interest groups and some scholars, continue to maintain that tort law and the tort system provide a fair and reasonable means to compensate the injured, deter negligent behavior, remove dangerous products from the market, and punish outrageous conduct. These advocates maintain that the tort system ensures a just and individualized process and guarantees all individuals their day in court. In their view, tort reforms ignore the injured patients, making recovery more difficult and diminishing awards when obtained.

Other Alternatives

The search for solution to the medical malpractice problem has so far concentrated on tort reform, including voluntary arbitration of medical malpractice claims, which is authorized by statute in 15 states and used by at least two major West Coast health care plans.

Because tort law litigation, even with reforms, appears incapable of yielding a permanent solution for the health care malpractice problem, arbitration and other ADR methods have been proposed. Available studies do indicate some advantages of arbitration in resolving such controversies, but several studies, summarized by the US General Accounting Office (GAO), do not indicate that arbitration significantly reduced the time for claim resolution, significantly reduced malpractice insurance costs, or slowed the rate of cost increases.[14-16] Other alternative solutions have therefore been proposed, including neo no-fault proposals (also termed "offer and recovery" elective no-fault, or guaranteed economic recovery); compensable event designation; and compensation systems, which would eliminate litigation and jury by establishing agencies outside the court system for claim resolution and injury compensation and that, in effect, incorporate mandatory binding arbitration into a structured institutionalized environment. Such administrative compensation systems may theoretically apply pure no-fault or may focus on medical error or nontort fault, as in the Swedish and New Zealand systems.[17,18]

Pure no-fault compensation of all adverse events is generally believed to be prohibitively expensive, as indicated in the California Medical Insurance Feasibility Study of 1974 hospitalizations,[19,20] which reported that only a small fraction of health care injuries are presently compensated. That study found that approximately 5 percent of hospital admissions involved iatrogenic injuries, 1 percent involved fault or negligence, less than 10 percent of injured patients filed claims, and only approximately 4 percent of injured patients obtained compensation under the tort system. The similar, but more comprehensive, Harvard Medical Practice Study of 1984 New York hospitalizations found that 3.2 to 4.2 percent of hospital admissions resulted in iatrogenic injury, 1 percent of injuries were fault related, one claim was filed per 7.6 adverse events, but only 1.5 percent (8 of 280) of negligent injuries in the study resulted in claims. The Harvard study also concluded, based on a number of assumptions, that pure no-fault compensation for iatrogenic injury might be economically feasible, although more claims would then be paid.[21-25]

A discussion of health care alternatives, other than tort reform and arbitration, follows. These alternatives generally either retain the tort system for some claims or replace tort litigation with administrative compensation for adverse events resulting from negligence, medical error, or nontort fault.

Neo No-Fault (Early Offer and Recovery System) This concept, formulated by Professor O'Connell of the University of Virginia, would give the alleged perpetrator of a tort the option of offering to pay the claimant's net economic loss and would, thereby, essentially foreclose tort litigation.[26] If the offer was not made or was unreasonable, tort litigation would remain an option. In the event a reasonable offer was made, but not accepted, changes in the burden of proof and other penalties would significantly decrease the chances of success in litigation. Among the objections to this concept are concerns that nonmeritorious claims might be encouraged, that frequency of claims and insurance costs might rise, that physicians would be faced with difficult decisions complicated by current requirements for reporting malpractice payments and settlements, and that tort litigation could still result in some circumstances.

Private Contracts Private contractual modification of substantive tort law and procedure to apply in potential disputes between patients and providers has been advocated by Professor

Havighurst of Duke University.[27] Such contracts are presently being used to provide for mandatory binding arbitration and to limit noneconomic damages in some health care plans. Other possibilities might be defining the standard of care, specifying appropriate credentials for expert witnesses, or mandating impartial experts in the event of a legal controversy. Another option might be to redefine liability using gross negligence, rather than ordinary negligence, as the standard.

However, the feasibility of this approach for general application to substantive law is not now apparent, although its use may increase with the development of managed care organizations. Concerns include the complexity of the malpractice problem, the potential of litigation to determine the scope and application of such contracts, and the probability of tort litigation if contracts are subsequently invalidated.

Designated Compensable Events   The enumeration and scheduling of specific adverse outcomes or events for compensation, initially introduced as medical adversity insurance, has been proposed by some legal scholars.[28] Such events would be compensated without a determination of fault, establishing a no-fault system to the extent of the events listed in the schedules. This no-fault approach has been advocated by Dr. Barry Manuel, whose "No-Fault Patient Compensation Model" has been introduced into the Massachusetts legislature several times.[29] Limited trials of this alternative are in progress under the National Vaccine Injury Compensation Program (1986), the Virginia Birth Related Neurological Injury Compensation Act (1987), and the Florida Injured Infants Plan (1988). This partial no-fault approach under the tort system provides significant advantages because of its departure from tort law and court-based litigation. Some adverse events would be removed from the litigation process and compensation expedited, but others not listed, not clearly identified, or under a plaintiff's option, would remain to be litigated.

Administrative Alternative Revising Tort   A fault-based administrative alternative proposal has been developed and published by the AMA/Specialty Society Medical Liability

Project.[30,31] This administrative compensation system is based on codified tort law and would eliminate the litigation process and the jury. A seven-member medical board, assisted by claim reviewers and hearing examiners, would expeditiously evaluate claims. The medical board would supply an attorney to assist the claimant for claims approved by examiners, and claimants would also be able to retain personal attorneys. Limited court appeal to the state court system would be possible. The medical board would also have disciplinary power, such as currently vested in state licensing authorities. Cost controls include the limitation of noneconomic losses, offset of collateral source payments, periodic payments of some awards, and elimination of joint and several liability. Economic and constitutional evaluations appear favorable. Disadvantages include the requirement of establishing individual fault or negligence as a prerequisite to compensation; the actual adoption of codified tort law, including a liberalized definition of negligence; and the expanded power of the medical board in the area of practice standards, physician performance, and provider discipline.

Administrative System Replacing Tort A Model Medical Accident Compensation System was developed by the Midwest Institute for Health Care and Law and published in 1988. It was introduced into the Kansas legislature in the 1989–1990 session.[8,10,32,33]

The proposed administrative system is based on Kansas Workers' Compensation Law, but is adaptable to any jurisdiction. The system is fault-based in retaining the concept of medical error or deviation from the standard of care, but requires no determination of individual fault or negligence. The framework includes a full-time three-member board, assisted by administrative law judges, expert review panels, the state court system for limited appeal, a quality review section, and a database section. The system eliminates the litigation process and the jury, as well as tort law and tort terminology. Benefits are based on actual or constructed earnings, with limitations on total payments as in workers' compensation. Cost controls include payment only for medical care, rehabilitation, and other economic loss; elimination of punitive damages; structured attorney fees; collateral source offset; reasonable statutes of limitations; periodic payment of awards; modification and termination of benefits, with changes in the status of beneficiaries; and elimination of joint and several liability. The economic evaluation of this system is favorable compared with the costs of the tort system. Constitutional evaluation is also favorable, because liberal construction and expeditious compensation of a larger number of injuries would supply the quid pro quo for replacing tort. Disadvantages of the system are largely related to the restrictive benefits of Kansas Workers' Compensation Law and can be modified, if desired.

Summary and Conclusions

The search for a solution to the medical malpractice problem has emphasized the need for change in the present court-based tort law litigation process for resolving claims. Available options fall between two unsatisfactory solutions: retaining the traditional tort system for all claims and replacing tort litigation with administrative no-fault compensation for all adverse events. Even though a recent study has suggested the economic feasibility of such no-fault compensation, one must question the desirability of compensating all adverse events, unless funding by new insurance methods can be developed. Tort reform and other intermediate options, which revise the tort system in varying degrees, are unlikely to result in permanent solution of the malpractice problem. The intermediate solutions, each of which revise tort to some degree, present advantages in that they depart from tort law and court-based litigation. The net benefit of such partial solutions, however, is diminished by the degree to which a dual system, part tort-part revision, retains the undesirable features of the current claim resolution process. For health care, the new ADR horizon may be administrative/agency compensation[34] in a system that removes prevention and compensation of health care injuries entirely from the law of torts, from the jury, and from court-based litigation.

117

Chapter II References

1. National Practitioner Data Bank Guidebook: US Department of Health and Human Service, Public Health Service, HRSA, Rockville, MD, Pub. No. HRSA-95-255

2. Oshel RE, Croft TE, Rodack J Jr.: The National Practitioner Data Bank: The first four years. Pub Hlth Rep, 110(4):383–394; 1995

3. Office of Inspector General, US Dept of Health and Human Services. National Practitioner Data Bank: Usefulness and Impact of Reports to Hospitals. Washington, DC: US Dept of Health and Human Services, 1993

4. Office of Inspector General, US Dept of Health and Human Services. National Practitioner Data Bank: Usefulness and Impact of Reports to State Licensing Boards. Washington, DC: US Dept of Health and Human Services, 5, 1993

5. Bovbjerg RR, Petronis KR: The relationship between physicians' malpractice claims history and later claims: Does the past predict the future? JAMA, 272(18):1421–1426, 1994

6. Smarr LE: Commentary malpractice claims: Does the past predict the future? JAMA, 272(18):1453, 1994

7. The Federation of State Medical Boards of the United States, Inc., 1995–1996, Exchange: Section 3: Licensing Boards, Structure and Disciplinary Functions

8. Halley MM, Fowks RJ, Bigler FC, Ryan DL (eds): Medical Malpractice Solutions: Systems and Proposals for Injury Compensation. Charles C Thomas, Springfield, IL, 1989

9. Spencer FC, Halley MM: The harmful effects of the "bad doctor" myth. Bull Am Coll Surg 75(6):6–12, 1990

10. Halley MM: Towards a solution to the malpractice problem. Surg Oncol Clin North Am 3(1):173–192, 1994

11. Morton J, "The Maine Demonstration Project: Using practice parameters as an affirmative defense, Bull Am Coll Surg 80(8): 30–33, 1995

12. Hyams JD, et al: Report to Physician Payment Review Commission: Practice Guidelines and Malpractice Litigation, Harvard School of Public Health, Boston, MA, January 25, 1994

13. Weiler PC: Medical Malpractice on Trial. Harvard University Press, Cambridge, MA, 1991

14. US General Accounting Office: Medical Malpractice: Alternatives to Litigation. Washington, DC, January 1992

15. US General Accounting Office: Medical Malpractice: Few Claims Resolved Through Michigan's Voluntary Arbitration Program. Washington, DC, December 1990

16. US General Accounting Office: Medical Malpractice: No Agreement on Problems or Solutions. Washington, DC, February 1986

17. Brahams D: The Swedish and Finnish patient insurance schemes. In Halley MM, Fowks RJ, Bigler FC, Ryan DL (eds): Medical Malpractice Solutions: Systems and Proposals for Injury Compensation. Charles C Thomas, Springfield, IL, 1989

18. Woodhouse Sir Owen: The New Zealand experience. In Halley MM, Fowks RJ, Bigler FC, Ryan DL (eds): Medical Malpractice Solutions: Systems and Proposals for Injury Compensation. Charles C Thomas, Springfield, IL, 1989

19. Mills DH: Report on the Medical Insurance Feasibility Study. Sutter Publications, Inc, San Francisco, CA, 1977

20. Mills DH: The case for and against pure no-fault. In Halley MM, Fowks RJ, Bigler FC, Ryan DL (eds): Medical Malpractice Solutions: Systems and Proposals for Injury Compensation. Charles C Thomas, Springfield, IL, 1989

21. Harvard Medical Practice Study Group: Patients, Doctors, and Lawyers: Medical Injury, Malpractice Litigation, and Patient Compensation in New York. Harvard University, Cambridge, MA, 1990

22. Brennan TA, et al: Incidence of adverse events and negligence in hospitalized patients. Results of the Harvard Medical Practice Study I. N Engl J Med 324:370–376, 1991

23. Leape LL, et al: The nature of adverse events in hospitalized patients. Results of the Harvard Medical Practice Study II. N Engl J Med 324:377–384, 1991

24. Localio AR, et al: Relation between malpractice claims and adverse events due to negligence. Results of the Harvard Medical Practice Study III). N Engl J Med 325:245–251, 1991

25. Johnson WG, et al: The economic consequences of medical injuries (implications for a no-fault insurance plan). JAMA 267(18)2487–2492, 1992

26. O'Connell JO: Neo no-fault reform: Settling for economic losses. In Halley MM, Fowks RJ, Bigler FC, Ryan DL (eds): Medical Malpractice Solutions: Systems and Proposals for Injury Compensation. Charles C Thomas, Springfield, IL, 1989

27. Havighurst CC: Malpractice reform: Getting there by private vehicle. In Halley MM, Fowks RJ, Bigler FC, Ryan DL (eds): Medical Malpractice Solutions: Systems and Proposals for Injury Compensation. Charles C Thomas, Springfield, IL, 1989

28. Tancredi LR: Designated compensable events. In Halley MM, Fowks RJ, Bigler FC, Ryan DL (eds): Medical Malpractice Solutions: Systems and Proposals for Injury Compensation. Charles C Thomas, Springfield, IL, 1989

29. Manuel BM: Is tort reform the answer? An alternative approach to end the malpractice crises. Mass Med 2:42, 1987

30. American Medical Association/Special Society Medical Liability Project: A Proposed Alternative to the Civil Justice System for Resolving Medical Liability Disputes. A Fault-Based Administrative System. American Medical Association/Specialty Society Medical Liability Project, January 1988

31. Todd JS, Hatlie MJ: The model medical liability and patient protection act. In Halley MM, Fowks RJ, Bigler FC, Ryan DL (eds): Medical Malpractice Solutions: Systems and Proposals for Injury Compensation. Charles C Thomas, Springfield, IL, 1989

32. Halley MM, et al: A medical accident compensation system: A model act. Kansas Med 89:259–282, 1988

33. Halley MM, et al: The model medical accident compensation act, part I and part II. In Halley MM, Fowks RJ, Bigler FC, Ryan DL (eds): Medical Malpractice Solutions: Systems and Proposals for Injury Compensation. Charles C Thomas, Springfield, IL, 1989

34. Halley MM: Alternative dispute resolution: The new horizon. Bull Am Coll Surg 77(3):21–26, 1992

III / RISK FINANCING

Editor's Note

Risk financing (insurance) continues to be a necessary part of most business endeavors in both the private and public sectors. Conceptually, the desirability of being insured stems from the need to protect a health care provider of surgical services from the risk of financial disaster in the event that injuries occur to a recipient of those goods or services.

Medical malpractice liability insurance provides those of us in the medical profession with just such a safety net. The changing nature of the practice of medicine today, particularly with regard to the sometimes unrealistic expectations of society, the rapid development of new technology, and the excesses of our legal system have forced surgeons to become knowledgeable in the area of medical malpractice insurance.

This chapter describes the evolution of the insurance system and the factors the surgeon should consider in selecting coverage. Additional mechanisms through which a surgeon can gain coverage, such as risk retention groups, joint underwriting associations (JUAs), and patient compensation funds (PCFs), are also described in detail. The forms of coverage, such as claims-made versus occurrence policies, are also explained. Finally, the special needs of residents with regard to insurance are also discussed.

Risk Financing

In the two decades from 1975 to 1995, ever-increasing claim costs resulted in dramatic increases in the cost of medical liability insurance. Premiums for most surgeons reached extraordinary levels and became a major portion of a physician's overhead. Although costs have varied at different rates in the past decade, the possibility of "runaway" verdicts continues to haunt the profession, underscoring the need for careful selection of insurance protection. Despite the moderation in the cost of insurance, it must be clearly understood that the frequency of claims and the severity of individual claims have continued to rise, though at a lower rate than had been predicted in the past.

The availability of insurance coverage is no longer a problem. In fact, in many states, surgeons have a choice of several carriers. The purchase of medical liability coverage is not without pitfalls, however, and a physician should have a clear understanding of the options that are available in order to make an informed and intelligent decision. Predatory pricing and the sudden appearance of premiums that vary greatly from those of established carriers should be viewed with great suspicion, especially in view of current low interest rates and the very real possibility that we may be entering a new cycle of escalating frequency and severity. In the past, loss trends across the country have been cyclical.

Differences in cost between the carriers may make the decision appear to be an easy one, but decisions about insurance coverage should never be based on cost alone. The financial security of the insurance company, the policyholder's access to state *guaranty funds* in the event of the company's insolvency, the commitment of the company to medical liability insurance, its philosophy about and disposition to resisting groundless claims, and whether the policy provides assurance that no case will be settled without the physician's consent are equally important considerations.

Insurance Carriers

Physician-owned insurance companies provide more than 60 percent of the coverage required by private practitioners in the United States, covering 177,000 physicians in 40 states. For the most part, these companies were started by state medical societies in 1975 and 1976, when the commercial insurance industry was largely abandoning the medical liability market. Although these companies may differ in organizational form, they all are owned and managed by physicians. With only a few exceptions, they are not in business to make a profit, typically use investment income to reduce premiums and sponsor risk management programs, and emphasize peer review among those they insure. The use of investment income to reduce premiums is very important because a 1 percent increase in investment income can result in as much as a 10 percent decrease in premiums. A disturbing recent trend with physician-owned companies is their efforts to reach into other states with different insurance mechanisms such as risk retention groups. This expansion may well lead to costly and poorly conceived infighting, which will not be in anyone's best interests and has the potential to leave policyholders without coverage that they believed to be present and had purchased.

Among commercial insurance companies that still are in the medical liability market, the St. Paul Insurance Company is the largest in terms of premium volume. Other commercial carriers tend to confine their medical liability business to a few states or, perhaps, to one specialty group.

As a result of the availability crisis of 1975, many states now require property and casualty insurance companies to share the medical liability risk through the formation of joint underwriting associations (JUAs). Over time, as the number of physician-sponsored companies has increased, these JUAs have come to be regarded primarily as a secondary resource, available to physicians who do not want to, or cannot, purchase insurance from other carriers. The JUAs do, however, remain the only source of insurance coverage in some states, including Massachusetts and Rhode Island.

So-called channeling programs also exist in several states. These programs provide for the coverage of a physician under the insurance of the hospital with which he or she is affiliated and share the limits of coverage with that hospital or perhaps with several hospitals. A physician-owned company may provide coverage for hospitals, and those physicians who have one of those hospitals as their primary affiliation may obtain a premium discount under a joint defense program.

In 1986, federal legislation permitted the formation of *risk retention,* or purchasing, groups to provide nationwide coverage for affiliated groups. Once licensed in one state, the insurance entity that provides this coverage can write insurance in all other states, without conforming to the normal regulatory requirements of those states. It should be noted, however, that state guaranty funds will not protect policyholders if such a company becomes insolvent.

Physicians whose claims experience is so adverse that they are unable to obtain coverage within their own state may seek coverage through so-called surplus line companies. However, these companies are not licensed by the state, and their premiums are significantly higher than state-regulated premiums.

Patient compensation funds (PCFs) also have been established in several states. These funds provide coverage for providers above a basic minimum of insurance purchased by physicians and hospitals. To participate in a PCF, insured physicians are required by the state to pay a special contribution in addition to their basic coverage. In Pennsylvania, for example, physicians must buy insurance coverage of $200,000 to $600,000, then pay a percentage of their premium (at this writing, 50 percent) to the fund, which provides an additional $1 million to $3 million in coverage. In Indiana, physicians are insured for $100,000 to $300,000, and the fund provides coverage of up to $750,000, the statutory limit on liability awards.

Limits of Coverage

In most states, the limits on primary coverage are $1 million for each occurrence and $3 million in the aggregate for all occurrences within the period the policy remains in effect, although insurers in several states offer single limits of $5 million (the limit may go as high as $10 million in a few states). Many hospitals require specified limits of protection as a condition of staff privileges, and this requirement has consistently withstood legal challenge. Hospital medical staffs also now frequently establish requirements for basic levels of coverage independently from their hospitals.

Although the high-risk surgical specialties of neurosurgery, obstetrics/gynecology, and orthopaedic surgery have the greatest exposure to costly settlements, *all* physicians, including those who are not surgeons, run the risk of very large verdicts. Therefore, each physician should determine the limits of coverage he or she requires based on consideration of all relevant circumstances and after careful deliberation and consultation with the physician's insurance broker, carrier, and, perhaps, personal counsel.

Forms of Coverage

In theory, physicians may purchase one of two available forms of insurance coverage: *occurrence* or *claims-made*. Occurrence policies provide coverage for all incidents that occur during the period covered by the policy, no matter when they come to light. Claims-made policies cover only those incidents that occur *and are reported* during the policy period. The initial cost of claims-made coverage is deceptively less expensive than occurrence coverage. In fact, because only about one-third of the incidents that occur in a given year are actually reported in that year, the charge for claims-made coverage in the first year will be only about one-third of the occurrence rate. Subsequently, usually in five to six years, claims-made rates rise significantly and eventually equal the occurrence rate. Thus, a mature claims-made policy may cost more than an occurrence policy. In addition, once a claims-made policy is canceled, physicians must have protection for incidents that occurred while the policy was in force, but which do not come to light until after cancellation. This protection is referred to as reporting endorsement coverage, or, more popularly, *tail coverage*. This coverage must be purchased at the time the claims-made policy expires and, in effect, converts a claims-made into an occurrence policy.

Physicians who purchase claims-made policies also need to be aware of policy terms related to the reporting endorsement. Most carriers provide an automatic, or free, reporting endorsement under certain circumstances, such as the death or disability of the policyholder or the retirement of the policyholder from medical practice after having been in the company's claims-made program for a specified number of years or having reached a specified retirement age. Unfortunately, a physician who finds it necessary to cancel a claims-made policy, because of a move to another state or a change in the nature of the physician's practice, will find the purchase of a reporting endorsement very expensive. For example, a physician in New York in the third year of a claims-made cycle would pay almost one-and-one-half times the present occurrence rate to purchase a reporting endorsement. Physicians considering entering a partnership or employment arrangement should be aware of this risk and clearly establish who will bear the cost of buying a reporting endorsement, should one become necessary.

As a practical matter, however, a physician's options may, in fact, be more limited than this discussion would suggest, inasmuch as many companies now offer only claims-made coverage.

Special Needs of Residents

Most residents are aware of the dangers of professional liability suits and the effect that threat has had on the practice of their specialty, but residents face other professional liability issues related to malpractice or risk management of which they may not be aware. Although less well recognized, these insurance issues can nonetheless have a significant impact on the resident's future ability to practice medicine.

Most residents assume that professional liability insurance will be provided for them by their residency programs. However, a resident needs to know more than simply whether liability insurance is provided. Other, perhaps more crucial, questions should be asked.

What type of coverage is provided by the program? Will claims arising out of the residency be covered if they are made after the resident leaves the program? As the preceding discussion indicates, occurrence coverage protects the resident for all claims resulting from the period of the policy, regardless of when the claim is made. Thus, a resident covered by an occurrence policy would be protected by all malpractice claims arising from the residency, even if, for example, a claim for an impaired infant arising out of an obstetrics residency were made years after the residency were completed.

In contrast, if the resident is covered by a claims-made policy, the insurance company has no obligation to cover claims made after the policy expires, and the resident is protected after leaving the residency program only if tail coverage has been purchased.

Residency programs throughout the United States are likely to provide either occurrence coverage or claims-made coverage for their residents; seldom do they offer both. Because the residency employment contract may not include information about professional liability insurance, a resident should make every effort to obtain and keep copies of the program's master professional liability insurance policy, as well as a written statement or certificate of the coverage provided.

In addition, recognizing that claims can be made years after a residency is completed and that some residency programs and insurance companies periodically purge their files, residents should obtain evidence of insurance for each year of their residency and retain this evidence in their files indefinitely.

Equally important, those who are covered by a claims-made policy should be sure that tail coverage is provided upon the completion of the residency, lest they find themselves with no coverage for claims made after the residency ends.

How much coverage is provided for the resident by the program is another important matter to determine, inasmuch as the coverage provided by some programs may be limited to a certain amount per incident and a certain aggregate amount. In some states, residents' liability is limited by statute or by treating residents as state employees. Other states have established PCFs that reduce the amount of primary insurance that is needed by a resident. Thus, it is impossible to generalize about what constitutes an inadequate amount of insurance for a resident. The question is further complicated by the fact that residents have little power to negotiate for greater amounts of coverage. Nonetheless, every resident should know the limits of his or her coverage and the requirements and special circumstances of the state in which the residency takes place.

Does the policy place any limitations on practice? Most residency liability policies are subject to certain restrictions or exclusions, and residents should be aware of them, because liability coverage will not be provided for claims resulting from activities that violate them.

The most common of these exclusions is for moonlighting activities—that is, events that may occur while the resident is practicing at a second job in another hospital. In general, the practice of moonlighting is not recommended, and residents should be discouraged from engaging in it for a variety of reasons. For one thing, few residency liability insurance policies provide coverage for these activities; therefore, residents who choose to moonlight would be well advised to investigate whether the second institution provides insurance coverage. If coverage is not provided, the resident must either obtain appropriate coverage personally or run the risk of being uninsured for any claims that could result.

What effect would a claim have on the resident's future ability to obtain liability insurance? Even residents whose coverage ensures that adequate amounts will be available to cover all claims resulting from the residency should be aware of an insurance practice known as surcharging or experience rating. Insurers frequently set higher premium rates on claim experience, either in the form of a surcharge in addition to the basic premium or a higher basic premium. Bowing to consumer demands and the belief that the malpractice crisis has been caused by a small number of so-called bad physicians, some insurance companies and state insurance commissions have applied these rating practices to malpractice insurance.

Because it is not uncommon for a plaintiff's attorney to file suit against all health care providers whose names appear in a plaintiff's medical chart, including all residents, a physician who has experienced a number of malpractice claims during residency should investigate the surcharging or experience rating practices of prospective insurance carriers and states prior to entering private practice. Neglecting to do so may mean finding that malpractice insurance is either unavailable or prohibitively expensive.

The entire issue of coverage for residents is worth careful thought, but should not be viewed with excessive alarm, because residents are not usually held to have the primary responsibility in a given case. Paying careful attention to your hospital's rules and regulations, promptly seeking consultation when appropriate, and cooperating with the risk management office are your best defense against adverse decisions.

An Additional Word of Advice

This treatment of the subject of medical liability insurance must, of necessity, be general in nature and is intended only to make the reader aware of the issues that should be considered in making intelligent decisions. Specific circumstances will, of course, vary from individual to individual and from state to state. Therefore, seeking the advice of the state medical society or local chapter of the American College of Surgeons is strongly recommended to those making choices involving liability insurance.

IV / RISK PREVENTION

Editor's Note

The cornerstone of risk prevention is the surgeon's technical and intellectual competence, which is an important and implied consideration in any discussion of this topic. Another very important factor is the development and maintenance of a good surgeon-patient relationship. This chapter discusses ways in which the surgeon can strengthen this relationship and minimize the possibility of litigation if there is an adverse patient occurrence.

The process of informed consent is explained in detail. Various aids that can be used to ensure that the process is appropriate and that the patient is truly informed are described.

The importance of providing adequate documentation is clearly and concisely outlined. In addition, certain guidelines that must be observed, particularly when an adverse event occurs in caring for a patient, are explained.

In an effort to help surgeons minimize the occurrence of missed communications, specific documentation systems that should be used in either the surgeon's office or in an ambulatory surgery center are outlined in detail.

The role of risk prevention as it relates to the department of surgery is discussed. Two major activities that are essential in minimizing risk in the department of surgery are credentialing and ongoing monitoring of patient care. Both are described in detail. The importance of clinical pathways, a modification of critical pathways used in industry, is presented. The use of the clinical pathways in

137

improving quality is thought to be a useful tool, in addition to being a cost-effective mechanism.

Finally, the special position that the resident occupies in the dynamics of quality assurance and risk management, and his or her role in the department in that regard, are discussed.

Surgeon-Patient Relationship

Patient confidence is essential to a satisfactory surgeon-patient relationship, and that confidence is likely to be directly linked to the patient's belief that the surgeon is competent, caring, compassionate, and concerned about the patient's outcome. Indeed, we can perform everything optimally in a given case yet have a less-than-desired outcome just as we can have a good outcome even though every decision during the course of the surgical illness may be less than optimal.

In the course of surgical care, adverse events are bound to happen. The Harvard Medical Practice Study in New York State estimated these adverse events to occur in 3.7 percent of hospital admissions. The majority of these adverse events (2.7 percent of hospital admissions) were not due to negligent care. Even though most adverse events are not the result of negligence, in our litigious society, surgeons must relate to patients in a manner that leads to a patient-physician cooperative interaction. Communication is the foundation upon which cooperative interaction is built.

In this process, family members of the patient are a potential hazard to the surgeon-patient relationship. Lacking assurance that the surgeon is concerned about the patient's outcome, family members can contribute to the patient's anxiety or suspicion, and the surgeon who is not aware of the importance of family concerns increases the risk of introducing a negative, or even adversarial, aspect to the relationship.

The task is not made easier by the fact that the surgeon does not always enjoy the benefits of an orderly, planned encounter. Indeed, the surgeon's first contact with the patient is as likely to occur in an emergency situation, in which the patient is unconscious or otherwise unreceptive, as it is in the course of a routine office visit. Whatever the circumstances of the encounter, it is imperative that the surgeon take care to communicate calmness and competence. To the patient or family member who is already experiencing the stress that is likely to be associated with the circumstances that necessitate the encounter, any careless word or gesture could be the one that triggers the erosion of the delicate surgeon-patient relationship. Therefore, every encounter with the patient, no matter how seemingly insignificant, warrants thoughtful assessment of its potential impact on that relationship.

The Office Visit

A patient's first contact with a surgeon frequently is through the receptionist who answers the surgeon's office telephone. The impression the patient receives in that encounter can set the tone for the relationship that is to follow. Politeness, of course, is absolutely essential, as is a tone of voice that engenders confidence. Any hint of impatience, disorganization, or flippancy must be scrupulously avoided.

In scheduling an appointment, the receptionist must be trained and prepared with appropriate questions to determine the patient's problem and realistically estimate the amount of time the patient will require. To facilitate information-gathering during the initial visit, the patient should be instructed to bring to the office all medications that he or she may be taking, as well as any laboratory reports and X rays related to the reason for the visit. The patient also should be asked to arrive 15 minutes prior to the first visit to allow time to complete registration forms.

Patients arriving at a surgeon's office for the first time are frequently ill and almost invariably anxious. When a person is in that state of mind, little is more disconcerting than the sight of an office reception area overflowing with waiting patients. Being required to wait beyond the appointed time to see the surgeon is almost certain to aggravate any negative feelings with which the patient is already grappling. Therefore, it is essential, to the greatest degree possible, that appointments be kept on schedule.

When delays are unavoidable—and every surgeon encounters such delays—every effort should be made to contact patients by telephone prior to their arrival to reschedule their appointments. When that is not possible and a patient has been kept waiting, taking time to *personally apologize* for the patient's inconvenience and explain the reason for the delay can go a long way toward defusing any resentment the patient understandably may feel. Doing so will, at the same time, avoid giving the appearance of arrogance that busy surgeons may too often inadvertently convey.

Of course, any patient who arrives with fresh lacerations or injury should be seen without delay, leaving the details of registration and identification to be dealt with after the urgency of the situation has been addressed. Delays in responding to a patient's urgent needs are as bad for good patient relations as they are for good patient care.

Once the consultation begins, the patient expects and should receive the surgeon's undivided attention. Taking steps to ensure that telephone calls and other potential sources of interruption are not allowed to interfere with the process is one tangible way to demonstrate the surgeon's genuine concern about the patient.

Beginning the consultation with a detailed history-taking can enhance that demonstration of concern. Any medical problem the patient has encountered, past or present, is important to that patient, and failing to provide an opportunity to talk about it can leave the patient with the impression that the surgeon is unconcerned or the consultation incomplete. This discussion also affords the surgeon the opportunity to communicate to the patient, through vocal intonation and body language, the attitude of concerned, reasoned, friendly, and professional interest that the surgeon should seek to convey. It is very important that the surgeon have good listening skills. As an initial step in the information-gathering process, the history-taking can also provide a logical introduction to the physical evaluation, thereby easing the transition to what can be a stressful experience for the patient.

Once the history-taking and physical examination have been completed, it is time for the surgeon to make treatment recommendations, recommendations that often will involve an operation. First, however, the patient must be advised of all the options that are available, including the option of relying on observation only. The surgeon's goal at this point should be to promote discussion of the available options with the patient, rather than to dictate a decision or press for one point of view.

Indeed, any indication of confusion or uncertainty on the part of the patient or family member should be a signal to the surgeon to proceed cautiously in asking for a decision. The importance of obtaining informed consent for any surgical procedure cannot be emphasized enough. The issue of whether or not consent was truly informed may subsequently be open to challenge if any question arises that the consenting party was under duress to make a decision.

Preparing Patients for an Operation

Helping the patient who elects to undergo a surgical procedure understand and deal with the implications of that decision affords the surgeon another opportunity to communicate caring and concern. Having an operation is likely to be a frightening prospect for many patients. Helping them understand and deal with their apprehensions is an excellent way to establish trust between patient and surgeon, creating a climate of understanding and cooperation, rather than one of fear and resistance.

The surgeon also can make an important contribution in helping the patient prepare for hospitalization. Because many patients are reluctant to confess ignorance of hospital procedures, the surgeon must assume responsibility for describing each event that is likely to occur, including the admitting process, laboratory tests, and the preoperative visits of nurses, anesthesiologists, or other consultants, as well as for discussing such matters as what medications the patient may be given and why they are required. No other source of information, no matter how informative and valuable, is likely to be as reassuring to the patient as a personal explanation by the surgeon. Similarly, while skilled assistants may provide information to patients that reinforces the information they receive from the surgeon, assistants should be viewed as supplements in the information process and never as substitutes for the surgeon.

Asking the patient to designate a spouse, parent, or other person to communicate with the surgeon on the patient's behalf in the immediate postoperative period is another way to provide support to the patient while strengthening the surgeon-patient relationship. The presence of loved ones often is seen as crucial to the patient's comfort and successful recovery. The experience is likely to be a far more positive one for all concerned if family members or concerned friends are briefed on such matters as when the patient will be taken to the surgical suite, how long the operation is likely to take, and where the surgeon will meet with them after completing the operation. Providing a detailed discussion of the outcome of the procedure as soon as it is completed in language that a layperson can understand is, of course, essential to nurturing trust.

The Postoperative Period

The period following the operation affords additional opportunities for establishing trust. With third-party payors now often mandating the number of days a patient can be hospitalized, many surgical patients are discharged sooner than in previous times. In addition, some procedures that once would have been performed while the patient was hospitalized are now performed on an outpatient basis. Thus, it is not uncommon for a patient to experience some event at home after an operation that nursing care might have resolved if the patient were hospitalized. In that event, patients are likely to seek the surgeon's advice. The frustration a patient can experience by having to deal with an impersonal answering service can quickly turn to anger, and that anger can undermine whatever rapport existed between surgeon and patient. Thus, simply remaining available throughout the postoperative period to answer questions and to provide assurance may be as important to a positive outcome as postoperative care itself.

Postoperatively, a pattern of consistency should be established. The surgeon represents the patient's security—an anchor at a time of pain and suffering. The patient should be better acquainted with his or her surgeon than with those on the surgical floor who care for the patient. Postoperative rounds should be made regularly, and, if possible, rounds should not be delegated to others. The patient has hired the surgeon. If all goes well, the patient may simply wonder at the surgeon's decreased attention once the surgical procedure has been completed, but any adverse event may lead the patient to ask if the complication could have been avoided if the physician had been more attentive after the operation.

The patient or the patient's family should not be abandoned when the outcome is poor. At these times, it is even more important to foster compassionate communication between physician and patient.[1] The surgeon should be available to address a patient's problem and plans for treatment.

Surgeon's Rights

The surgeon, while addressing the rights of the patient, is also entitled to certain rights, such as the right to restrict the scope of specialty practice. If required treatment is beyond his or her specialty, the surgeon has the obligation to refer the patient to an appropriate specialist. The surgeon also has the right to limit practice to a certain geographic area or community; to be unavailable, provided that a competent substitute has been designated; to determine the time and frequency of appointments; to refuse to make house calls; and to refuse a request for what may be considered a less appropriate method of treatment.

Consent and the Process of Informed Consent

Informed consent is a consent obtained after adequate disclosure.[2] What defines adequate disclosure differs throughout the United States. Because obtaining consent is so important, every surgeon, with the help of the state medical society, ACS chapters, or private counsel, should identify the consent requirements that apply in the state in which the surgeon practices and take steps to ensure that the surgeon's practice complies with those requirements. However, it is almost universally agreed that the patient should be given pertinent information about the proposed treatment in each of the following categories: (1) the diagnosis, (2) the nature and purpose of the proposed treatment, (3) the prognosis if the proposed treatment is carried out, (4) the risks associated with the proposed treatment, (5) the feasible treatment alternatives (as well as the likelihood of success and the risks associated with each), and (6) the prognosis if the treatment is refused.

The process of obtaining informed consent should not be viewed as just signing a consent sheet. Ideally, the process of consent starts when the patient and surgeon first meet to discuss a problem. The surgeon-patient relationship stressed in the previous section is important. Consent is a continuing education process that results in a joint decision to pursue a specific treatment plan. Both participants—the surgeon and the patient—are on the same team battling the same enemy: disease or disability. Both hope for the best result, but neither has unrealistic expectations. The

145

signing of the consent form is merely a formality, signifying that the goal of full disclosure has been accomplished.

Some physicians mistakenly believe that the process of informed consent is necessary only for surgical and other invasive procedures. In fact, informed consent is required for all treatment, whether therapeutic or diagnostic, invasive or noninvasive, surgical or medical. Therefore, whatever the recommended treatment, a frank discussion between surgeon and patient about treatment alternatives may be necessary, even in the event that no treatment is recommended.

Failure to obtain a patient's informed consent is legally excused in only three instances.

First, obtaining informed consent is excused when a legitimate medical emergency necessitates immediate treatment, but the patient is unable to give consent and no one who is authorized to consent on behalf of the patient is readily available. In such an event, the surgeon should document the nature of the emergency and the need for immediate treatment, obtain a consultation to confirm that a medical emergency exists, note the reasons why the patient could not give consent, and record the efforts made to locate and obtain the consent from the patient's next of kin.

Second, informed consent is also legally excused when therapeutic privilege to withhold information is applicable. However, surgeons would be well advised not to rely on therapeutic privilege because the courts have been reluctant to apply it. Therefore, the surgeon who is absolutely convinced that frank disclosure would interfere with treatment must take extreme care to document the reasons for that opinion, obtain a consulting opinion confirming the reasonableness of the conclusion, and communicate with the patient's next of kin. In making disclosure to the next of kin, surgeons should carefully consider the patient's rights to confidentiality and privacy.

Third, some patients do not want to be informed about such matters as the risks and complications of a surgical procedure or its prognosis. In that event, it is essential to obtain the patient's signature on a written statement of that fact.

146

To meet informed consent requirements, discussion of the risks and benefits and alternatives to a treatment must take place before the treatment is rendered. More importantly, the discussion must take place before the patient signs a consent form. By signing the consent form, the patient acknowledges that the necessary information has been conveyed and, where required by state law, that the patient has had adequate opportunity to ask questions and have them answered in a satisfactory manner.

For a number of reasons, the surgeon's office is the ideal setting in which to hold a discussion of and obtain consent for operation. Obtaining consent and initiating treatment at two different times is more likely to enable the patient to adequately consider his or her decision, thus reducing the risk that a question subsequently may arise regarding whether the patient was pressured to proceed with treatment or given insufficient time in which to consider relevant information. In addition, the surgeon retains greater control over the circumstances in which the consent is obtained and therefore should be better able to implement protocols to ensure adequate disclosure and documentation of the process.

Obtaining consent in the surgeon's office also reduces the likelihood that a patient can claim that the surgeon was unavailable to discuss the treatment and answer questions, or that the consent form was signed while the patient was under the influence of medication, as is more likely in the hospital setting, and was not cognizant of what was being signed. Nor is the patient likely to be able to claim, as some have, that the consent form was just another of the many forms he or she was asked to sign on admission to the hospital and that the patient therefore had not realized what was being signed. The presence of a nurse in the room at the time of a surgeon's discussion with the patient offers additional confirmation. In the office setting, the nurse can be asked to sign the consent form as a witness of the circumstances under which it was obtained.

Any surgeon who has performed a procedure hundreds of times is likely to have difficulty recalling exactly what one particular patient was told. Thus, if the surgeon's recollection were challenged, it would be extremely difficult to provide assurances that the surgeon could accurately recall in detail a conversation that might have taken place years earlier. In the event of a lawsuit, therefore, a surgeon will be able to testify only as to what is customarily told such a patient, while the patient who has undergone a surgical procedure only once may be believed to be able to recall the conversation in detail. For these reasons, it would be wise for the surgeon to make a note of the explanation given to the patient, particularly that portion related to the general nature of the risks involved.

Many patients prefer to include family members in a discussion of planned treatment, and, therefore, it is recommended that one or more family members be present at this time, with the patient's permission. If, for some reason (for example, in the case of a very old or infirm patient), the surgeon believes it necessary, the family may also be conferred with in the absence of the patient. These conversations would, of course, be duly noted in the medical record. Due consideration, however, should be given to the patient's prior expression of a desire for confidentiality. Remember, also, that it is the decision of the competent patient, and not that of the family, that is paramount.

Because only the surgeon has sufficient information on the patient's background, expertise needed to evaluate risks, ability to answer patients' questions, and knowledge of why one form of treatment has been recommended over others, the courts have concluded that the surgeon is responsible for obtaining a patient's informed consent, rather than the hospital or its nurses. In most states, therefore, it is the surgeon's ultimate responsibility to provide patients with sufficient information to permit them to give an informed consent. A physician who merely includes an order to get a consent form signed, together with other preoperative orders, would have a difficult time successfully mounting a defense against a claim of lack of informed consent if the information conveyed by the nurse was inaccurate or inadequate.

The Joint Commission on Accreditation of Healthcare Organizations (JCAHO) requires the hospital record to contain evidence that the patient's consent to treatment was obtained. Most hospital attorneys advise nurses to refer patients' questions to their surgeon and to discourage an uninformed patient from signing the hospital's consent form. In the interest of their own protection, nurses also are advised to record patients' requests for information about scheduled treatment and referrals for such information to the patient's physician.

The Consent Form

In most states, verbal consent to treatment is valid. However, this form of consent makes it difficult to prove exactly what was said, thereby placing the surgeon at a disadvantage in the event of a subsequent lawsuit. The physician would suffer the same disadvantage if verbal consent were documented only by an entry in progress notes or office records. The more prudent course is to follow the process of informed consent, which includes, but is not limited to, documenting a patient's consent on a form that details the information disclosed to the patient and to have it signed by both patient and surgeon and witnessed by a hospital or office nurse.

To protect against liability for lack of informed consent, each surgeon's office should develop a series of standard consent forms for each procedure that is regularly performed by the surgeon. Although some physicians rely on a single generalized consent form indicating the patient's consent for "medical treatment" and stating that "the risks of the procedure have been explained" to the patient, such a form would be of little value in proving the exact nature of the disclosures made to the patient. A consent form that is specifically tailored to the procedure to be performed conclusively establishes exactly what disclosures were made, and thus can be a significant deterrent to an informed consent claim.

Any surgeon who doubts the value of developing consent forms that detail the specific risks of the procedure to be performed would do well to consider the size of the judgment that might be awarded in the event that a complication of an operation arose, and a jury concluded that the risk of the complication should have been disclosed. In fact, as a general rule, the more elective the procedure and the greater the number of therapeutic alternatives, the more detailed the disclosure should be. Every consent form should disclose the risks of death, brain damage, and paralysis to a patient who is to undergo general anesthesia.

Using a consent form that has been drafted by an attorney and endorsed by the state medical society and that conforms to other consent forms in use throughout the state should be advantageous to the surgeon in the event of litigation. Each state, through its courts or legislature, has developed its own informed consent doctrine. For that reason, although a court in one state may have concluded that a certain risk need not be disclosed, that fact is no guarantee that a court in another state will reach the same conclusion. Many states do not dictate exactly what is required in a consent form.

The following general principles should be kept in mind when drafting a consent form:

1. Use medical terminology supplemented with a clear explanation of each medical term in language a layperson can be expected to understand.

2. All commonly occurring risks of the procedure should be listed, including those associated with anesthesia. When possible, the anesthesiologist should personally advise the patient of anesthesia risks. If it is unclear whether or not a particular risk should be included, it is wise to err on the side of disclosure.

3. A risk should never be minimized by describing it in the consent form as something that is extraordinarily rare or unlikely to occur. The words "simple," "uncomplicated," or "minor" should never be used to describe a procedure, and every consent form should include a statement that no result has been guaranteed.

4. With rare exceptions, the use of statistics should be avoided, as it may be argued that national statistics may be misleading if the physician's own experience varies from the norm.

5. The fact that a patient has been given an informational brochure or shown an audiovisual aid should be noted on the consent form.

6. The patient should be asked to acknowledge in writing that the information disclosed has been understood, that an opportunity to ask questions has been provided, and that all questions have been answered to the patient's satisfaction.

7. Ideally, the signatures of both patient and surgeon should be required on the consent form to establish that both were present for the discussion, and the time and date on which the discussion occurred should be indicated.

8. Each consent form should conclude with an omnibus consent provision, such as the following, from the ACS *Patient Safety Manual*[3]:

> **4. Complications; Unforeseen Conditions; Results**
>
> I am aware that in the practice of medicine, other unexpected risks or complications not discussed may occur. I also understand that during the course of the proposed procedure(s) unforeseen conditions may be revealed requiring the performance of additional procedures, and I authorize such procedures to be performed. I further acknowledge that no guarantees or promises have been made to me concerning the results of any procedure or treatment.

It should be noted that such a provision may be legally worthless and must never be used as a substitute for discussing foreseeable contingencies and noting them in the consent form. However, its inclusion in the consent form may serve as a deterrent to legal action.

Practical Approaches to Disclosure

As a practical matter, of course, the informed consent doctrine poses a practice management challenge, seeming to demand more time for discussion with each patient than the busy physician's time might permit. One possible solution in the case of patients who are seen in the physician's office prior to having an operation is to establish a protocol for disclosure that enlists the assistance of office staff members.

Essential information on the proposed procedure, the therapeutic alternatives, and their risks can be conveyed to the patient through the use of informational aids, such as a well-designed brochure or videotape. Pamphlets, videos, and other forms of informational aids are, of course, commercially available for this purpose. However, in-house production of information tools allows for easy and economical updating. The aid need not be elaborately or expensively prepared—printed material can be no more complicated than a stapled set of typewritten pages, while a videotape may simply show the physician at his or her desk talking to the camera as though he or she were talking to a patient.

Once such aids are available in the office, a patient who is to undergo a procedure can be referred to a member of the office staff, who can provide written materials to the patient or schedule a viewing of audiovisual material. Next, you might want to give the patient the consent form to read and then provide an opportunity for the patient to raise any questions about the procedure. When the information-giving process has been completed and the consent form signed by the patient, the title of the information aid used should be noted on the consent form, together with the name of the office employee who can attest to the fact that these steps were taken. It is also recommended that each time an informational piece is updated, copies of earlier versions be maintained on file so that they can be used to document exactly what information was conveyed to a given patient. It must be stressed, however, that the dialogue between the patient and the surgeon is mandatory, regardless of the informational aids.

Developing informational aids does require an initial investment of time and effort, but that investment is likely to be very quickly recouped in the form of more efficient use of the physician's time. At the same time, informational aids will help keep patients both better and more consistently informed.

Obtaining Consent in Special Circumstances

Obtaining appropriate consent may be a more complicated process when the patient is a minor, mentally ill or deficient, sedated, in shock, or in great pain. Requirements vary from state to state, but it is likely that such circumstances will require that disclosures be made to and consent obtained from the patient's parent or legal guardian, or that the patient's own consent be supplemented by that of another person authorized by law to give consent.

Other circumstances that require special treatment include the need to obtain consent for transplants, sterilization, abortion, experimental therapy, and the removal or withholding of life-support systems. In such special cases, it is strongly recommended that the surgeon obtain legal counsel that is directly relevant to the matter at hand from a qualified attorney.

Finally, the surgeon should be aware that each case brought to litigation is decided on its particular facts and in accordance with the perceived credibility of the various witnesses who testify. For those reasons, unless the highest appellate court of a state determines—as a matter of law, rather than on the evidence presented at the trial—that a particular risk need not be disclosed, courts (even those in the same state) may arrive at conflicting decisions.

Proper Documentation—The Medical Record

Medical records, both hospital and office charts, are extremely important in the management of risk. In addition to documenting the care given to a patient, medical records serve as the vehicle for communicating data needed by all members of the patient's health care team, charting the course of care rendered in the hospital, and outlining plans for the patient's present and future care.[1]

Medical records also have legal status, and as such, they are a fiduciary responsibility and may become a legal document for later review. Required by the government, the records also must satisfy requirements outlined by the Joint Commission on Accreditation of Healthcare Organizations and in hospital bylaws.

What is not written in the medical record is legally presumed not to have occurred. In fact, to paraphrase R. S. Brittain, writing about medical-legal cases in *The Practicing Surgeon's Perspective*: Reality is not what happened or what you say happened; reality is what is in the medical record.[4]

The medical record is invaluable as a patient care tool. When carefully and meticulously kept, the record also can be an indelible line of defense in these litigious times. D. Danner wrote in *Medical Malpractice: A Primer for Physicians*, "In the courtroom, medical records are witnesses whose memory never dies."[1]

Care must be taken, however, to ensure that medical records will meet the rigorous tests to which they would be put if presented

155

in the courtroom. Toward that end, the surgeon should approach recordkeeping with certain suggestions in mind.

- **All entries should be neat, legible, and written in ink.**

  A well-kept chart enables the health care provider to reconstruct the patient's course of treatment and demonstrate that the care provided to a patient was in accordance with accepted medical practice.[1] Therefore, a physician must always maintain complete and adequate records, including records of important negative events.

- **Each entry should be signed with the physician's first and last names and professional designation.**

- **Each entry should note the date and time it was made.**

  Entries should be made in a timely fashion and in chronologic order.

- **Each page of the record should be dated and labeled with the patient's name.**

- **Inappropriate skipping of lines or spaces should be avoided.**

  If a blank space remains at the end of an entry, a line should be drawn through it.

- **Only standard abbreviations and symbols should be used, and ditto marks and initials should be avoided.**

  Records should be written in accepted medical terminology, and abbreviations should be avoided.

- **Supplemental pages may be used, if necessary, to record missed notes, which should be indicated as late entries.**

- **Medical records should be restricted to statements of fact.**

All entries to the medical record should be pertinent, relevant, and objective.[5] The recording of impressions or tentative diagnoses should be avoided; however, if they must be recorded, they should be clearly labeled as such. Opinions and descriptions of treatment plans should be backed by statements of relevant facts, and explanations should be given for choices and decisions made. For example, if certain diseases have been ruled out, that fact should be recorded to indicate to anyone who may later review the chart that treatment alternatives were considered in the course of determining the plan that was followed.

- **Medical records should never be altered.**

  Medical records must never be altered. If any corrections or additions must be made, they should be added to the chart in regular sequence, with appropriate reference to the previous entries. This procedure is strongly recommended, because changes in records, such as notes added and comments entered out of order, can easily be detected. Where corrections must be made, one line should be used to cancel incorrect entries and the time and date of the cancellation noted, together with the initials of the person making the change. Appropriate corrections should be entered chronologically, and care must be taken to avoid giving the appearance that the records have been tampered with.[1] Altered records, if at issue, are easily detected by experts and can substantially weaken a physician's defense in court in the event of a dispute.[5]

The following items should all be documented in the medical record:

- **All missed appointments and other indicators of possible lack of patient compliance**

  Any problems that develop in the course of a patient's

157

care must be addressed in the medical record. These notes should be consistently recorded, not only in their statements of facts but also in writing style. In other words, the notes should never be suddenly expanded upon or take on a defensive tone.

- **The dates of all referrals and return visits**

  If the physician has any questions about the care of the patient, he or she should be sure to obtain appropriate consultations. Those consulting opinions, which can be extremely valuable if questions later arise about the conduct of patient care, should be duly recorded.[4]

- **Content of all telephone calls**

  The time and content of all telephone calls should be noted. Telephone conversations conducted after the surgeon's regular office hours should be documented immediately after their completion. Details of the conversation should be subsequently entered into the office chart and initialed. Surgeons who take telephone calls for another surgeon should provide details or summaries of them that can be transmitted to the office of the patient's regular surgeon.

- **All prescriptions written and refills needed**

  The name of the drug, the dosage, the directions for taking the medication, and the number of pills or tablets should be recorded, as well as the number of refills.

- **Verbal follow-up care instructions**

  Instructions given to the patient must be recorded in the chart and signed.

- **Distribution of educational and informational materials to patients**

  Medical records should be as complete as possible. All instructions or informational materials given to the patient should be identified in the record.

- **Poor clinical outcomes and treatment plans for complications**
- **Explanations for any instances in which the notes made by the physician and those entered by the nurse do not agree**

  Care should be taken not to eliminate the nurse's notes; rather, the physician should write a follow-up note in appropriate chronologic order, making reference to the discrepancy and explaining it.[1]

What should *not* be recorded in the medical record are any personal and disparaging remarks or statements that imply cause and effect. The medical record has no place for comments that blame procedures performed by other personnel for a particular series of events.

Office and Outpatient Settings

As an employer, the surgeon establishes office procedures, a style of communication with patients, risk management techniques, and medical record policies. This chapter sets forth a checklist of areas in which special attention may ensure a good physician-patient relationship.

Office Procedures

Telephone Etiquette

At all times, office staff need to be consistently courteous and helpful in dealing with patients. It is also essential that staff are aware of the need to consult with the surgeon if they are unsure how to respond properly to a call when the patient says it is an emergency. In any event, such calls must invariably be handled without delay.

Any instructions that staff give to patients must be pursuant to protocols that have been developed in advance with the surgeon. *All telephone calls asking for advice or instructions must be documented in the medical record, with the specific question and response recorded.*

Prescription Renewal

The surgeon's office should have established prescription renewal procedures. If office personnel are delegated this task, procedures should specify that the surgeon give verbal approval and that the surgeon note that approval in the patient record.

Filing and Charting Test Results

Medication and telephone logs should be maintained in the office, including a record of calls received at home, transcribed promptly into the patient's chart, then signed or initialed by the surgeon. All laboratory and x-ray reports should be initialed and dated by the surgeon before filing in the patient record. *The surgeon should promptly and personally notify the patient, either by telephone or letter, of any positive results* and should document the notification in the chart. Failure to do so could result in an indefensible delay in diagnosis and treatment.

Written drug dosages must be kept in the record. Any calculations for mixing drugs also must be recorded, followed, and administered consistently.

Staff Training

In-service training sessions for office and ambulatory care staff should be held on a regular basis, including instructions for compliance with Occupational Safety and Health Administration (OSHA) and the Americans with Disabilities Act (ADA).

Both surgeon and staff should be careful to ensure that a staff member is present during any physical examination of such a nature that it could be misinterpreted by the patient. Both surgeon and staff should be sensitive to any remarks or actions that might raise a concern of potential sexual harassment.

Waste Disposal and Office Facilities

Detailed procedures for disposal of infectious waste materials, such as contaminated dressings and used needles, must be written and carefully followed, both in the office and ambulatory care facility. This waste disposal plan must be consistent with OSHA standards. Hazardous substances should be labeled. Controlled substances should be stored securely, and access to them should be strictly controlled. Outdated medications must be discarded. The office, restrooms, and other facilities should be in compliance with the ADA.

Emergency and Disaster Plans

Mock Code Blue emergency and disaster plans should be written, and these disaster plans should be readily accessible to staff members. The staff should be familiar with the location and use of Code Blue equipment, and such equipment must be kept in working order.

Missed Appointments

Missed appointments should be documented in the patient chart. Patients who miss appointments should be contacted by telephone to learn the reason for their absence and to reschedule the appointment, if appropriate. If the appointment had been made for the purpose of communicating laboratory, test, or x-ray results, the patient should be contacted by letter. For important positive test results, a registered letter, return receipt requested, is the most cautious way to reduce the risk of litigation.

Inquiries

All inquiries from attorneys or third parties, subpoenas, depositions, and other legal materials should be managed directly by the surgeon, not by office staff. Some county medical societies and local bar associations may have prepared guidelines for responding to these inquiries.

Billing

The surgeon should be notified before any collection action is instituted on a delinquent account, because the surgeon alone may know of a circumstance, such as patient dissatisfaction with a treatment, that would argue against pressing for payment.

Incident Reporting

Any incident involving patient, office staff, or physician that would indicate patient dissatisfaction with care, whether observed or overheard, should be documented in the record and signed or initialed by the surgeon. Any incident that appears to put the surgeon at risk of a suit should then be reported to the professional liability insurance carrier and, if the incident occurred in the hospital, to the hospital risk manager.

The surgeon should be familiar with state laws and regulations regarding reportable diseases, cases of domestic violence or other abuse, and AIDS. All testing and reporting for AIDS must be in compliance with state confidentiality requirements.

Patient Termination

If a surgeon believes that it will be impossible to continue caring for a patient, the surgeon can terminate all nonemergency treatment. Notification should be by certified mail, with return receipt requested. State that the surgeon is no longer willing to continue treating the patient and allocate a reasonable amount of time to permit the patient to locate a new surgeon before care is finally terminated. The office should also indicate willingness to assist the patient in finding another surgeon, if so requested, and should transfer records promptly to the new surgeon. These precautions are important to prevent the patient from claiming abandonment. These procedures are not necessary for patients who are no longer in need of the surgeon's care.

Quality Assurance

The surgeon's office should have procedures to ensure that patients have 24-hour access to surgical care, with night and weekend coverage arrangements that are available to the office staff, the answering service, and/or specified on a recorded message accessible through the office telephone number. Emergency instructions should be included on any such message.

The surgeon should keep up with all state and specialty continuing medical education requirements. Documentation of significant certifications and recertifications should be displayed or available in the office.

All laboratory testing must be performed in compliance with applicable Clinical Laboratory Improvement Amendments (CLIA) regulations. All radiologic and other testing procedures must be carried out in conformance with state and federal statutes and regulations concerning self-referral.

For all managed care contracts, the office should be conversant with applicable quality assurance and utilization management protocols, and office procedures should be in compliance with them. Where parameters of care, clinical pathways, protocols, or standards are required, the surgeon and the office staff should be familiar with and in compliance with these guidelines.

At a minimum, office record systems should identify patients who need preoperative clearance, laboratory work, antibiotics, or radiologic studies, and there should be a follow-up system to ascertain that the patient obtains all of these. Similarly, follow-up plans for each patient should be documented in the office record, both in the interest of good patient care and to forestall any future claim that the patient was never so instructed.

Patient Rapport

Communication

The surgeon should take time to listen carefully to each patient. Through their conversation and deportment in the office, the surgeon and all office staff should show that the concerns of the patient are important to them. Office staff should avoid frivolous conversation or any appearance of inattention to the patient's needs.

Surveys show that the length of time a surgeon spends with a patient is a key factor in patient satisfaction. Interpreters should be available, if needed, to assist patients who do not speak the same language as the surgeon. The surgeon should give the patient an adequate explanation of the need for any expensive or unpleasant tests, procedures, or medications. The surgeon should be sure that the patient has the information necessary to properly prepare for tests and examinations and to understand the results. The surgeon and office staff should be compassionate in the handling of fear, grief, and death.

Medical Records

Medical records should be legible, never backdated, and *never altered.* When an error is made, it should be corrected by drawing a single line through it, initialing and dating the correction concurrently, never backdating it. Care should always be taken to carefully document the site of a lesion or condition, especially on preoperative histories and permits. (See previous sections of this chapter.)

Informed consent can be significantly enhanced if the following information is included in the medical record: A GENERAL description of the disease entity and procedure, a list of ALTERNATIVES in procedures, and a brief list of the more common RISKS associated with the procedures, as well as the risks to the patient if the procedure(s) is not done. Any material used for elucidation of the discussion should be listed.

Patient Right of Self-Determination

Any patient who has signed a durable power of attorney or a living will should have this document kept on file, and it must be consulted if, at some time in the future, the patient becomes legally incompetent to make decisions about further treatment options.

Office Surgery

The surgeon who performs office surgery should be sure that procedures performed in this setting are generally consistent with his or her hospital privileges. Any sedation to be used should not run the risk of respiratory depression unless the patient is adequately monitored, with resuscitation equipment available and office personnel trained to respond properly in the event of emergency.

Office personnel should be instructed in the proper handling and labeling of specimens, should be familiar with the laboratories with which relevant managed care plans currently contract, and should have systems in place for promptly and reliably obtaining results.

Physician Assistants and Advanced Nurse Practitioners

Surgeons who work with physician assistants or advanced nurse practitioners must be aware of their potential liability. These collaborative relationships must be structured, using written practice protocols, job descriptions, and written contracts, to enable all parties to agree on their respective responsibilities. Patients should be made clearly aware at all times whether they are seeing a surgeon or a nurse practitioner, and the surgeon should be available for consultation at all times.

Health care services delivered by each professional should be within the scope of practice for both, as defined by state law. Still, suits that arise out of the activities of either PAs or advanced nurse practitioners are more than likely to include the surgeon. For this reason, all members of the team should become familiar with each other's style of practice and should consistently work closely together.

Departments of Surgery

In the hospital setting, the department of surgery has an excellent opportunity to reduce the risk of professional liability actions by carefully overseeing and continuously improving the clinical work of department members. This process can be divided into three major activities: (1) credentialing of department personnel, (2) monitoring patient care data and outcome review, and (3) standardization of patient care through use of patient care plans called "clinical pathways," which decrease variation from accepted surgical practice. The goal of each of these activities is to improve the outcome of surgical care in the hospital.

Credentialing

Credentialing is the process by which the medical staff determines that its physicians have the training, skill, and judgment to deliver high-quality care. It is an ongoing activity that involves all members of the department, beginning with evaluation of new members and continuing with the reappointment of established members at two-year intervals and credentialing for performing new procedures. Credentialing is particularly important in the surgical specialties because of the potential adverse consequences of invasive procedures. The department chairperson or department executive committee is responsible for evaluating the information in the credential files. Their recommendation is then transmitted to the credentials committee, which in turn recommends clinical privileges to the medical staff executive committee. A credentialing process cannot arbitrarily deny clinical privileges to appropriately trained individuals based upon their department assignment; for example, gastrointestinal endoscopy being performed only by gastroenterologists to the exclusion of appropriately trained surgeons.

Initial evaluation of candidates for the department of surgery must be done carefully and comprehensively. Licensure must be confirmed. Gaps in training must be explained. Missing letters of recommendation need to be tracked down. Subtle innuendos in letters of recommendation need to be investigated further. It is easier to deny an appointment to the department than revoking privileges at a later date. Initial appointment to the department is based on five criteria: current licensure, relevant training and/or experience, current competence, medical ethics, and health status. Completion of an approved residency with a letter from the program director or board certification is adequate documentation of relevant training. Current competence is more difficult to assess. Letters of recommendation are often bland and uninformative. There should be some information included about the types of procedures performed by the applicant, the appropriateness and outcomes of those procedures, and the applicant's technical skill and judgment. This kind of detailed information often can only be obtained by requesting a surgical list or by a telephone call to the applicant's former program director or surgical colleagues.

An applicant who has satisfied basic criteria can be appointed on a provisional basis with privileges in specified disciplines. The provisional staff member may require evaluation by a proctor or supervisor. The duty of the proctor is to observe and report his or her findings to the department chairperson. Although the proctor *may* intervene in a case, with or without the consent of the surgeon who is being proctored, the proctor most often is only an observer. Case law has in fact established that the proctor is not obligated to intervene and cannot be liable for the outcome of the case. Some portion of the proctorship should be done by members of the department who are not in partnership with the provisional member. An adequate number and sufficient variety of cases, especially high-risk cases, should be proctored before relief from proctorship is granted. These requirements for relief from proctorship are defined in the department rules and regulations.

Credentialing is an ongoing process. Reappointments to the department of surgery are not automatic, but are made after review of the member's credential file. Reappointments are recommended by the department chairperson, using the same basic criteria as the initial appointment. In addition, the credentials file will contain information about the member's adherence to department regulations, use of current privileges, and results of peer review. Some modification of the member's clinical privilege list may occur at the time of reappointment, due to the changing practice of medicine, the development of new procedures, or the demonstrated competence of the practitioner.

Granting of privileges for new procedures can be particularly troublesome in rapidly changing surgical specialties. As demonstrated in the field of operative laparoscopy, there is patient demand for new technology, and surgeons are eager to practice newly acquired skills at a time when: (1) the training requirements are not well established; (2) experienced proctors may not generally be available; and (3) the effectiveness and the risks of the new procedure are not fully known. Currently, there is no simple or generally accepted solution to this problem. The credentials committee and the department chairperson should be familiar with the recommendations of specialty organizations with regard to specific new procedures. The most experienced members of the department should assume a leadership role in monitoring the performance and outcomes of the new procedures. The department members wishing to provide new technology should demonstrate a sincere and determined effort to obtain good training.

Monitoring Patient Care Data/Outcome Review

Although much of the quality improvement process has been described and mandated by JCAHO,[6] it can and is supposed to be tailored to meet the goals of the organization. If the department meets its objective, the patient outcome should improve and the risk of litigation decrease. The requirements of JCAHO—and the needs of the department—can be met in a variety of ways, but good quality improvement initiatives have the following features in common: (1) The plan or process of care is a written document developed and adopted by the department members and the chief of surgery. (2) Performance of the established process is measured. (3) Patient outcomes are measured by objective data, such as wound infection rates and the frequency of stroke following carotid endarterectomy. (4) Important adverse trends in patient outcomes are detected early, and corrective action is taken.

In the past, the focus of quality improvement has been on retrospective case review. This outgrowth of morbidity and mortality rounds remains, in its modern form, an important method of monitoring patient outcomes. The department first adopts a set of indicators, which are used by the medical records department to detect adverse outcomes and to select charts for review. Examples of these generic indicators are return to surgery within 24 hours or readmission to the hospital within 30 days of the surgical procedure. A committee of department members is appointed to review these charts on a regular basis and to report their findings to the department. This same committee also reviews incident or occurrence reports submitted by other departments. Most often, review of these charts finds only routine complications which are found to be acceptable and properly managed. At times, the department may detect adverse trends, such as a rising wound infection rate, and then more in-depth analysis of the problem is required.

The department also now has a responsibility to monitor patient care and outcomes in other ways that go beyond the morbidity and mortality review. Routine patient care, as well as adverse events, can be checked on a regular basis. Computer systems can provide rapid accumulation and analysis of ongoing patient care. With the advent of computerized data analysis, the department should implement *continuous patient data collection*, if feasible. Patterns of drug usage and the use of blood products by the department members should be monitored. Are antibiotics used appropriately, in the correct dosage and frequency? Are the appropriate laboratory tests obtained during drug therapy, such as creatinines and drug levels during administration of the aminoglycosides or platelet counts during heparin therapy? Surgical procedures must also be screened for appropriateness. In other words, even if the procedure was performed well and without complication, why was it performed? Was the procedure necessary and properly selected? Should the patient have had coronary bypass instead of angioplasty, for example? What is the rate of cesarean section or normal appendectomy? Appropriateness applies to diagnostic procedures as well, such as upper and lower endoscopy. Finally, the department should target certain operations for more in-depth surveillance. These operations are those which are either high-volume or low-volume and high-risk. Specific criteria are selected for monitoring each operation, and data are then collected by medical records personnel. For example, the rate of conversion of laparoscopic to open cholecystectomy, the incidence of retained stones, and the frequency of intraoperative cholangiography might be followed. In the review process, benchmark results are defined by the department, such as a 3 percent stroke rate after carotid thromboendarterectomy, and then more in-depth review could be done when this "threshold" is crossed.

In recent years, there also is growing recognition that bad outcomes of patient care can occur because of poorly designed patient care processes as opposed to human error. To this extent, patient outcomes may be improved and malpractice litigation avoided by redesigning those processes. The theory of total quality management, TQM,[7] grew out of Japanese industry and has been broadly applied to problems encountered in providing quality health care. TQM recognizes that the success or failure of a surgical procedure depends on many factors that go well beyond the control of the surgeon. The surgeon is playing only one role in a complex team effort that includes such services as preoperative evaluation and teaching, intraoperative and postoperative specialty nursing, laboratory and radiology services, and discharge planning. A careful, comprehensive analysis of all those factors helps to improve patient outcomes. Such an analysis is best performed in multidisciplinary committees, to which the department of surgery sends its representatives. The process of TQM is continuous, and reanalysis and redesign occur as necessary. The members of the department of surgery thus collaborate with other specialists and nonphysicians in a systematic and organization-wide effort to improve quality of care.

Clinical Pathways

For many hospital admissions, particularly elective surgical procedures, coordinated patient care plans have been developed and utilized. In most institutions these are referred to as "clinical pathways." A clinical pathway in the department of surgery is the optimal, daily sequence of events followed by the usual patient undergoing a specific surgical procedure. Clinical pathways were originally designed to minimize the cost of hospitalization in the era of managed care, but they have also proven to be useful tools in improving patient outcomes as well. The pathway lists all the important details of a complex hospitalization, such as preoperative teaching and laboratory testing, criteria for removal of lines and tubes, duration of prophylactic antibiotics, timing of physical therapy, discharge planning, and aftercare. The members of the department of surgery, including residents where available, play an important role in working with the administration, nursing staff, and ancillary medical personnel to develop the pathway. The pathway description, standardized order sets, and patient education material need to be written. When properly designed, pathways may both improve patient care and be cost-effective. Adopted by the entire department, pathways work to cut costs by eliminating the unnecessary laboratory tests and procedures that may have become a routine practice for some physicians. They ensure that an adequate amount of pre- and postoperative testing is done at the right time. Patient education and discharge planning, which are often forgotten until too late in the postoperative course, are initiated in a more timely fashion. Pathways make certain that important aspects of postoperative care, such as removal of a Foley catheter, are not omitted or delayed because the order was not written. The patient, his or her family, the nurses, and residents all have a better understanding of the fairly rapid progression of events in the postoperative period. Hospital stays are thus often significantly shortened. One of the authors (JEF) has had experience with clinical pathways for complicated procedures, such as total colectomy, ileal pouch, and anal anastomosis for ulcerative colitis and familial polyposis. He has found that the length of stay can be diminished by approximately one to one-and-a-half days without higher complication rates or unplanned returns to the hospital due to premature discharge. The chairman of the department of surgery should be vigorous in encouraging the adoption of clinical pathways, which often improve patient care as well as the financial position of the department.

Avoiding Professional Liability

The department chair should take an active role to avoid professional liability among the staff surgeons of the department. New members of the staff, but often older members as well, have not had formal training or exposure to the concepts of avoiding professional liability. The chair should encourage the staff to become familiar with this manual, which is made available to all Fellows of the American College of Surgeons. An educational program on avoiding professional liability should be set up, possibly with the help of the hospital's risk management office or its risk management attorney. Concepts such as obtaining proper informed consent and good communication with patients and their families should be emphasized. Regular monitoring of patient care data and retrospective case review, as previously discussed, is essential. When adverse outcomes occur, the hospital's risk management staff is notified and become involved to try to minimize the possibility of malpractice litigation.

Most importantly, when the department chair becomes aware of practices within the department that fall below the standard of care, the chair must promptly take corrective action. Often, counseling the involved physician or requiring additional training will be sufficient to change the practice pattern. Some practices may be considered a threat to patient safety. The department chair should not hesitate to institute a restriction of clinical privileges if necessary to protect patients from an adverse outcome, even when such action will generate a report to the National Practitioner Data Bank. Department members who participate in peer review activities and who must make these kinds of difficult decisions are immune from antitrust and defamation suits, as long as there is just cause for their action and as long as medical staff bylaws, rules, and regulations are written to comply with federal guidelines (HCQIA)[7] and are carefully followed. At times, the department may need to seek the opinion of experts outside the local community. This situation arises when there are no other surgeons on staff trained in the specialty being reviewed or when the reviewers are perceived to be motivated by economic competition. Some state chapters of the American College of Surgeons or of subspecialty organizations can provide such impartial expert peer review. Outside review is time-consuming, often expensive, and usually not necessary. If it provides an extra measure of fairness to the parties involved and allows the department to make the right decision, then the extra effort and expense are well justified.

The Resident

During the past several years, much has been written regarding professional liability and its effects on physicians, other medical care providers, third-party payors, health care recipients, government health programs and their creators, and legislative bodies. Although significant attention has been directed to physicians in general, little heed has been paid to residents or fellows in training.[8] In fact, the only single source of professional liability information that is devoted exclusively to residents has been compiled by members of the Department of Professional Liability of the American College of Obstetricians and Gynecologists (ACOG).[9] That source, with the permission of ACOG, serves as the basis for this discussion.

Accountability and Liability

The climate created by the current level of concern about professional liability has influenced how residents are taught, what they are taught, the breadth of experience that is available to them, the amount of responsibility they are allowed, and who teaches them.

All residents practice as trainees under the supervision of others, whether or not they are licensed. Supervision is performed by attending staff, clinical faculty, more senior residents, residency program directors, and the staff of the hospital or other institution at which the training occurs. Although those who supervise resident trainees are usually held accountable for their acts, the resi-

177

dents themselves also may be held responsible for their own actions.

Failure of a resident or a resident's supervisor to inform a patient of the resident's status may result in causes of action for fraud, deceit, misrepresentation, assault and battery, and lack of informed consent. Patient acceptance or refusal of medical service from the resident also should be documented.

The major source of liability for the resident is failure to meet appropriate standards of care. Residents must never forget that they may not be fully trained to provide all procedures and treatments and, therefore, should perform only those for which they have been fully trained.

Both the supervising physician and the resident are responsible for providing high-quality care to a patient.* Therefore, it is essential that they establish and maintain appropriate communication, particularly if either believes a patient's condition requires expertise beyond that of the resident. In such cases, it is the duty of the resident to inform the supervising physician of the urgency and scope of the patient's problem and to be particularly attentive to the patient's feelings. Should problems arise, the patient should already be aware of the resident's status and the fact that another physician may have to step in to care for the patient.

---

* The legal theory of vicarious liability states that responsibility for the acts of the resident lies not only with the resident, but also with the physician who directs or supervises him or her. Thus, the supervisor can be held legally responsible for the resident's actions. The physician's responsibility for the resident's actions arises out of the concept of an agency relationship. Under that concept, one person becomes the agent of a second person when the first person has been authorized to act for or represent the second. The partners in such a relationship are also referred to legally as "the master" and "the servant." The relevant legal doctrine—"Let the master speak," known as *respondeat superior*—holds that supervising physicians may be vicariously liable for the negligent acts of their residents.

This theory of law may also extend beyond the clinical faculty member to any physician who works with a resident, based on the legal concept of "the borrowed servant" or "the captain of the ship." Under these doctrines, one party may be liable for the acts of an employee of another if negligence occurs while the employee is under the first party's direction or control. (For further discussion, see Chapter II, pages 46–53.)

Resident-Patient Communications

Physicians always must clearly and honestly explain the nature of the services they can provide in terms that patients can comprehend. They must make sure that the patient has thoroughly understood the information that has been conveyed. Residents especially must always be sure to explain their status as a trainee to the patient, emphasizing that the care they provide is constantly supervised by the attending physician, who remains ultimately accountable for the care. The patient, of course, has the right to refuse treatment by a resident, but a good communicator can help the patient understand the advantages of receiving dual care, and a healthy, honest relationship can be the outgrowth of that exchange.

Always being willing to spend enough time with patients to answer their questions and address their concerns is an excellent way to demonstrate that the physician is the patient's ally.

When a resident is a participant in the **informed consent process**, a resident must be aware of the steps to be followed: obtaining and disclosing all relevant facts; thoroughly explaining alternatives and reservations; ensuring that patients thoroughly comprehend information, advice, and instructions; and answering all questions. Proper implementation of these steps should make it possible to obtain a validly informed consent. For further discussion of informed consent, see pages 145 to 153.

More recently, some jurisdictions have enacted specific informed consent laws. The resident needs to know these laws if they exist in the area in which the training is being done.

A resident's responsibilities do not necessarily end with treatment or operation, but also involve follow-up care, which may include follow-up visits and providing instructions to the patient. Ideally, all instructions to the patient should be detailed in writing and a copy placed in the patient's medical record for future reference.

Every resident should check hospital procedures to determine the kind of consent form that is preferred by the institution.

179

Most importantly, every resident must be aware that all treatment must be backed by evidence of consent—whether oral or written, expressed or implied— granting permission for the resident to proceed or evidence that the treatment was provided under circumstances in which consent could not be obtained.

Hospital Setting

The great majority of events leading to liability claims against physicians take place in the hospital setting. For that reason, it is especially important for residents to recognize their proper role in the treatment of hospitalized patients and in the institution's risk management program.

Typically, the resident plays a *supporting role* as part of a team functioning *under the supervision* of an attending physician. In some instances, however, the resident may function as a patient's primary physician. Whatever the circumstances, the resident must continually strive to achieve the dual goals of increasing patient safety and reducing risk.

From the resident's perspective, risk prevention in the hospital should begin with the resident's first encounter with a patient. Often the resident is the first person to discuss with the patient the reason for the hospitalization. Therefore, it is the resident's responsibility to fully explain to the patient all of the information needed regarding hospitalization, including the reason for admission, the recommended treatment, treatment alternatives, and the potential risks and complications thereof.

Nothing is as likely to lead to litigation as the patient's surprise and disappointment with the treatment received. Therefore, as is the case with the supervising physician, it is vitally important for the resident to convey to the patient any possibility of complications or changes in expected outcome. For example, a patient who can be expected to experience fever, infection, or an extended hospital stay after an operation is far less likely to be disturbed by those events if the patient has been properly forewarned about the possibility. By the same token, a patient should always be advised if a procedure could entail risk or not achieve the desired result. Any patient who suffers a complication requires adequate time, attention, and information to understand what has occurred. Never is the resident's alertness and demonstration of concern for the patient's welfare more important than under such circumstances.

The resident should keep in mind that many patients are under a great deal of stress and, therefore, may not be able to immediately grasp all of the information being conveyed. For that reason, a written summary of information relayed verbally may help give the patient and interested family members the opportunity to review and digest that information. The original discussion also should be followed by a later opportunity to ask questions and clarify any misunderstandings or misconceptions that may remain.

Videotaping is becoming an increasingly accepted activity that carries with it inherent dangers. Because video cameras are so common, staff might be complacent in a camera's presence, but must remember that both their actions and comments are being recorded permanently.

Virtually every hospital, of course, has established rules and departmental protocols to ensure the delivery of uniformly high-quality patient care. In the interest of both preventing patient injury and minimizing the risk of liability, every member of the health care team must clearly understand the hospital's systems and protocols. Any failure on the part of the resident to comply with hospital policies is open to interpretation as a violation of the standard of care. Knowing, understanding, and complying with hospital policies is therefore as much in the interest of the resident as it is in that of the patient and hospital. Because national standards of care for specialists in training are being increasingly accepted, residents would also be wise to familiarize themselves with national guidelines, although hospital departmental protocols are likely to be more stringent than those national guidelines.

Some states have enacted into law practice parameters for specific procedures. The resident should be aware of these. These laws are intended to protect the physician from liability if the parameters are followed. The resident should be aware of any such statutes in the state.

Managed Care

Managed care throughout the United States is growing at an ever-increasing rate. And, indeed, an ever-enlarging number of residents will find themselves practicing within managed care facilities. The resident should be familiar with these new areas[10] of contract liability, assumed third-party liability, gatekeeper liability, practice liability, and administrative liability. Currently, the courts have not definitively sorted out the obligations of members of these new systems, because a minimal number of physicians have been involved in liability under managed care, but federal appellate courts have not held managed care companies liable for malpractice. Basically, these decisions have held the physician responsible for informing the patients of the amount of medical care coverage provided by the managed care facility. Physician response to managed care restrictions on care coverage could set up the physician for liability suits.

Risk Management in the Outpatient/Office Setting

Medical care is being provided in outpatient settings with increasing frequency. Because so many surgical procedures are now performed on an outpatient basis, a physician's initial contact with a patient today is more likely to occur in a physician's office than in the hospital. Whatever the setting, all contacts with patients should be conducted in the same manner that is expected in hospital practice, including the informed consent process and its essential discussion of risks, benefits, and alternatives to the proposed procedure or treatment, together with appropriate documentation of that discussion.

Patients also should be routinely informed of all test results, whether normal or abnormal, and these discussions noted in the patient's record. In addition, it is appropriate to provide the patient and/or family member with personalized instructions for continuing care. Such instructions also should be documented in the patient's record.

Resolving Ethical Issues

The American Medical Association's principles of medical ethics provide that: "A physician shall in provision of appropriate patient care except in emergencies be free to choose whom to serve, with whom to associate, and the environment in which to provide medical services."

This principle gives physicians the right to choose their patients and refuse to render treatment that they consider morally or medically inappropriate. As supervised trainees, residents are not usually free to choose whom they will or will not see as patients. As a result, residents may be confronted with situations that require difficult decisions, such as being asked to perform a procedure that is beyond their expertise, encountering a complication they have not yet been trained to deal with, being asked to participate in or perform a procedure they are morally opposed to, or observing an impaired or incompetent physician attempting to provide patient care.

Wise residents should be prepared to address such situations before they occur. A good way in which to do so is to determine whether the residency program, department, or hospital already has developed procedures for dealing with problem situations. Residents also should be well versed in departmental protocols for the various procedures that are performed in the department so that they know what should and should not be expected to occur. Another good idea is to obtain copies of departmental policies and procedures and the institution's bylaws to determine the proper chain of command within an institution. Finally, the resident should be aware that, whatever the formal protocols and chains of command, problem situations have arisen ever since medicine first was practiced. Even where formal mechanisms to address such situations are not available, informal mechanisms may be.

If these protocols were to be exhausted, without providing a resolution of the problem, and if withholding care would result in greater harm to the patient than would attempting to provide it, residents should continue to treat the patient to the best of their ability, subsequently documenting in the medical record the steps that were taken to find substitute or additional care.

Today, given the many ethical questions that complicate even everyday medical practice, many residents will likely be forced to confront medical situations that raise personal moral issues of varying degrees. Where the potential exists for conflict, supervising physicians should be advised of the situation early in the residency program so that there is ample opportunity to make appropriate alternate arrangements. Any refusal on the part of the supervising physician to accede to a resident's request not to perform a procedure that is morally objectionable to the resident may be appealed through the appropriate chain of command.

Finding oneself caring for patients alongside a chemically impaired or incompetent physician poses another kind of moral dilemma for the resident. Lacking specific guidelines on how to proceed, any residents who may find themselves in these situations can only follow their own best judgment, remembering always that their patients' welfare is their overriding concern. Many institutions now have established formal channels through which an impaired or incompetent physician can be assisted in finding help.

Of course, an emergency situation is likely to preclude the resident's ability to consult with others about such a problem. In that event, if the physician's impairment is causing immediate harm to the patient, the resident may assert authority over that physician and subsequently seek assistance from senior hospital staff.

Insurance Checklist for Residents[11]

When signing contracts, residents should determine the following five items as they apply to the professional liability insurance provided for them in their residency programs:

1. The type of coverage provided by the residency program.

2. Whether the coverage for claims during residency will be provided if those claims are made after a resident leaves the program.

3. Dollar amount of insurance coverage and the dollar amount of tail coverage, if applicable.

4. Any and all limitations on practice contained in the insurance policy.

5. What effects claims might have on the resident's ability to obtain liability insurance in the future.

Even if residents are provided with a policy that ensures appropriate coverage during residency, "surcharging" or "experience rating" may be used by some insurance companies or state insurance commissioners when the physician applies for future malpractice insurance.

National Practitioner Data Bank[11]

Four types of reportable adverse actions are reported to the data bank: (1) licensure actions, (2) clinical privilege actions, (3) professional society membership actions, and (4) payment of a claim against a practitioner.

The law requires that "whoever makes the payment in satisfaction of a claim for medical negligence must notify the data bank. This essentially means that the hospital or insurance carrier will notify the data bank of a payment on behalf of a resident. If, for any reason, a resident ends up making a payment directly to the patient, he or she is also legally required to report to the data bank. Failure to do so can result in a $10,000 penalty. Reporting by the hospital or insurance company of their payments on a resident's behalf does not relieve the resident of the responsibilty of reporting his or her own payments. While such a situation is extremely rare during residency, it may occur for a suit filed after the residency program is completed."

When the data bank receives a report regarding a malpractice payment, it will send the physician or resident a "practitioner notification document." The resident should check the accuracy of all information at this time. Do not delay. A formal dispute with the data bank must be filed within 60 days of the process date shown on the document. There are very specific procedures for disputing data bank reports.

Chapter IV References

1. Danner D: Medical Malpractice: A Primer for Physicians. The Lawyers Co-operative Publishing Co, Rochester, NY, 1988

2. Palmisano DJ, Mang HJ, Jr.: Informed Consent—A Survival Guide. Invictus Publishing Company, New Orleans, 1987

3. American College of Surgeons: Patient Safety Manual: A Guide for Hospitals and Physicians to a Systematic Approach to Quality Assurance and Risk Management. Written for the American College of Surgeons by Bader & Associates, Inc, Rockville, MD, 1985

4. Brittain RS: The Practicing Surgeon's Perspective. Presented at Professional Liability Update, 75th Clinical Congress, American College of Surgeons, Atlanta, GA, October 17, 1989

5. Hirsh HL: Conferences on Legal-Medical Issues. International Conferences of Huntington Station, New York, July 5–17, 1989

6. Joint Commission on Accreditation of Healthcare Organizations: Manual for Hospitals. Joint Commission on Accreditation of Healthcare Organizations, Chicago, IL, 1990

7. Health Care Quality and Improvement Act of 1986 (HCQIA), PL 99-660

8. Committee to Study Medical Professional Liability and the Delivery of Obstetrical Care: Medical Professional Liability and Delivery of Obstetrical Care, Vol 1. National Academy Press, Washington, DC, 1989

9. American College of Obstetricians and Gynecologists: Professional Liability: A Resident's Survival Kit. American College of Obstetricians and Gynecologists, Washington, DC, 1989

10. Manuel BM: Physician liability under managed care. J Am Coll Surg, 182(6):537–546, 1996

11. Council on Resident Education in Obstetrics and Gynecology: Professional Liability for Residents. American College of Obstetricians and Gynecologists, Council on Resident Education in Obstetrics and Gynecology, Washington, DC, 1993

V / CLAIMS MANAGEMENT

Editor's Note

Claims management is the process that occurs following the filing of a claim based on a patient's real or perceived injury. The surgeons who are the defendants in a medical malpractice action must become active participants in this process. This chapter discusses how a surgeon should choose and work with an attorney, particularly in the areas of deposition and trial. In addition, specific suggestions as to how a surgeon might handle various difficult situations are reviewed.

The fact that the surgeon should approach the process of giving a deposition with caution and confidence is emphasized. In addition to understanding the need to answer questions carefully, the surgeon must develop a sense of confidence through careful preparation to be fully knowledgeable about the data to be discussed. It is pointed out that this cautious but confident approach to the deposition must be combined with a disciplined demeanor that carefully avoids any expression of anger, irritation, or other types of inappropriate behavior.

It is also noted that the experience of going through a trial— especially if it is the surgeon's first exposure to that process and if he or she is handicapped by a lack of familiarity with courtroom procedures—can be uncomfortable and unpleasant for the surgeon. The basic principles a surgeon should follow are described in detail.

In addition, the settlement process as one aspect of claims management is presented. Factors that should be considered by the defendant surgeon are described.

Finally, the important practical aspects of asset protection are discussed. Generic guidelines and common misconceptions are discussed, as is the suggestion that the surgeon might seek additional advice.

Surgeon-Attorney Relationship

General Considerations

Civil litigation is the legal process that begins when a defendant receives a summons, usually together with another document, a complaint. This event gives official notice that a lawsuit has been filed and that failure to respond will result in judgment by default.

For most physicians, participating in a lawsuit, especially as defendants, is both an unfamiliar and uncomfortable process. Both unfamiliarity and anxiety are serious handicaps, which is the major reason these sections concerning the attorney, the deposition, and the trial are especially important. The personal experience of the authors of this section (MH and FS) are especially significant. MH is both a clinical cardiothoracic surgeon and an attorney (J.D.) with a long interest in professional liability. His book, *Medical Malpractice Solutions: Systems and Proposals for Injury Compensation,*[1] was published in 1989. FS, also a clinical cardiothoracic surgeon, is chairman of a large department of surgery and chairman of the Professional Liability Committee of the American College of Surgeons. He has had both a long interest and extensive personal experience with professional liability over the past 25 years. He has personally been the defendant in six jury trials and won four. One was lost for a small sum, and one with a brain-injured child was settled for an annuity with no admission of liability. These detailed personal experiences provide the background for the general statements described in this chapter.

The usual procedure in a malpractice suit is for the plaintiff to file a formal document (the complaint or petition) in the appropriate court. This action initiates the lawsuit and identifies the defendant—in this situation, the physician. The complaint usually states the nature of the claim or allegations and the relief requested, (monetary damages). The defendant is then served with the summons and complaint, and the defendant must reply within a specific period of time. When a summons is received, the defendant physician must notify his or her insurance company immediately, as is usually described in the policy. Preparations can then begin for the timely filing of documents and other defense considerations. The documents and defense are handled by an attorney, with appropriate communication with the defendant physician. The insurance company ordinarily selects the attorney; if you are self-insured, you must obtain your own.

Most physicians have little or no experience with courtroom trials, which is a serious handicap, for it makes the physician vulnerable to intimidation from nonmeritorious lawsuits. Unfortunately, unwarranted lawsuits are common, in some states representing more than half of all suits filed. Therefore, most surgeons can expect to be sued one or more times during their surgical career. Several methods have been tried in different states to minimize or eliminate these nonmeritorious suits, but, to date, no successful method for screening out these unwarranted suits has been found. Only through the ability of the physician and the attorney to mount an effective defense can intimidation be avoided. On a more positive note, however, national data have shown repeatedly that a physician will win at least 80 to 90 percent of lawsuits in cases that go to trial, especially with careful preparation and no obvious malpractice.

Knowing that the courtroom experience is an unfamiliar one, but that with ample preparation a successful result can usually be obtained, the importance of active participation by the physician with the attorney from the very beginning of the lawsuit is obvious. A key principle is that the physician be an *active* participant, not simply passively following instructions from the attorney. This subject is addressed further in the section entitled "Working with the Attorney," but, in brief, legal evidence in a courtroom trial evolves from answers to the questions asked. Just as the physician cannot ask questions, but can only respond to the questions asked, deciding what questions *should* be asked to develop the key points is a complex intellectual process, requiring both legal and medical expertise. Because the attorney is not widely experienced in medicine, the active role of the physician in helping decide what questions should be asked is a key one, which emphasizes both the importance of intensive preparation and active participation from the start. Simply passively awaiting instructions from the attorney about what to do next is grossly inadequate.

This intense, active participation to develop the defense requires a great deal of time, work, and intellectual effort. It is very similar to preparing for a board examination in a medical specialty, requiring hours of careful tabulation, analysis, and memorization of pertinent data that describe all the events with the patient's illness and treatment. Preparation is worth every minute of effort.

As discussed in Chapter II, malpractice is legally a charge that the physician deviated from proper care of a patient, and this deviation resulted in injury to the patient. In medicine, answers to many major questions are simply unknown, such as the causes of cancer, atherosclerosis, or hypertension. Hence, deciding what caused an unexpected complication is often difficult and uncertain. The problem could be an unusual complication of the disease; it could be a simple mishap, such as a fall in the bathroom; or it may be malpractice. If the exact cause of the complication is unknown, recognized experts may sharply disagree.

A peculiarity of the American civil system of justice is that uncertainties about what caused the problem are ultimately resolved by a jury trial. The United States is the only country in the entire world where such cases are resolved by a jury. The decisions are made by laymen whose judgment must be based upon the conflicting testimony of so-called expert witnesses. This fact reiterates the importance of the active role of the physician, because the jury's decision is made both from the facts presented and from the jury's assessment of the credibility of opposing opinions presented by the plaintiff and the defendant. To repeat, using the principles outlined in this section, a physician can—with careful preparation combined with an appropriate amount of effort and study—win the vast majority of lawsuits without obvious merit.

Selecting an Attorney

Usually the insurance company carrying the physician's insurance will select and assign an attorney. The physician is usually consulted beforehand to approve the attorney selected. The physician should then meet with the attorney as soon as possible to develop an effective working relationship. It is particularly important for the physician to judge as best as possible the attorney's competence in professional liability, because experienced *defense* attorneys are less common than experienced plaintiff attorneys. In medicine, specialists evolve from years of training in a residency training program designated for that specific purpose. In law, however, such specialized training programs do not exist; expertise must be acquired by personal experience. Hence, the importance of determining the attorney's previous experience with professional liability is obvious. Asking the attorney how often he or she has worked with other physicians, hospitals, and insurance companies in the same geographic area can be helpful.

The most valuable information usually comes from consulting with colleagues who have had experience with litigation. If, for unknown reasons, a young, inexperienced attorney has been assigned, a more experienced attorney should usually be requested. A great deal of the effectiveness of an attorney depends upon prior experience. Usually the insurance company will make every effort to comply with the physician's request.

In large legal firms, a junior attorney may be initially assigned to evaluate a case, collect basic facts, and perhaps conduct the deposition, with the plan that a more senior attorney will conduct the trial. In general, except for initial fact-finding, this arrangement is a mediocre one for the physician. The effectiveness of an attorney depends both upon his or her detailed familiarity with all of the data, as well as having developed a close working relationship with the physician. This situation greatly enhances the ability to think of effective questions to ask as events occur during the trial. Simple legal expertise in the courtroom, per se, is inadequate.

A second attorney, usually termed a personal attorney, may be of value for the defendant physician in several circumstances. Although personal attorneys seem to be retained in only a minority of cases, the most common situations making such representation advisable are the following:

1. Lawsuits in which the damages grossly exceed the amount of insurance policy limits.

2. Any claim in which the insurance carrier has advised the physician that insurance coverage is in debate or questionable.

3. When, for whatever reason, the physician wants to settle a case and does not want a trial under any circumstances, or if the physician chooses to go to trial and the insurer is inclined to settle.

4. When the defense counsel appointed by the insurer feels another attorney would be helpful.

5. When the physician feels uncomfortable with defense counsel, he or she may want a personal attorney to advise as to the quality of services being provided.

6. Any claim that would probably affect the physician's licensure or staff privileges.

Working with Your Attorney

As repeatedly stated, the physician must be an active participant in the entire litigation process, which requires both a lot of personal study and a lot of work with the attorney. The degree of study required, "the homework," is often woefully underestimated. Like preparing for a specialty board examination, hours of careful tabulation, analysis, and memorization of pertinent data are required.

The legal evidence in a lawsuit is principally the patient's hospital chart and the physician's office records. Because these records are legal evidence, they cannot be used as personal notes. Hence, the important first step is for the physician to obtain a personal copy of the entire hospital chart, even if it is a few hundred pages long and requires several hundred dollars to duplicate. The physician's entire office records should also be duplicated, so that they can be marked, indexed, and notated as a personal working copy. The original records, of course, must be submitted at trial and *cannot* be marked or altered in any way.

Once the personal copy of the hospital chart has been obtained, it should be carefully scanned, page by page, with appropriate notes and indices made for reference. This excercise is both time consuming and laborious, but highly effective. Considerable harm to a physician's case can occur at trial if the plaintiff attorney questions the physician about data in the patient's chart with which he or she is not familiar. The *entire* record, including progress notes, nurses' notes, and other items, must be scanned for significant information. These data should then be memorized, similar to preparing for an examination. Only by such complete familiarity with the data can a physician not only answer questions effectively, but also consider what points should be developed at trial in the cross-examination process.

A similar, though less laborious, process should be done with personal duplicates of all office records, committing the key data to memory. Unless the physician has personal copies of both the hospital chart and the office records, an effective review cannot be done, because the hospital chart and office records cannot be marked or cross-indexed in any way.

This tabulation and study of pertinent data should be done before the first detailed meeting of the physician with his or her attorney. This first meeting is educational, both for the physician and the attorney, each learning from the other the key issues in the defense of the case. The amount of time required for this meeting cannot be predicted with any certainty; so a large block of time should be set aside, preferably in the late afternoon or early evening. Scheduling a short meeting during the working hours of a busy day is woefully inadequate and invites disaster. Obviously, a physician should never accept a restriction on the amount of time used for preparation by the attorney. The attorney is functioning as the physician's employee through the insurance company and will be reimbursed whether the attorney wins or loses. The physician, however, is on trial for both money and reputation and should allocate as much time as possible for preparation and expect the attorney to do likewise. Usually, the attorney is more than willing to devote all the time needed, while the physician is reluctant. This attitude must be avoided.

Expert witnesses on the subject being litigated are essential for an effective defense. The physician should assist the attorney in identifying and contacting appropriate experts, based on personal knowledge or information supplied by colleagues. Once chosen, the expert witness must be given a complete copy of the records and other pertinent information. At times, the attorney may want to arrange a joint meeting with the physician and the expert witness to discuss various aspects of the case.

The major pre-trial activities that allow both parties to discover information about the opponent's case are called *discovery*. These activities include written interrogatories, request for production of documents, physical and mental examinations, and deposition. Interrogatories consist of a series of questions submitted by one party to the opponents and must be answered in writing, under oath, within a certain time period. Responding to such questions obviously requires consultation with your attorney. Other fact-finding activities may or may not be used, depending upon the judgment of the attorneys. A most important discovery procedure, *deposition*, is discussed in the next section. Deposition has been called the plaintiff attorney's "deadly weapon."

How often the physician and attorney should meet before the deposition will vary with the complexity of the case, ranging from one or two meetings to several. The number required is immaterial; the goal is complete and thorough preparation.

The Deposition

General Considerations

The deposition is the standard legal procedure commonly used before a courtroom trial. It is primarily a fact-finding inquiry by the plaintiff attorney to discover any facts that would be *applicable* in the case being litigated.

In general, this process is one-sided for the plaintiff. The plaintiff attorney can ask a wide range of questions, while the defendant physician can simply answer as best he or she can unless the attorney objects.

Neither a judge nor jury is present, and the plaintiff attorney has a wide latitude for questioning, far more so than at trial. The only restriction is that the line of questioning could conceivably lead to "admissible evidence." One casual description of the overall procedure is a "fishing expedition" by the attorney.

The physician should answer questions as concisely as possible, without elaboration. The physician should not elaborate in a futile attempt to educate the plaintiff attorney with the hope of having the suit dismissed. Theoretically, the physician is required to answer, as best as possible, all appropriate questions. In unusual circumstances, if a physician refuses to answer a question, the plaintiff attorney can adjourn the deposition and request a court order requiring the physician to answer.

The deposition is usually conducted in a conference room of the law offices of one of the attorneys, either the plaintiff or the defense. The atmosphere is semi-formal; participants include the plaintiff attorney, the defendant physician and defense attorney, attorneys for any co-defendants, and a court reporter. Although the atmosphere may seem somewhat relaxed, the physician should regard the entire procedure soberly and seriously. The physician has little to gain, but a lot to lose, and may seriously injure the case with unplanned improper testimony. The answers by the defendant are given under oath and may be subsequently introduced at trial. To some extent, the deposition "freezes" the physician's testimony. If contradictory statements are made at trial, the physician's statements in the deposition can be used either to impair his or her credibility or actually impeach testimony. Hence, the deposition is essentially a "mini-trial" with the potential for little to gain but a lot to lose.

Preparation for Deposition

As described in the preceding section about the physician working with the attorney, detailed study and preparation are essential, requiring a lot of time and effort. The entire procedure should be viewed with the same gravity as a courtroom trial.

The description in the preceding section ("Working with Your Attorney") should be reviewed about study of personal copies of the hospital record and office notes. These working copies should *not* be brought to the deposition, however, because any material present at the deposition may be obtained by the plaintiff attorney and used accordingly. Hence, the physician responds to questions from memory, referring to the hospital record or the official office notes, as necessary. The importance of careful analysis and memorization of data beforehand is obvious.

The importance of detailed planning between physician and attorney was emphasized in the preceding section. A meeting immediately before the deposition is essential, again reviewing key points that may develop in response to the questions that will probably be asked.

Legal Considerations

In planning for a deposition, it is important to emphasize what is and what is not malpractice. Malpractice is defined as a significant deviation from the standard of care, with the added stipulation that this deviation caused injury to the patient. The standard of care is the quality of care that would be given by a reasonably competent practitioner in that specialty, not exceptional care. An error in judgment, unless significantly inferior to that of the usual community physician, does not by itself constitute malpractice.

The plaintiff must clearly demonstrate that this deviation from the standard of care caused injury to the patient. The deviation, per se, is not malpractice, unless a demonstrated injury occurred as a consequence. Hence, the physician should rarely, if ever, **admit** that the deviation from a standard of care caused the patient injury. This approach will be pursued by the expert witness for the plaintiff. If you agree under oath that your deviation from the standard of care caused the injury, you essentially have become the expert witness against yourself.

In general, the physician should restrict his or her answers, as much as possible, to the care given to the patient, not the broad subject of the disease being treated. To do otherwise has the defendant physician assuming the role of expert witness. If you make broad general statements to demonstrate your breadth of knowledge, they may be subsequently used against you.

Maintaining a Professional Demeanor

The physician should maintain a formal, professional demeanor while answering questions slowly, thoughtfully, and concisely. Do not be overtly hostile or combative, nor appear careless or bored. The intense sober concentration that is required is somewhat similar to participating in a chess tournament. Distracting comments or questions, such as jokes, gratuitous compliments, abuses, or insults, should be viewed as hazardous distractions that could interrupt the physician's concentration on the subject and should be briefly acknowledged or simply ignored. It is most important that the physician be disciplined beforehand not to become angry or irritated, no matter what the provocation. Under no circumstances should the physician attempt to argue with the plaintiff counsel. Some questions naturally irritate, annoy, or anger, but all of these emotional reactions distract from the intensity of thinking. Becoming angry might be fully justified, but the impaired concentration that follows can lead to improper or hazardous answers to subsequent questions, which become part of the legal testimony. The plaintiff attorney benefits, not the physician.

After a puzzling or complex question, the physician may pause to provide time for the defense attorney to object. If the attorney objects, the physician should simply listen until the objection is decided. If the physician becomes fatigued or distracted from a long series of questions, he or she can request a recess.

Answering Questions

The defendant physician can only answer questions asked by the plaintiff attorney. The physician cannot ask questions and, in general, cannot comment, except in answer to a specific question. The plaintiff attorney may request that general comments, separate from the answer to the question asked, be stricken from the testimony, unless the information is helpful to *the plaintiff's case*.

The two key requirements for effective testimony at a deposition are thorough familiarity with the pertinent data, coupled with an understanding of what to answer, how to answer, and what not to answer. In many ways, what not to say and what not to answer are almost equally important as what answers are given.

Answers to questions should be simple, thoughtful, and specific, based upon written statements in the patient's chart or the physician's notes. The most concrete answer is one that can be validated by what has been documented in the notes in the hospital chart or the office records.

A second type of answer is based on *specific memory*; a physician clearly remembers the events about which the question is asked. Usually, specific-memory answers are based on recent events or vivid circumstances that the physician remembers clearly.

Questions about events in the remote past that are neither documented in the record nor remembered specifically should be answered in general terms, such as, "My routine practice in such circumstances is...." A physician is certainly not realistically expected to remember such details. Under no circumstances should the physician guess or speculate as to what was specifically done with a patient. Such statements are of dubious validity and are often contradictory. Simply answer, "I don't remember the specific event. My usual routine is _____; otherwise, I don't remember."

Answer the Question—Do Not Lecture

It should be repeatedly emphasized that the deposition process is a wide-ranging, fact-finding inquiry by the plaintiff's attorney to discover material that might subsequently be used at trial. The deposition is primarily for the plaintiff's benefit; the physician has little to gain, but can seriously harm his or her case by gratuitously providing important information previously unknown to the plaintiff. The physician should not attempt to elaborate and impress the plaintiff counsel with personal knowledge and skill, hoping that the case will be terminated. Similarly, natural instincts to teach or explain should be restrained; simply answer the question. This advice merits repeated emphasis: *Simply answer the question.* Do not volunteer information, attempt to educate the attorney, or correct erroneous statements unless absolutely necessary.

Complex, Deceptive Questions

The professional skill of the plaintiff attorney in many ways depends upon the nature of the questions that he or she can formulate. Answers to these questions create evidence upon which the case is decided. A wide range of complex, misleading, or deceptive questions may be used in an attempt to mislead or trap the unwary physician. This type of question contrasts sharply with the usual type of question a physician asks a patient when simply seeking facts.

Many good examples of hazardous questions are discussed in the 1988 publication by Danner, *Medical Malpractice: A Primer for Physicians*.[2] Unless the question is clear and the answer obvious, the physician can simply state, "I don't understand," or "I don't know," or "I don't remember." Alternately, ask that the question be rephrased.

Several examples of misleading or tricky questions are as follows:

"Yes or no"   A complex question may be followed with a firm request in a dictatorial tone, "Simply answer, yes or no!" Such questions are designed so that either answer is hazardous. An exaggerated example of such a question is, "Have you stopped beating your wife?" The proper response to such questions is to simply reply that the question must be rephrased, because it cannot be answered with a simple, "Yes or no."

Ambiguous   Questions that are ambiguous can be interpreted in different ways and should simply be rejected, with the request that the question be rephrased or, "I don't understand." A so-called "leading" question is one that instructs or suggests to the witness what answer is desired, or one that embodies the answer sought in the question. For example, "As this wound infection resulted from absence of prophylactic antibiotics, should antibiotics be routinely given?" Answering the question as formulated agrees with a key point that the wound infection resulted from lack of antibiotics and essentially admits that a deviation from a standard of practice caused the patient's injury. The physician has unwittingly testified in favor of the plaintiff.

Hypothetical   Be particularly wary of a hypothetical question, such as, "Let's assume such and such." This statement is essentially a discussion of the subject, not the patient. The attorney is using you as plaintiff's expert witness. Such questions are best avoided by restricting comments to the care of the particular patient. Expounding on the subject of the disease being treated is seldom helpful and has serious hazards. A similar type of question may be initiated with a casual, "Well, off the record, let's assume such and such...."

Another deceptive phrase is the preamble, "With a reasonable degree of medical certainty, such and such...." This type of statement is hazardous, because it can be subjected to a wide variety of interpretations. For example, "With a reasonable degree of medical certainty, vomiting is consistent with a diagnosis of appendicitis." Such a statement is true, but misleading. Vomiting is also consistent with innumerable conditions, such as cerebellar tumors or pregnancy. It is far more precise to answer in terms of probability, such as 5 to 20 percent, by saying, "Approximately ____ percent of patients with appendicitis experience vomiting."

Authoritative Textbook Another common trap used by plaintiff attorney is to ask if a physician recognizes a textbook as "authoritative." This question should rarely be answered with a simple, unqualified "yes," for any deviation of the physician's performance from what is recorded in the textbook is an admission of deviation from authoritative practice. Textbooks, in general, should simply be described as helpful references, but only one of many sources of information. Some parts are helpful, some are not.

The Trial

General Considerations

A courtroom trial is very different from virtually any activity a physician normally does in the practice of medicine. Most of a physician's work is with the diagnosis and treatment of a patient's disease, trying either to cure the problem or to make the patient more comfortable. A courtroom trial, however, is an adversarial experience in which allegations are made and facts are presented. Sharp, even bitter, controversy often develops about the significance and interpretation of the facts, often with legal maneuvers that can distort their meaning or suppress their presentation altogether. This situation is usually quite different from anything the physician has previously experienced. It may be a brutal, depressing experience for both the patient and the physician. More than once, a trial has been described as "the ultimate form of civilized warfare." A detailed discussion of the psychological trauma attendant to a trial is described in Chapter VI.

A unique aspect of a trial is that the courtroom procedure is not only a search for the facts, but often includes different forms of attack on the reputation of the physician. There are four well-known methods for such an attack. The most obvious and most common method is to *challenge the physician's* **competence**. If the physician is clearly well-trained and competent, a second avenue of attack is to *charge the physician with* **carelessness**. "He is well trained, but simply so busy, he can't pay attention to details." "Everyone makes mistakes!"

The third method, highly effective with contradictory testimony, is to *impair* **credibility**, which is usually done by demonstrating inconsistencies in testimony, especially between the pre-trial deposition and the court testimony. Thus, the deposition and the careful pre-trial reviews of the deposition are essential. If contradictory testimony can be demonstrated, the implication is that the physician's memory is faulty. Blatant dishonesty is rarely charged.

A fourth method, discussed in more detail in the section on "Maintaining a Professional Demeanor," is to *challenge* **compassion**, portraying the physician as an indifferent, noncaring, wealthy entrepreneur.

The physician can anticipate attack and abuse in any or all of these four categories. The type of response, discussed in the subsequent section on professional demeanor, is crucial. Arousing emotions in a witness by intimidation, provocation, or guilt evocation are well-established questioning techniques. The jargon is to *"rattle the witness!"* Hence, no matter how irritating or unwarranted abusive statements may be, under no circumstances must the physician become visibly angry. Anger, no matter how justified, arising from provocative, abusive questions may ultimately harm the physician and help the plaintiff. As discussed in subsequent paragraphs, abusive, irritative questions can be used to the physician's benefit if dealt with properly.

On a more positive note, with careful planning and full knowledge of pertinent data concerning the case, combined with an understanding of courtroom procedures, the physician can win at trial the majority of all suits in which no obvious malpractice exists. As stated in the introduction to this section, one of the authors (FS) has personally been the defendant through six jury trials, settling one for an annuity for a brain-injured child with no admission of liability, losing one small case, and winning four, all of which concluded unanimously in the defendant's favor.

Planning and Preparation

During the trial of a complex, hazardous lawsuit, the physician should virtually stop the practice of medicine and plan on being in court 80 to 90 percent of the time. Well-meaning advice, such as "You will be called as little as possible, so you can continue to work with your patients," sounds reassuring, but is often disastrous.

Being present in court most of the time is essential for two major reasons. An important factor influencing the credibility of a physician's statements before a jury is the personality of the physician. In brief, "Is the physician the type that jurors respect and would seek for their personal illness?" "Does the physician seem compassionate and concerned that the patient sustained an unforeseen complication or irritated and angry at an unjust assault on good intentions and reputation?" The proper demeanor must be conveyed by appearance, as well as by words. The jury is spending a lot of time with the case to make a decision. It is naturally irritating to observe that the physician doesn't even have enough concern to come to the courtroom. There is no substitute for being regularly seen by the jury, soberly observing and listening to everything that is said.

The other major reason for being present is to listen carefully to all testimony in order to detect statements that could be useful in the defense. In complex cases, transcripts of the testimony given in the earlier days of the trial can be obtained and studied in detail. The basic charge is deviation from the standard of care and that the alleged deviation from the standard of care resulted in injury to the patient. The attorney is an expert in legal matters, while the physician is not; however, the physician is knowledgeable in medicine. Hence, the physician should carefully listen for erroneous or contradictory statements about medical facts or events that can subsequently be examined by the attorney when questioning either the plaintiff, expert witness, or the defendant physician. The physician is not only looking for key points, but trying to help decide what questions his or her attorney could use to demonstrate contradictory or erroneous statements. The attorney, of course, is the final judge of the best approach to follow.

Trial is an intense intellectual process of concentrating carefully on the evolving events and looking for clues that could be helpful. The senior author of this section (FS) found major clues in two of four trials (that were won), which were subsequently developed by his attorney and clearly played a decisive role in discrediting the testimony of the expert witness for the plaintiff. This intense intellectual process is the principal reason that a physician must be a very active participant in the entire legal proceeding, starting from the receipt of the summons to the conclusion of the courtroom trial.

The basic preparation for the trial is essentially the accumulation, careful study, and memorization of all pertinent data, already described in the sections entitled "Working with Your Attorney" and "Preparation for Deposition." Hence, this information will not be repeated here. As often stated, the intensity of the work and intellectual effort is almost identical to that involved in planning for an oral examination for specialty board certification.

The close physician-attorney relationship that was initiated at the beginning of the case, and further developed through the pre-trial deposition, is crucial at this time. In complex cases, the physician and attorney need to meet each day and discuss the developments and plans for the subsequent day, either during the day in court or that evening. The physician virtually retires from the practice of medicine during trial.

Maintaining a Professional Demeanor

The importance of maintaining a formal professional demeanor, despite irritation or abuse, cannot be overstated. This advice was emphasized in the preceding section, "The Deposition." During the deposition, a calm sober demeanor is necessary to avoid distraction from clarity of thinking. In the courtroom trial, demeanor is even more important because of the emotional impact the appearance and attitude of the physician have on the jury. The demeanor of the physician should be that which a juror respects and admires: appropriately formal, courteous, not smiling; events are neither funny nor humorous, especially to the injured patient. The physician is neither unduly humble or agreeable, compliant or subservient, nor fearful or hostile. Courteous professional demeanor should be maintained, no matter what abuse, admirably demonstrating "grace under pressure." Responding to continued abusive questions with proper grace and dignity may significantly help the physician, for the jury sympathetically admires the ability to maintain composure and will likely become angry with the attorney's persistent abuse.

As stated earlier, the four major aspects of a physician's reputation that may be questioned are competence, care, credibility, and compassion. All of these should be embodied in the physician's demeanor and behavior.

Competence is displayed by answers that are clear and certain, expressed with confidence, without equivocation or obvious arrogance.

Care is shown by demeanor, thinking carefully, answering slowly and deliberately, and avoiding flip statements, snappy answers, or brisk retorts.

Credibility is demonstrated primarily by the consistency of the physician's statements, stating clearly what he or she knows, does not know, or does not remember.

Compassion is exemplified by the overall behavior in court, demonstrating a serious appropriate concern for the distress of the patient that led to the lawsuit, rather than displaying anger or irritation at what the physician considers unjust accusations.

A useful pre-trial preparation is to envision a steely discipline that says, "I will not be baited into anger with abusive, distorted questions." To repeat again and again, **do not become visibly angry!** With particularly abusive questions, the defendant should pause before answering.

Testimony

A basic principle of effective testimony is termed *persuasive speaking*, with positive clear comments that underline their credibility. Answering questions in court is quite different from answering the same questions during the deposition. In the deposition, the goal is to answer questions without providing excessive information to the plaintiff attorney. Hence, questions are answered clearly and as briefly as possible. In court, however, the physician is speaking directly to the jury, a lay audience who must interpret opposing statements both by what is said and by their assessment of the credibility of the speaker. The physician should speak directly to the jury, with eye contact that connotes sincerity and credibility. This type of behavior is diametrically opposed to that of the aloof, indifferent physician who unemotionally recites the facts in answer to a question. When feasible, answers should be given that can be elaborated upon if further understanding can be helpful. For example, if an elaborate answer is useful, a direct question can be answered with "Yes, for five distinct reasons. They are as follows...." This type of elaboration, of course, is not given at the deposition but is valuable at trial, not only indicating the importance of the data, but the physician's overall knowledge of the subject. Often the plaintiff attorney will try to interrupt such answers. If necessary, the defense attorney can provide another opportunity for the physician to elaborate during cross-examination of the physician.

Repetition

Important facts in the physician's defense should be repeated as frequently as possible during answers to different questions. The jurors are instructed not to make notes, so frequent repetition of important facts is valuable.

Clarity of Communication

Clarity is another important method for better understanding by the jurors, who are laymen with little medical knowledge. In some circumstances, a blackboard or other visual aids may be used to illustrate complex medical issues, not only clarifying the point in question, but also demonstrating the physician's overall knowledge of the subject.

The methods of giving specific answers to questions in a trial are identical to those described in the section on "The Deposition." That section should be read when planning for a trial, because some of the same guidelines are applicable in both situations. In brief, the most concrete, specific answers are those that are documented in the patient's hospital chart or the office records. Precise answers may also be possible for events that the physician clearly and specifically remembers. Certain events in the distant past can usually only be partly recalled. In no instance should the physician speculate; such speculation is not only of dubious value, but easily leads to contradictory statements. The best answer is to describe "my usual practice" or to simply state "I don't recall."

The same advice given about complex, deceptive questions in the section on deposition testimony is, of course, equally applicable in the courtroom.

Questions are usually asked about textbooks. Such questions include what textbooks are used, which are "authoritative," and similar questions. The physician may comment on opinions in the different textbooks, displaying not only familiarity with the material, but the independence of his or her own thinking. Of course, the trap to avoid is accepting any textbook in its entirety as being "authoritative." This trap can usually be avoided by answering in general terms, such as "Like several excellent textbooks, some are helpful in some areas, but not in others. No one is completely authoritative."

The Plaintiff Expert Witness

This section concerns the important role of the defendant physician in analyzing and, hopefully, discrediting the qualifications of the expert witness for the plaintiff, a key element in the entire case. Guidelines for the behavior of the physician when testifying as an expert witness and not as a defendant, are not described in this

215

section, but are detailed in three other publications (two from the Professional Liability Committee of the American College of Surgeons in 1988 and 1989).[3,4,5]

The testimony of the expert witness for the plaintiff is crucial for the plaintiff's case, because the jury, as laymen, cannot determine independently the quality of the medical care, but must evaluate the conflicting testimonies of expert witnesses for the plaintiff and the defense. A potential for serious abuse currently exists in the legal qualifications for an expert witness. A few states have addressed this problem with specific remedial legislation. This subject has also been discussed in detail in two publications from the Professional Liability Committee of the American College of Surgeons.[3,5]

In brief, the decision as to what qualifications are required for an expert witness is a legal one, not a medical one. A medical organization can describe appropriate qualifications, but these are simply recommendations with no legal authority, unless enforced by the court system.

The current abuses with "unqualified" expert witnesses arose from difficulty in past years of finding any expert witness of any kind for the plaintiff. The broad, excessively liberal rule arose that any person with a medical degree might qualify to testify, regardless of specialty or background.[1] Improvements have come, but serious defects remain. Today, in many states, physicians may testify in a case even though their training in that specialty is meager, and they may not have actively practiced the specialty for several years, if ever.

This background is described in some detail to explain that many "experts" have limited training and experience with the specific medical condition being litigated. In some states, the expert witness is known in advance, and a deposition may be taken or a background search can be made to determine what type of testimony the expert has given in previous similar trials. In other states, however, the identity of the expert witness is not known until a court appearance to take the witness stand.

Usually, from experience, the "professional" expert witness has acquired an imposing presence on the witness stand, appearing wise, reflective, and scholarly—a true "expert." This presence may be accompanied by an orotund, authoritative manner of speaking, designed, as in theater, to convey the impression of authority and wisdom. However, the simple fact that the plaintiff has employed a professional expert with little, if any, experience in the matter at hand can be exploited with great benefit by a vigorous cross-examination by the defendant's attorney.

The defendant physician has a key role in analyzing the knowledge and reasoning of the plaintiff expert, because the defense attorney cannot judge the witness's medical knowledge or the validity of the conclusions. This analysis may be one of the most critical elements in the entire trial. If the physician knows the data and the subject in detail, erroneous or unsound conclusions by the expert may become apparent. The basic question is, "Are the conclusions supported by the pertinent data?" These analyses can subsequently be used by the defense attorney in cross-examination to seriously discredit the qualifications of the expert. To repeat, this type of analysis can best be done by the physician, knowing both the data and listening to the testimony. Possibly, it could be done by the expert witness for the defendant, but the defendant's expert usually has not heard the majority of the preceding testimony.

One of the authors (FS) has personally used this approach effectively in two major trials, both of which reached a verdict in favor of the defendant.

One suit concerned a plastic surgeon who underwent a cardiac operation for a prosthetic valve replacement. Subsequently, a mild diplopia and Horner's syndrome evolved, and the surgeon retired on total disability, with the claim that his impaired vision prevented him from performing surgery. A CAT scan (computerized axial tomogram) of the brain demonstrated a linear opacity in the wall of one of the two vertebral arteries proximal to their junction at the base of the brain to form the basilar artery. The charge was that a fragment of vascular catheter (an "angiocath") had broken off at operation and embolized to the vertebral artery, even though such an episode had not been recorded, nor had a similar episode ever been recorded. The most probable explanation was that the eccentric opacity in the wall of the vertebral artery was a form of calcification. Despite the dubious validity of the entire charge, the case, over a period of years, proceeded to trial.

During the trial, a visual display of the anatomy of the base of the brain showed the anatomic course of the vertebral and basilar arteries and their relationship to the cranial nerves innervating the musculature of the eye. The plaintiff expert witness testified that the opacity in one vertebral artery caused the neurologic deficit. Study of the anatomic drawings made it apparent that an opacity in the wall of one vertebral artery, regardless of type or source, could not possibly injure a cranial nerve to the eye, because the cranial nerves for the eye muscles (III, IV, and VI) arise from the brain stem at the level of the basilar artery, not at the level of the vertebral artery more proximally. Incredibly enough, this simple anatomic fact had not been recognized previously by several consultants over a period of years. Its subsequent emphasis was clearly significant in reaching a favorable verdict for the defendant.

Another example occurred in a trial in which the charge was that the use of the antibiotic clindamycin (Cleocin) following a cardiac operation led to pseudomembranous colitis, severe dehydration, and shock. The patient survived with a temporary ileostomy, followed by colon reconstruction. The cardiac operation had been performed before the relationship between clindamycin and enterocolitis was widely known; the origin of the disease from *Clostridia difficile* had not been established. The expert witness for the plaintiff stoutly asserted that the patient had been neglected for days, with improper fluid replacement, resulting in progressive dehydration and shock resembling cholera. The neglected fluid replacement that produced severe dehydration and shock was denounced in strong theatrical terms as malpractice.

Study of the patient's hospital chart in detail showed that proper hydration had been given, the patient's fluid balance was satisfactory, and the blood urea nitrogen,which had been measured daily, was normal. Knowing that the blood urea nitrogen is quickly elevated as a result of a decrease in renal blood flow produced by dehydration, the defense attorney questioned on cross-examination whether the expert witness knew what the blood urea nitrogen was before he made such sweeping conclusions about days of neglect from improper fluid replacement. Simply asking the question quickly revealed the expert's carelessness and seriously impaired his credibility. A successful verdict for the defendant was soon forthcoming.

In summary, the expert witness for the plaintiff plays a key role in the entire case. He or she must demonstrate to the jury that the care provided by the defendant physician was "substandard" and that this deviation from accepted medical practice caused the plaintiff's injury. If the testimony can be discredited with proper questions on cross-examination, the case for the defense is greatly strengthened. Effective questions by the defense attorney may demonstrate the expert's lack of knowledge of the specialty, a careless review of the patient's record, or improper conclusions from the data available. As said earlier, this careful analysis is a crucial responsibility for the defendant physician; it can seldom, if ever, be done by others unless they know the data and the entire case thoroughly and have heard the majority of preceding testimony.

Complaining, after the trial, of deceptive, misleading, or inaccurate testimony by the expert witness, which may seem downright fraudulent, is virtually futile. The trial court has the responsibility for accepting the qualifications and testimony of the expert witness. Unless this testimony is discredited *at trial* and unless gross perjury can be proved later, virtually nothing can be done.

Settlement

Settlement, an important part of the litigation process, usually occurs in the pretrial phase, but it may also occur at subsequent stages of the lawsuit. Although no exact figures are available, it is estimated that 90 to 97 percent of all civil litigation, including medical malpractice actions, ends in settlement or dismissal before trial. Legal scholars and commentators overwhelmingly agree that settlement is desirable and should be encouraged.

A settlement made between the parties to an incident or a claim involved in a lawsuit is an agreement that resolves the legal dispute. It results in a final disposition of a case without a decision on the merits. Usually, payment is made to the plaintiff in exchange for a release, which is a legal document that absolves the defendant from all past, present, and future liability in connection with the incident or claim. Settlement agreements should, of course, be in writing, because an oral agreement, even if legally adequate, would likely be the subject of further disputes at a future time. Settlement agreements are governed by contract law and should be drafted by an attorney, based on contract law principles. Most jurisdictions do not require that the agreement be filed with the court or that its contents be made public in any way, so that the terms of the agreement may remain confidential. Most releases specifically state that settlement by the defendant does not constitute an admission of fault.[6,7]

The provisions of malpractice insurance policies may permit the insurer to settle without the concurrence of the insured physician, but ordinarily the physician has some control over the process, as contained in the clauses of the insurance policy. Some malpractice insurance policies promise that a physician's consent will be obtained before a settlement is offered or provide a mechanism to appeal an insurance company's decision to settle. Other companies retain complete control of the decision and may not even inform the physician until the settlement is made. Another approach is to allow physicians to refuse a settlement, but then to limit the insurance company's subsequent liability to the amount of the settlement offer. A present trend toward group policies may further complicate this process, because an organization under such a policy may settle a claim without the physician's knowledge to avoid the nuisance, risk, or expense of litigation.[8]

Considerations in Settlement

In arriving at a decision to settle a legal controversy, a number of factors must be carefully weighed. The objective advice of the defense attorney retained by the insurance company is usually the final determinant. However, in the event of disagreement, or if potential conflicts of interest exist, a personal attorney, as discussed in the section on surgeon-attorney relationship, may be advisable.

The process of deciding whether settlement should be offered will include the following considerations: probability of winning or losing at trial; presence or absence of legally actionable negligence; severity of the patient's injury and disability; type and quality of available experts who will face each other on behalf of the plaintiff and defendant in the "battle of the experts"; location or venue of the lawsuit (for example, whether it will be tried in a conservative rural area or a liberal, more plaintiff-oriented urban center); factors that might engender sympathy in the jurors and influence them to award large sums for pain and suffering; adequacy or inadequacy of the available medical record; and presence of alterations of the record, which might result in the loss of an otherwise defensible case. A consideration that is sometimes ignored is the unpredictability of the jury verdict, perhaps resulting in a large award in excess of insurance limits, when a more favorable settlement might have been obtained initially.

Other increasingly important considerations relating to settlement are malpractice reporting requirements to state licensing authorities, other administrative bodies, and, most notably, the National Practitioner Data Bank. Currently, settlement must be reported to such entities, as well as on subsequent credentialing and recredentialing applications for hospitals and any prospective employers or organizations. The practical effect of such reporting requirements is to discourage settlement, because defendants may choose the chance of a favorable jury outcome and thus avoid the negative implications of the reporting process.

Factors *Favoring* Settlement

The law favors settlement. Generally, settlement promotes judicial economy; expedites claim resolution; removes the uncertainties inherent in a trial; conserves the parties' resources that would otherwise be spent on court costs, legal fees, and other expenses; and is socially desirable in that it ends discord and potentially minimizes dissatisfaction with the legal process.

Each participant in a lawsuit has reason to prefer settlement. The **judge,** eager to clear the court calendar and dispose of cases, may require the parties to participate in a pretrial settlement conference or in other alternative dispute resolution methodology. The **insurance carrier** wants to limit the cost of defense. The **plaintiff attorney** considers settlement a victory, inasmuch as it ensures compensation for the client and for the attorney's time and effort, thus avoiding the "litigation lottery" that a trial represents. The **defense attorney** also wants to avoid the uncertainty of a jury verdict. The **defendant physician** saves the time, energy, and emotional trauma demanded by the litigation process and avoids the danger of a verdict in excess of the physician's insurance coverage.

How Settlement Is Reached

Parties have great latitude in working out a means to resolve their justiciable controversies, so that many disputes can be resolved without prolonged, expensive, and emotionally traumatic litigation. The process includes many possibilities, some within or a part of the litigation process itself. On the other hand, a number of extra-judicial possibilities are available, which do not require the usual litigation formalities.

Incident Settlement

Settlement of an incident may occur when the possibility of a claim is first identified. Here, the physician may play a primary role, although attorneys are also essential and the insurance carrier must, of course, always be notified, be in agreement, and be willing to participate. For an incident that occurred in a hospital, the hospital risk manager should also be involved, or at least notified. Settlement will then depend on the response of the insurer, the hospital, and the parties, and may include treatment of the patient at no cost in exchange for release or some amount of compensation paid to the patient.

Settlement After Lawsuit

After a lawsuit is filed, the attorneys play a primary role. Plaintiff attorneys frequently make a monetary demand upon the defense attorney, to which the defense attorney then responds with rejection, acceptance, or a counteroffer. Negotiations may continue until the parties arrive at a settlement and may be made at any time, even if settlement negotiations have previously broken down. The insurance carrier, of course, plays a critical role and retains authority to negotiate settlements. The defense attorney may only accept, demand, or counteroffer settlement with the consent of the insurance carrier. The defendant physician's role depends upon the provisions of the insurance policy. Thus, it is important that physicians be aware of the terms of their respective policies. Settlement continues to be a factor even after a verdict has been rendered, as well as during the appeals process. At such times, both parties will attempt to minimize their losses and replace continuing uncertainty with a definitive outcome.

Although settlement within the litigation process usually occurs following direct negotiations between the attorneys, the judge may also take a direct role that may be in the form of informal discussions or suggestions in an attempt to resolve disputes. The judge may actually become a mediator, may speak directly to the parties or to the attorneys, and may require and structure conferences to attempt resolution.

Alternative settlement techniques within the litigation process are also encouraged by the courts.[9] These are known as court-annexed alternative dispute resolution (ADR) and include mediation designed to encourage parties to identify their differences and resolve them; mandatory nonbinding arbitration; summary jury trials in which each attorney presents the case to a jury drawn from the regular jury pool and where the subsequent verdict is then used in the settlement negotiations; the use of court-appointed neutral experts, which is permitted by federal and most state courts; and other alternatives that use neutral evaluation of the controversy.

Other Methods of Resolving Controversies

Other methods for resolving or settling disputes without the involvement of courts are known as freestanding alternative dispute resolution (ADR). This methodology may use litigation procedures, as well as other freestanding procedures, that are not a part of the litigation process. Such procedures include settlement of cases without filing a lawsuit; mini-trials, based on procedures to which the parties agree; binding arbitration; conciliation or mediation, which involves the assistance of impartial third parties; fact finding by another party for identification of issues; private judging, where the dispute is submitted to a former or retired judge for resolution; and a combination of the various methods.[9,10]

Conclusions

Realistic and objective assessment of the option of settlement at any stage of the claim, either before or after the filing of a lawsuit or the rendering of a verdict is a continuing consideration. This multifaceted, ongoing process should operate to expeditiously resolve an indefensible, or perhaps a borderline defensible, claim. A final decision should be made objectively, based on the factors previously noted, as well as on the advice of the defense and personal attorneys.

Protecting One's Assets

Strategies for dealing with one's personal finances should include timely planning for the protection of past, present, or future assets from judgment creditors or creditors in bankruptcy proceedings. Such considerations are essential, because nonexempt assets are available to creditors for the satisfaction of a debtor's obligations and are thus at risk to the extent an award for compensatory or punitive damages is not covered by insurance.[11]

The risk of a judgment in excess of insurance coverage is particularly evident in the increasing severity of jury awards in medical malpractice cases, where awards averaged in excess of $1.4 million, ranging as high as $90.3 million, in the period 1988 to 1994. Jury Verdict Research data indicate that 26 percent of awards for doctor malpractice in those years were $1 million or higher, 13 percent were $2 million or higher, 8 percent were $3 million or higher, and 4 percent ranged from $5 million to more than $10 million.[12] Although most awards against physicians appear to be ultimately settled for amounts within insurance limits, the usual limits are well below the larger awards. An evaluation of this risk to personal assets and its potential consequences includes an integrated consideration of insurance, property ownership, business relationships, creditors' rights, and bankruptcy, as well as personal quality assurance and risk management.[13]

General Considerations

The legal rules protecting assets from judgment or bankruptcy creditors vary from state to state and differ under federal or state law. An appropriate program must address the applicable law in a particular state, personal factors, and various special circumstances. The program should be part of an integrated financial plan, covering the entire range of an individual's assets, and must not be driven exclusively by considerations of the malpractice problem.

Most importantly, planning and implementation of a program must occur well in advance of any specific creditor problems to avoid allegations of fraudulent transfer and possible return of assets to the reach of creditors or to the bankruptcy estate. Property transfers should be based on reasons other than simple protection from creditors, and adequate records of all transactions should be maintained. Further considerations should include unexpected events, such as possible future deterioration of family relationships (for example, divorce) and the potential personal liabilities of the "safe spouse," who may actually be vulnerable through professional or business activities, membership on boards of directors, or participation in a variety of organizations.

It must be emphasized that there is no single correct method, no uniform "generic" plan for asset protection. Each program is necessarily unique and should be based on an overall financial plan formulated with competent professional advice. The plan should integrate insolvency planning with other considerations, including insurance, tax planning, estate planning, and gifts to a spouse or children.[14–18]

Common Misconceptions

Several commonly held erroneous beliefs are worthy of specific mention. The short discussions of each topic are designed to present a brief overview of problems and possibilities for asset protection, as a basis for further discussion with appropriate advisors.

1. **Not carrying liability insurance ("going bare") will prevent lawsuits.**

   There is no objective basis for this belief. Should a lawsuit occur, the absence of insurance would require substantial personal expenses for defense costs, while personal and business assets can certainly be reached by creditors. Additionally, the risk of underinsurance is also substantial. Although it is widely believed that carrying low levels of insurance may reduce claim frequency or claim severity, this has not been established by objective data. It is also possible that lack of liability insurance may jeopardize a discharge in bankruptcy if sufficient funds to pay malpractice judgment creditors are not available.

2. **Carrying an "adequate" amount of liability insurance will prevent possible personal liability.**

   This concept is false, because multimillion-dollar verdicts and awards are increasingly common, resulting in potential liability in excess of insurance coverage. The risks of a judgment above one's insurance limits are reduced, but not avoided, by adequate insurance coverage.

3. **Jointly titled assets are protected from the creditors of one owner.**

   This assumption is false. Assets owned separately by one spouse are not reachable by creditors of the other spouse, and assets owned separately by children, as under Gifts to Minors or Transfers to Minors Acts, are not reachable except by the children's creditors. Joint ownership, however, subjects these assets to creditor claims, except in states permitting the protection of tenancy by the entirety between spouses, and litigation may result for the determination of the individual interests. Examples of jointly held property subject to claims against one owner include joint bank accounts, certificates of deposit, money market or mutual funds, savings accounts, brokerage accounts, joint accounts with children, and nonexempt real estate.

4. **Organizing as a corporation protects individuals from personal liability.**

This statement is only partially true. The corporate structure does result in limitation of liability for shareholders. Individuals, however, remain personally liable for their own acts, as well as vicariously for the acts of others in certain circumstances. Corporate shareholders may be personally liable if improprieties in corporate organization or function permit a court to "pierce the corporate veil," thus removing the protection of the corporate structure. The corporate entity itself is subject to liability for its conduct and for the acts of its employees.

5. **Assets may be rendered judgment-proof from creditors, while you still maintain control and enjoyment of the assets.**

This assumption is false. Protective transfers can remove assets from the reach of creditors, and enjoyment of such assets may still be possible, but any degree of retained control over assets will probably permit creditors to reach them. The fundamentals of asset protection can be axiomatically stated as "Do it early—give up control."

Creative management, which changes ownership and relinquishes control of assets, includes gifts to the spouse or children and the establishment of trusts that give control of assets to a trustee who administers the interests of the beneficiaries. Effective gifts, of course, are irrevocable. Trusts must be irrevocable to be effective for the protection of assets, but may be short-term, permitting asset reversion to the grantor after a period of years.

6. **Retirement assets, including ERISA-qualified or other plans, such as corporate pension plans, deferred compensation plans, Keogh plans, or individual retirement accounts (IRAs), cannot be reached by creditors.**

   This assumption may or may not be true, depending on state laws, federal law, court decisions, and other factors, which result in variable and incomplete protection for retirement plans. The United States Supreme Court, however, has held that qualified plans meeting the requirements of the federal Employee Retirement Income Security Act (ERISA) are protected from bankruptcy and other creditors.[18,19]

7. **Bankruptcy is a fairly simple process that permits a fresh start.**

   While bankruptcy may be a valid consideration in the event of a judgment in excess of insurance and property owned, the process should not be considered simple. A fresh start does result, but the final outcome will probably significantly affect one's lifestyle, through direct effects on assets and indirect effects on personal and business relationships, as well as credit ratings.

Conclusions

Adequate and timely planning for the protection of assets from possible future creditors, sometimes termed insolvency planning, can substantially reduce the risk of loss. The implementation of such a program requires advice from competent professionals who are knowledgeable in the laws of the particular state, detailed individualized considerations, and integration of general financial, tax, and estate planning. Asset transfer must occur well before the threatened claim, suit, or bankruptcy and must avoid circumstances permitting challenge on the basis of fraud upon creditors.

Chapter V References

1. Halley MM, Fowks RJ, Bigler FC, Ryan DL: Medical Malpractice Solutions: Systems and Proposals for Injury Compensation. Charles C Thomas, Springfield, IL, 1989

2. Danner D: Medical Malpractice: A Primer for Physicians. The Lawyers Co-operative Publishing Company, 1988

3. Spencer FC: The expert witness: One surgeon's opinion. Bull Am Coll Surg 73(5):11–14; 43, 1988

4. Rovit RL, Hauber C: The expert witness: Some observations and a response from neurosurgeons. Bull Am Coll Surg 74(7):10–16, 1989

5. Professional Liability Committee of the American College of Surgeons. Bull Am Coll Surg 75:(6), June 1989

6. American College of Obstetricians and Gynecologists: Litigation Assistant: A Guide for the Defendant Physician. Washington, DC, 1987 (reprinted in Bull Am Coll Surg 72(5):26–44, 1987)

7. Haydock RS, Herr DF, Stempel JW: Fundamentals of Pretrial Litigation. West Publishing Co., St. Paul, MN, 1985

8. Anderson ER and Gold J: Are you covered? Am Med News 38(46):12–15, 1995

9. Fowks RJ: Arbitration. In Halley MM, Fowks RJ, Bigler FC, Ryan DL (eds): Medical Malpractice Solutions: Systems and Proposals for Injury Compensation. Charles C Thomas, Springfield, IL, 1989

10. Halley MM: Alternative dispute resolution:The new horizon. Bull Am Coll Surg 77(3):21–26, 1992

11. Hokanson D, Stevens J Jr., Koesten S, Schmidt RN, Woods R, Kirkland R, Meyer J: Protecting your assets from lawsuits. Seminar sponsored by Shook, Hardy and Bacon and Creative Planning, Inc., Kansas City, MO, October 1989

12. Shenker B, Fisher J (eds): Trends in Health Care Provider Liability. LRP Publications, Horsham, PA, 1994

13. Halley MM: Avoiding malpractice liability. Bull Am Coll Surg 73(9):5–13, 1988

14. Malpractice: Can you really protect your assets? In Medical Economics for Surgeons, pp 92–100, 1989

15. Penrod J: How to protect your assets. In Postgraduate Course 19, Professional Liability/Risk Management and Legal Preparedness. American College of Surgeons, 76th Annual Clinical Congress, San Francisco, CA, October 1990

16. Perdo JR Jr., Borders JR: Legal criteria in relating to individual protection of assets in the context of an increasing liability crisis. In Postgraduate Course 19, Professional Liability/Risk Management and Legal Preparedness. American College of Surgeons, 75th Annual Clinical Congress, Atlanta, GA, October 1989

17. United States Code (USC) 100 et seq

18. Burg B: Asset protection: Moves to make before you're sued. Medical Economics, pp. 57–69, Nov 13, 1995

19. *Patterson v. Shumate*: 112 S.CT.2242 (1992)

VI / THE PSYCHOLOGICAL TRAUMA OF A MEDICAL MALPRACTICE SUIT: A PRACTICAL GUIDE

Editor's Note

Surgeons who are named in medical malpractice suits frequently experience a great deal of stress. This chapter discusses the wide range of emotions that are commonly observed in surgeons who are faced with the trauma of being sued.

The emotional or physical symptoms the surgeon can expect to experience are outlined for each step of the process—from the time of the initial complaint, during the period of litigation, and after the suit has been resolved. Methods for coping with the psychological trauma that is associated with each phase of a medical malpractice suit are described in detail.

The need to obtain social support, maintain self-esteem, and master the content of the case are explained as being important factors in dealing with the first phase of this stressful experience. Moreover, an explanation is provided as to why sharing concerns with a spouse, family, and friends, while attempting to be patient through the course of this frustrating ordeal, and maintaining control of the daily work schedule are essential in minimizing anxiety during the resolution process.

It is pointed out that the surgeon should realize that some change in his or her practice pattern is a common occurrence following completion of the suit. The importance of seeking professional support when indicated is emphasized, particularly for the defendant surgeon who loses the case.

A surgeon may practice the highest level of competence in a surgical specialty, implement the latest directives in risk management strategies, and still be named in a medical malpractice suit. Research has shown that the overwhelming majority of sued physicians experience some emotional disequilibrium as a result of being named and that the degree of symptomatology experienced is often not related either to the merits or to the outcome of the suit.

Physicians expect and are accustomed to a high level of stress in their work. If, however, there is too much stress, an individual's ability to function optimally can be markedly compromised. Being named in a medical malpractice suit may generate such an overwhelming degree of added stress for doctors that symptoms may develop, affecting every aspect of their personal and professional lives.

The Psychological Stress Associated with a Medical Malpractice Claim

Although recent data indicate that medical malpractice claims against primary care physicians for failure to diagnose have increased dramatically, surgical specialty continues to be the most significant predictor of claim vulnerability, and surgical complications continue to be the most frequent medical malpractice allegation.

Surgeons expect and are somewhat accustomed to a high level of stress. The ordinary stressors associated with their work usually provide sufficient challenge for them to perform at an optimal level. When there is insufficient stress or challenge, boredom and inefficiency can occur. Conversely, excessive stress or challenges that extend beyond one's abilities can cause the surgeon to become overwhelmed and, on occasion, immobilized.

For most physicians, being named in a medical malpractice suit represents an added stressor that generates emotional disequilibrium, affecting every aspect of their personal and professional lives. As a result, the surgeon's family also suffers from the impact of litigation for the entire length of the process and beyond. In addition, there is evidence that physicians who experience a claim-producing event are twice as likely to experience an additional claim within the next 12 months. It is conceivable that the unattended effects of litigation render the physician more vulnerable to claim. Unless the impact of this stress is recognized and an effort made to diminish its effects, surgeons' work as well as their personal and family lives may be negatively affected.

Surgeons and Risk Management Education

Risk management education is geared toward reducing the possibility of harm to patients, as well as minimizing liability when injury occurs. The aim of risk management education is to help physicians identify those events and situations in practice over which they can exert some control. It should also include the recognition of the psychological and physical effects of litigation, as well as strategies that can be used in coping.

Control is essential to the performance of medical work, and restoring control is one of the primary ways of diminishing the stress of litigation. Since physicians do not—and, in fact, cannot—control every dimension of their practice, any effort to identify aspects of their work subject to oversight helps to strengthen their feelings of control over their environment. Risk management, therefore, plays a very important psychological function when it equips the doctor to deal with the emotional repercussions of being named in a claim, in addition to identifying controllable practice behaviors.

Surgeons do benefit from risk management courses. This fact is especially evidenced by a reduction in the payout amount when a claim occurs. Risk management reinforces the importance of good records, good communication with staff and patients, efficient and effective office procedures, in addition to recognizing and dealing with the stresses associated with litigation, and enables surgeons to function as good defendants.

Even though surgeons practice with the highest level of competence and implement the latest directives in risk management strategies, however, they may still be the subject of a malpractice claim, largely because of the intrinsically risky nature of their work.

The Psychological Impact of Litigation

Two major factors are central to understanding the psychological impact of litigation. First, physicians tend to share common personality features associated with compulsivity: a tendency to doubt themselves, a vulnerability to guilt feelings, and an exaggerated sense of responsibility. These characteristics enable us to be caring and conscientious in our work with patients. They work against us, however, when we are sued for malpractice.

Second, current medical malpractice law is fault-based. An accusation of having failed to have met the standard of care must be initiated to begin the process that allows for compensation to be paid. The object is to establish the legal criteria essential to assessing fault and assigning responsibility for the perceived injury. This accusation represents an attack on the surgeon's sense of self. Because of their compulsive personality features, surgeons are vulnerable to feelings of hurt and anger, as well as damaged self-esteem.

The litigation process, therefore, is designed to establish whether the physician had control over the events in question and, if so, how much control. This process exacerbates the ongoing tension that most physicians consciously or unconsciously feel regarding control: the constant effort to balance feelings of vulnerability and fallibility, on the one hand, against the external and internal pressures to be infallible and omnipotent, on the other.

This process, once begun, has a life of its own and may take many years to resolve. During this period, physicians respond best when they are shown strategies that enable them to help themselves regain control, rather than those that increase feelings of dependency. The aim is to prevent long-term problems and impairment. Rapid interventions are necessary to restore equilibrium so that the physician can return to the optimal conditions for medical work, which is the source of positive feelings of self-esteem and self-worth.

General Strategies for Dealing with Litigation

Three areas of intervention for coping are based on the premise that litigation is a stressful life event. It is, therefore, similar in impact to other serious life events, such as the death of a family member, divorce, or severe loss of any kind. In all of these instances, an emotional reaction is normal and predictable in the process of returning to psychological equilibrium.

Using these broad suggestions, physicians can generally devise their own specific coping strategies and adapt them to their own circumstances.

Social Support Is the Single Most Effective Intervention in Any Serious Life Event Discuss your feelings about the event with whomever you feel most comfortable. It may be your lawyer or claims representative, and/or your spouse, family members, a trusted associate, and staff. Empathic responses from those with whom we live and work are enormously supportive and restorative.

Because of the nature of litigation, your lawyer will counsel you not to talk to anyone about the case so as not to jeopardize your defense. This is good legal advice. However, a psychological need also exists. Care, therefore, should be taken in whom you confide and what is said. What you need to do is talk about your feelings of anger, frustration, and hurt with those who have some understanding of your experience. This person is most often one's spouse and, additionally, a fellow physician who has already gone through the process. Support of this kind diminishes the feelings of isolation that follow being singled out by an accusation of malpractice.

Feelings of Personal Mastery and Self-Esteem Are Necessary to Do Good Work Self-esteem increases when we are able to exert proper control in our lives. Although physicians have some degree of control within the medical environment, litigation draws us into a process over which we have little control. This situation makes most people feel anxious and vulnerable to feelings of impotence and dependency.

Often, the allegation charges that we did not exert sufficient, or even absolute, control over the event in question. Because most of us are cognizant that we have limited control and that we struggle daily with this reality, the accusation, whether based on reality or not, generates feelings of failure, guilt, shame, and anxiety.

The accusation of having failed to perform competently is especially painful for highly trained and highly motivated physicians. During the long process, through depositions, expert testimony, and other legal maneuvers, your professional integrity will be challenged repeatedly, causing a resurgence in the feelings of doubt, low self-esteem, and shaken self-confidence.

To counteract these feelings, you need to focus on actions that strengthen your feelings of control in your personal and professional life. If your office procedures or personnel are inadequate or faulty, now is the time to correct the situation. If you are ambivalent about the amount of time you devote to your family, reevaluate your priorities and change your schedule. If aspects of your practice make you anxious, alter them. Listen to your inner feelings of comfort versus anxiety and learn to be kind to yourself and to those with whom you live and work.

Additional suggestions you may find helpful: master the content of your case; work to improve your competence; review the literature related to your case; take courses in subjects relevant to the case; participate in professional activities, such as hospital committee work, teaching, or preparing a grand rounds; and implement risk management suggestions into your office procedures. Many doctors begin to review cases and offer to serve as expert witnesses, not only to familiarize themselves with the legal system, but also to lend support to fellow physician defendants. All of these activities can increase your sense of self-esteem and of affiliation with peers and counter the feelings of lack of control.

Change the Meaning of the Event Most serious life events are perceived as overwhelming catastrophes. These events must be gradually reevaluated and reconceptualized in order to identify responses that are useful and possible. A charge of malpractice suggests that you have failed in your duty and, in a commonly accepted distortion, that you are a "bad doctor." Despite a growing public understanding of the medical malpractice system as one of compensation rather than of competence, myths about the sued doctor remain. Patients want the doctor to be human and, at the same time, to perform "perfectly."

The challenge for the defendant physician is to reconceptualize your own understanding of litigation so that you achieve some peace of mind and equilibrium about the experience. Only then can you begin to take steps that enable you to feel good about yourself within the context of being sued. Most physicians need their self-perceptions to return to pre-litigation status in order to function as a good defendant. To defend yourself actively, you need to feel that you are good, caring, and competent, rather than a "bad physician."

The daily challenge to the defendant physician is to believe in yourself and know that you continue to practice as a competent and caring physician. This attitude demands not only physical effort but psychological energy, using a range of psychological mechanisms, to develop and maintain a mindset that guides your behavior. You may have to work to keep thoughts of the litigation out of your consciousness or identify ideas or thoughts that "get you back on track." One idea helpful to many is to recognize that very good physicians may, in the course of their work, have outcomes that result in a perceived need for compensation. Charging negligence is often the only way to obtain that compensation. Some comfort is afforded by the fact that negligence is not assessed in most instances, and, in the large majority of cases, no settlement is paid.

Additional Suggestions

Every malpractice suit is unique, and every physician responds in his or her own way. In the event that more than one suit has been filed against you, each one of these cases is also unique. For most physicians, a previous claim does not result in a "thicker skin"; the feelings of emotional disequilibrium and hurt still occur. The experience of previous claims, however, often enables the physician to gain control and to cope effectively more rapidly. There is also good evidence that a previous claim enables the physician to utilize more effectively the risk management strategies that decrease risk both of further claim and the amount of indemnity paid.

When a complication or unanticipated poor outcome occurs that eventually results in the filing of a medical malpractice suit, the physician often suffers anxiety and apprehension, as well as feelings of shame and guilt. The legal complaint only substantiates the physician's worst fears.

The Complaint

What Can I Expect?

An Immediate Reaction   The wording of the complaint often generates a feeling of being stunned, misunderstood, immobilized, and/or of anxiety and frantic activity. This initial reaction is followed by intense feelings of anger and rage. Most physicians feel strongly that the charges filed against them are inappropriate and unjust. The complaint usually charges that the doctor has failed to provide the appropriate level of competent and professional care to the patient. Such an accusation results in feelings of hurt and narcissistic injury so often described by physicians as "devastating." These are normal reactions to a major assault on one's sense of integrity.

Feelings That Are Intense and Sometimes Conflicted In some instances, the complaint may generate overwhelming feelings of guilt and self-accusation, which may or may not be justified. It may take a considerable period of time, with input from legal, insurance, and medical expert advisors, to determine whether or not the case has any substance.

A Lengthy Process   A lawsuit may take many years to resolve. You would be well advised to inquire about the expected length of time for adjudication of malpractice suits in your jurisdiction.

What Can I Do?

Contact Your Insurer and Follow Directives Too many physicians are driven to activities that are not in their best interests, such as talking with the plaintiff's attorney or talking to the aggrieved patient. You must understand that such activities are often driven by your emotional reactions. The legal system, into which you are reluctantly drawn by the complaint, is governed by rules that operate quite differently from that of the medical environment. Ask your claims representative and legal counsel to acquaint you with the litigation process and to specify your expected role in it.

Observe Your Reactions to the Litigation Doctors, as a group, tend to deny or rationalize symptoms and fail to seek help in a timely fashion. The most common symptom experienced by physicians is insomnia, which can be the source of major disruption in the family's life. The doctor may deny the problem; the spouse, because their sleep is affected as well, insists on addressing the problem. In these circumstances, physicians tend to self-medicate or obtain informal consultations with an associate, who may or may not be objective. Carefully assess your use of alcohol, which is often used to self-medicate during stressful periods.

Obtain Appropriate Consultation If Indicated If either physical or emotional symptoms develop that do not resolve themselves within a week or two, obtain consultation from an appropriate source. Do not self-diagnose or self-medicate. If you do not have a personal physician, this is an ideal time to obtain one.

During the Process

After the initial stunned feelings have diminished, the physician is generally reassured by legal and insurance counsel to go back to work and "don't worry about it." Approaching the process of litigation with such lack of concern and equanimity, however, is not an easy task.

What Can I Expect?

The Periodic Resurgence of Emotional and/or Physical Symptoms Almost every physician develops some symptoms at some time during the process. Most often, these symptoms are anxiety and depression, such as insomnia and lack of energy. A range of somatic symptoms, such as gastrointestinal disturbances, headaches, and sexual dysfunction, are also common. About 15 percent of physicians experience the onset or exacerbation of a diagnosable physical illness, such as coronary artery disease or hypertension.

Your Usual Coping Strategies Don't Work   Most physicians maintain good physical and psychological health. Many rely on exercise or other diversions to maintain equilibrium in the face of stress. Many doctors who regularly run or engage in other athletic activities find they discontinue them, due to lack of energy or temporary preoccupation or disorganization after being named in a malpractice suit.

Exacerbations and Remissions of Anxiety   During some of your ongoing medical responsibilities, such as covering in the emergency room or for an associate whose patients you do not know, you may feel increased anxiety. This feeling occurs because, in these instances, you feel less control. In addition, you may become anxious when exposed to similar challenges or medical situations that gave rise to the claim against you. These experiences can unnerve even the best functioning physician, and the connection between the situations and your anxiety need to be recognized. Only then can you effectively deal with them.

Increased Feelings of Anger and Frustration   The litigation process ebbs and flows, punctuated with cancellations, delays, and continuances. The case may almost fade from your psychological radar screen for months, when suddenly your lawyer contacts you to begin work on some motion or deposition. All the initial anger, insomnia, and anxiety about the case can reemerge.

What Can I Do?

Observe Yourself and Your Behavior   Physicians tend either to actively or unconsciously put out of their minds any physical or psychological discomfort to the point that, perhaps, for the moment, the source of the distress does not even exist. This denial is a necessary and useful mechanism that enables physicians to minimize their distractions and maximize their concentration. Denial can be destructive, however, if extended to ignoring personal physical and emotional symptoms such as chest pain, insomnia, weight loss, or loss of interest in family or work. Sexual problems also need to be recognized and dealt with so that needless misunderstandings and insensitivities can be avoided.

Watch for Changes in Your Personal and Professional Relationships Maintaining relationships is one of the most crucial challenges during the long period of litigation. The first advice offered by your insurer and attorney is not to talk to anyone about your case, which is legally understandable and represents good legal advice. Lack of communication, however, is psychologically bad advice, because it introduces defensiveness and withholding that will ultimately inhibit the intimacy and openness necessary for smooth-functioning relationships. If your personal relationships become strained, either at work or at home, you need to find ways to share the feelings associated with your suit.

The Spouse Is the Single Greatest Source of Support for the Majority of Sued Physicians Most spouses are well able to understand the various difficulties of the process and want to help in whatever way they can. To do so, however, they must know how you feel and what is happening, which means you have to talk with them about it. When the spouse is excluded, the strain on both parties can increase dramatically. If the relationship was already compromised before the litigation event occurred, the pressure can increase dramatically. Divorce is not an altogether infrequent complication of litigation. On the other hand, a relationship that is strong and trusting strengthens as a result of this added stressor, and many physicians describe how the experience brought them closer to their spouses and families.

The most difficult problem for many spouses during the litigation period is having to abandon their loved one to a process that is intrinsically adversarial and the source of so much pain and hurt. Many remark that they cannot believe that a patient would accuse their spouse of negligent behavior when they know their spouse to be such a dedicated, responsible, and caring physician. Through the years, the spouse and the family have often borne a heavy burden in allowing the physician to render competent care to patients. Frequently, the spouse must host the party, attend the children's performances or ball games, or conduct other family events alone, because the physician is fulfilling a duty to the patient. On a rational level, the spouse knows that the accused physician is traveling a lonely journey and that the defense of one's integrity can only be done on an individual basis. Meanwhile, the spouse is left to feel lonely, abandoned, and outside of things and at the same time is often the object of displaced anger, frustration, and shifting moods. The physician needs to understand that both of you feel hurt and challenged by the malpractice action.

The children should also be made aware of the problems you currently face. The kind and amount of information you share with them is highly dependent on their ages. Young children need to be appropriately reassured and not burdened by the event. They need to know, however, that their parent is particularly stressed so that if and when regrettable behaviors occur, they can be understood in context. Older children can be the greatest source of support to a parent.

Recognize the Intent of Some of the Legal Maneuvering Doctors often fail to understand that the plaintiff's counsel wants you to be angry, frustrated, and "off balance." If, with the help of your lawyer, you can understand that such legal maneuvering is often aimed at getting you to settle, you can begin to gain more control over the situation. Deciding whether or not to settle can be an agonizing and highly individual decision. It is important to listen to your insurer and legal counsel. It is also important to consider your own personality, as well as input from your spouse, family, and associates. Additional professional considerations need to be carefully reviewed, including the long-term implications of various reporting sequelae in the decision to settle.

Consider Realistically the Assessment of Legal and In-surance Counsel If you find yourself feeling increasingly anxious, self-accusatory, and guilty, your work will clearly be compromised. Sometimes, the poor outcome that is the basis of the claim can be attributed to the actions of the doctor. On other occasions, physicians accuse themselves of failing to meet the standard, when outside experts and legal counsel determine that the case is defensible. In both of these instances, psychiatric consultation may be indicated to enable the physician to work with counsel toward effectively assessing the case.

After the Resolution

As with so many other life events, when the litigation is resolved, life goes on, but is forever changed. Physicians agree that winning is always better than losing. Although most cases result in the vindication of the physician, this is not always the outcome. Most often, the doctor's feelings about career, work, patients, and self have been transformed by the experience.

What Can I Expect?

Lingering and Often Conflicted Feelings Those who win can experience pervasive feelings of having been unjustly accused, of wasting countless hours and days, and of going through something that was of no lasting benefit to anyone except the attorneys. Those who lose can have persistent feelings of injured self-esteem and depression. For some, symptoms persist. For others, a new surge of positive energy infuses both their personal and professional lives.

What Can I Do?

Seek Consultation If Psychological or Physical Symptoms Persist Professional help may be especially indicated when the judgment has been against the physician. Psychological consultation can aid in exploring the persistent negative feelings and in making reasonable plans for the future.

Recognize That Physicians Experience a Common Set of Lingering Concerns   Some physicians become phobic about treating certain kinds of patients or medical conditions, as well as performing certain procedures. Adapting your practice to your level of stress tolerance is not always easy in today's work environment. Good patient care, however, demands that the physician have a degree of comfort and feeling of control in as many aspects of practice as possible. This situation may require consultation about the pace of or possibility of resuming your pre-litigation practice level.

You should take whatever steps are necessary to practice the kind of medicine that you feel you can provide most effectively and to organize your life in a way that affords sufficient gratifications from both your personal and professional life.

Conclusion

For both physicians and their families, litigation is a stressful life event and, for some, the most stressful experience of their entire lives. The more quickly this fact is recognized, assessed, and addressed, the more quickly they can return to psychological and physical health. This recovery usually can be accomplished by physicians and their families if they can be equipped with strategies to implement themselves.

A major source of assistance is from medical organizations, which recognize that litigation is a common experience and that to be named in a suit is usually not a reflection of the physician's competence. This assistance can include developing avenues of support that further enable their individual members to regain control over the work environment. Surgeons who are well-integrated into and supported by the medical community, both locally and nationally, will be more quickly able to regain their level of performance and satisfaction in providing medical care for their patients.

GLOSSARY

abandonment

Termination of a physician-patient relationship without reasonable notice and without an opportunity for the patient to acquire adequate medical care, which results in some type of damage to the patient.

***ad damnum* clause**

The part of a plaintiff's complaint that states the damages that are claimed.

admissible evidence

Evidence that may be properly introduced in a legal proceeding. The determination as to admissibility is based on legal rules of evidence and is made by the trial judge or a screening panel.

ADR

See *Alternative Dispute Resolution.*

adverse action*

(1) action taken against a practitioner's clinical privileges or membership in a professional society, or (2) a licensure disciplinary action.

affidavit

Voluntary, written statement of facts made under oath before an officer of the court or before a notary public.

agency

Relationship between persons in which one party authorizes the other to act for or represent that party.

allegation

Statement of a party to an action, made in a pleading, setting out what the party expects to prove.

alternative dispute resolution

Alternative dispute resolution, also called ADR, is a method or methods of resolving legal dispute outside the tort system.

answer

A legal document that contains a defendant's written response to a complaint or declaration in a legal proceeding. The answer typically either denies the allegations of the plaintiff or makes new allegations as to why the plaintiff should not recover.

appeal

The process by which a decision of a lower court is brought for review to a court of higher jurisdiction, typically known as an appellate court.

appellate court

The court that reviews trial court records. Appellate courts review the transcript of the trial court proceedings and determine whether errors of law were committed by the trial court.

arbitration

The submission of a dispute to one or more neutral persons for a final and binding decision; usually displaces trial by judge and jury, but is based on the same substantive rules of law.

assault

Intentional and unauthorized act of placing another in apprehension of immediate bodily harm.

battery

The unauthorized and offensive touching of a person by another. In medical malpractice cases, battery is typically contact of some type with a patient who has not consented to the contact. Battery can be either a civil or a criminal offense.

breach of contract

Failure, without legal excuse, to perform any promise that forms the whole or part of a contract.

breach of duty

Any violation or omission of a legal or moral duty.

burden of proof

The necessity or duty of affirmatively proving a fact or facts in dispute. The plaintiff typically has the burden of proof.

capitation

A payment system whereby managed care plans pay health care providers a fixed amount to care for a patient over a given period.

captain of the ship

An older doctrine whereby the surgeon in charge of a medical team is liable for all the negligent acts of the members of the team.

captive insurance company

See *Insurance Company, Captive Insurance Company.*

carrier

An insurance company.

case

An action or cause of action; a matter in dispute; a lawsuit.

causation

Existence of a connection between the act or omission of the defendant and the injury suffered by the plaintiff. In a suit for negligence, the issue of causation usually requires proof that the plaintiff's harm resulted proximately from the negligence of the defendant.

certificate of merit

A tort reform mandated by law in several states that requires the plaintiff or the plaintiff's attorney in a medical malpractice case to file an affidavit or other sworn statement with (or shortly after) the complaint, stating that the case has been reviewed by a qualified expert who determined that, on its face, the case is not frivolous.

circumstantial evidence

See *Evidence, Circumstantial Evidence*.

claim

In common parlance, any demand for compensation. What constitutes a claim that must be reported to an insurance company varies, but is always defined in the policy.

claims-made insurance policy

Provides coverage for claims arising from incidents that both occur and are reported to the insurance company while the policy is continually in force. A claims-made policy is in force beginning with the starting date of the initial policy period and continues in force from that date through each subsequent renewal. When a claims-made policy is terminated, future claims arising from incidents that occurred during the policy period are not covered. See *Tail Coverage*.

clinical pathways

Clinical pathways were originally designed to minimize the cost of hospitalization in the era of managed care, but they have also proven to be useful tools in improving patient outcomes. The pathways list all the important details of a complex hospitalization, such as preoperative education and laboratory testing, criteria for removal of all lines and tubes, duration of prophylactic antibiotics, timing of physical therapy, and discharge planning.

collateral source rule

A rule of law that prevents a court from subtracting any payments that the plaintiff has received from such sources as workmen's compensation, health insurance, government benefits, or sick pay benefits from the damage award.

common law

That body of law that was passed down to the colonies by the British legal system and has been interpreted and refined by case law, as opposed to statutory law.

community standard rule

See *Locality Rule*.

comparative negligence

See *Negligence, Comparative Negligence*.

compensable medical injuries

Defined medical injuries that would be compensated according to a schedule of benefits. Several tort reform proposals advocate an insurance mechanism that would remove medical malpractice cases from the court system into an administrative system that would compensate designated compensable events. See *No-Fault Compensation*.

compensation

Money payment for damages for the injury sustained proximately by a plaintiff caused by a defendant.

no-fault compensation

A method for compensating persons injured during the course of medical treatment, regardless of whether the injury was caused by the negligence or the fault of a health care provider.

compensation fund

See *Patient Compensation Fund*.

complaint

A legal document that is the initial pleading on the part of the plaintiff in a civil lawsuit. A complaint is sometimes known as a declaration. The purpose of this document is to give a defendant notice of the alleged facts constituting the cause of action. The complaint is usually attached to the summons.

confidentiality

The status of information transmitted during the course of a physician-patient relationship. The right of the patient to prevent disclosure of communications made between the patient and physician is also termed doctor-patient privilege. This privilege may not be recognized in all jurisdictions and may be limited in others.

consent

Voluntary act by which one person agrees to allow another person to do something. "Express consent" is that directly and unequivocally given, either orally or in writing. "Implied consent" is that manifested by signs, actions, or facts or by inaction and silence, which raises a presumption that the consent has been given. It may be implied from conduct (implied-in-fact), for example, when someone rolls up his or her sleeve and extends his or her arm for vein puncture; or by the circumstance (implied-in-law), for example, in the case of an unconscious person in an emergency situation.

consultation

Formal request by an attending physician of a medical specialist in a field for which information is sought. Ordinarily, a legal duty to consult arises when, after a reasonable length of time and effort on the part of the attending physician, the diagnosis is unusually difficult and uncertain, the therapy is ineffective, or the patient requests a consultation. To be legally sufficient, a consultation requires that the consultant personally examine the patient and the patient's records. A referral is to be distinguished from a consultation—a referral involves the transferral of the complete responsibility for the care of the patient to the specialist, whereas in a consultation, the attending physician retains primary responsibility.

contingent fee

A fee agreement between the plaintiff and the plaintiff's attorney, whereby the plaintiff agrees to pay the attorney a percentage of the damages recovered.

continuous quality improvement (CQI)

See *Total Quality Management (TQM)*.

contract

Obligation that binds the involved parties to perform the terms of the agreement that they have reached, providing that there was a mutual meeting of the minds.

contributory negligence

See *Negligence, Contributory Negligence*.

court reporter

A professionally trained stenographer who transcribes deposition or trial testimony.

court trial

A trial without a jury, wherein a judge determines the facts as well as the law. Also called a bench trial.

damages

The sum of money a court or jury awards as compensation for a tort or breach of contract. The law recognizes certain categories of damages, including general, punitive/exemplary, and special damages.

general damages (noneconomic)

Typically intangible damages, such as pain and suffering, disfigurement, interference with ordinary enjoyment of life, and loss of consortium (marital services).

punitive/exemplary damages

Damages awarded to the plaintiff in cases of intentional tort or gross negligence to punish the defendant or act as a deterrent to others.

special damages (economic)

Out-of-pocket damages that may be quantified, such as medical expenses, lost wages, and rehabilitation costs.

decedent

A dead person, usually the injured person, who would have been described as the plaintiff if still living.

defendant

The person against whom a civil or criminal action is brought.

defense attorney

The attorney who defends the person who is sued (defendant).

department

An organizational unit of the hospital or of the medical staff.

deposition

A discovery procedure whereby each party may question in person the other party or anyone who may possibly be a witness. Depositions are conducted before the trial under oath and are admissible at trial under certain circumstances.

directed verdict

Ruling by the trial judge that, as a matter of law, the verdict must be in favor of a particular party. A verdict is usually directed as a result of a clear failure to meet the burden of proof, sometimes referred to as a failure to establish a *prima facie* case. See also *Prima Facie Case*.

direction

Authoritative policy or procedural guidance for the accomplishment of a function or activity.

disability

Want of capability to perform an act. Incapacity for the full enjoyment of ordinary legal rights, actually because of a prior demonstrated impairment.

discovery

Pretrial procedures to learn of evidence in order to minimize the element of surprise at the time of trial. These typically include interrogatories and depositions, but can also include requests for admission of facts and requests for genuineness of documents.

discovery rule

A limitations statute does not begin to run until a patient knows, or reasonably should know, of an injury and also is aware, or reasonably should be aware, that the injury was wrongfully caused. See also *Period (Statute) of Repose* and *Statute of Limitations*.

dismissal

A legal denial. To dismiss a motion is to deny it; to dismiss an appeal is to affirm the judgment of the trial court.

doctor-patient privilege

See *Confidentiality*.

due care

Required degree of reasonable or ordinary observation and awareness that a person has and owes to another person by virtue of a special relationship or circumstance. Applicable as a standard of conduct in most personal injury cases, but not in medical malpractice cases, where the standard is that of a reasonable, qualified physician practicing the same specialty as the defendant.

duty

An obligation recognized by the law. A physician's duty to a patient is to provide the degree of care ordinarily exercised by physicians practicing in the same community or area of specialization.

Employment Retirement Income Security Act (ERISA)

ERISA exempts self-insured health plans from state laws governing health insurance, including contribution to risk pools, prohibitions against disease discrimination, and other state health reforms.

entity representative*

An individual empowered by an eligible entity to submit reports or queries to the National Practitioner Data Bank (NPDB). The entity representative certifies the legitimacy of information in a query or report submitted to the NPDB. In most cases, the entity representative is an employee of the eligible entity (such as an administrator or medical staff director).

evaluation

The review and assessment of the quality and appropriateness of an important aspect of care. The review and assessment is designed to identify problems and/or opportunities to improve care and, when they exist, to develop plans to solve the problems or take the opportunities to improve care.

evidence

All the means by which any alleged matter of fact, the truth of which is submitted to investigation at trial, is established or disproved. Evidence includes the testimony of witnesses, introduction of records, documents, exhibits, objects, or any other probative matter offered for the purpose of inducing belief in the party's contention by the judge or jury.

circumstantial evidence

Facts or circumstances that indirectly imply that the principal facts at issue actually occurred.

experience rating

The practice of basing insurance premiums on past loss history.

expert opinion

The testimony of a person who has special training, knowledge, skill, or experience in an area relevant to resolution of the legal dispute.

expert witness

Person who has special training, knowledge, skill, or experience in an area relevant to resolution of the legal dispute, which is beyond the average person's knowledge, and who is allowed to offer an opinion as testimony in court.

federal court

Federal courts are another system of trial and appellate courts and, like state courts, only accept certain types of cases. Malpractice cases generally are not filed in the federal courts unless a patient is from one state and the health care provider from another state.

fee-for-service care

The traditional payment method in health care, under which providers bill separately for each component of health care services.

fiduciary

Person in a position of confidence or trust who undertakes a duty to act for the benefit of another under a given set of circumstances.

fraud

Intentionally misleading another person in a manner that causes legal injury to that person.

frequency of claims

Refers to the number of claims that are filed. Frequency and average severity of claims are the fundamental variables used in determining insurance premiums. See *Severity of Claims*.

future earnings

Element of damages involving the specific "loss" of earnings that would probably have been made during a given future time had it not been for the injury that is the basis of the lawsuit.

gag rule

Prohibits physicians from communicating freely with their patients regarding the quality of care, administrative and procedural issues, financial incentives, and so on, of the managed care company.

gatekeeper role

The term given to the function of a primary care practitioner in monitoring the need for, and coordinating patient referrals for, specialized care or other services not rendered by the primary care provider.

general damages

See *Damages, General Damages (Noneconomic)*.

Good Samaritan statute

Statute enacted to encourage individuals to stop and assist victims of accidents by granting immunity from liability for any negligence resulting from attempts to give such emergency aid, without the expectation of payment.

guaranty fund

Established by law in every state, this fund is typically maintained by the state commissioner of insurance to protect policyholders in the event that their insurer becomes insolvent or otherwise unable to meet its financial obligations. The fund is usually financed by an assessment against all property and casualty insurers regulated by the state.

guardian

Person appointed by a court to manage the affairs of and to protect the interests of another who is adjudged incompetent by reason of age or physical or mental status and is thereby unable to manage his or her own affairs.

health care entity*

Health care entities include hospitals and other organizations, such as HMOs, that provide health care services and engage in professional review activity through a formal peer review process for the purpose of furthering quality health care.

HMO (health maintenance organization)

Any organization that, through an organized system of health care, provides or ensures the delivery of an agreed upon set of comprehensive health maintenance and treatment services for an enrolled group of persons for a prepaid fixed sum.

group model HMO

A contractual arrangement between a corporate managed care organization and an independent group practice, under which members of the group practice provide health care services to individuals insured through the managed care organization. Ordinarily, the group practice is not restricted from providing services to individuals not insured by the particular managed care organization. Sometimes a contract may contain negotiated provisions dealing with whether the group practice may contract with competing managed care organizations.

staff model HMO

A managed care entity, in which physicians and other health care providers are employed by the corporate managed care organization (unless state law prohibits such employment) and provide health care services only under the auspices of the managed care entity.

hold harmless clause

A contractual arrangement whereby one party assumes the liability inherent in the situation, thereby relieving the other party of responsibility. See *Indemnity*.

house staff

Individuals, appropriately licensed, who are graduates of medical, dental, osteopathic, or podiatric schools; who are appointed to a hospital professional graduate training program that is approved by a nationally recognized accrediting body approved by the commissioner of education; and who participate in patient care under the direction of licensed practitioners of the pertinent clinical disciplines who have clinical privileges in the hospital and are members of, or affiliated with, the medical staff.

hypothetical question

A form of question put to a witness (usually an expert witness, but also a defendant or plaintiff) in which things that counsel claims are or will be proved are stated as a factual supposition, and the witness is asked to respond, state, or explain the conclusion based on the assumptions and question.

immunity

In civil law, protection given certain individuals (personal immunity) or groups (institutional immunity) that may shield them from liability for certain acts or legal relationships. Ordinarily, the individual may still be sued, because immunity can be raised only as an affirmative defense to the complaint, that is, after a lawsuit has been filed.

impairment

Measurable dysfunction of a person.

important aspect of care

Clinical activities that involve a high volume of patients, entail a high degree of risk for patients, and/or tend to produce problems for staff or patients. Such activities are deemed most important for purposes of monitoring and evaluation.

incapacity

Inability and preclusion of exercising an inherent right or carrying out a transaction because of a legal impediment or impairment.

incident report

A written report by either a patient or a staff member that documents any unusual problem, incident, or other situation for which a patient or staff member wishes to have follow-up action taken by appropriate administrative or supervisory personnel.

indemnity

Agreement whereby a party guarantees reimbursement for possible losses.

indicator

A defined, measurable variable used to monitor the quality or appropriateness of an important aspect of patient care. Indicators can be activities, events, occurrences, or outcomes for which data should be collected to allow comparison with the threshold for evaluation related to each indicator. Indicators are often guidelines for care or practice that include objective clinical criteria based on authoritative sources, such as the clinical literature and consensus panels.

informed consent

A legal doctrine that requires a physician to obtain consent for treatment rendered or an operation performed; without an informed consent, the physician may be held liable for violation of the patient's rights, regardless of whether the treatment was appropriate and rendered with due care. See *Battery*.

insurance

Written agreement (the insurance policy) wherein, for premium payments, the insurance company (the insurer) promises to compensate the policyholder (the insured) for losses that occur as defined in the agreement.

insurance company

A company, also known as a provider or a carrier, that is licensed by a state to sell some or all types of insurance.

captive insurance company

An alternative insurance mechanism in which a corporation, hospital, or group of such entities forms its own insurance company. These captives are typically capitalized by their parent(s), are professionally managed, and issue insurance policies modeled after those used in the commercial market. These insurance policies are issued to risks that include, but are not limited to, the founding parents. Captives are typically located offshore and have favorable tax and regulatory treatment, compared with those of domestic insurers.

intent

Voluntary function of a person's mind in purposely performing a perceivable act.

interrogatories

A discovery procedure in which one party submits a series of written questions to the opposing party, who must answer in writing under oath within a certain period of time. The answers are admissible at trial under certain circumstances.

IPA (independent practice association)

A contractual arrangement between a corporate managed care organization and an individual physician or group of physicians, in which the individual/group agrees to provide certain health care services to those insured through the managed care organization.

JCAHO (Joint Commission on Accreditation of Healthcare Organizations)

The Joint Commission on Accreditation of Healthcare Organizations is a private, not-for-profit organization dedicated to promoting health care through a voluntary accreditation process.

joint and several liability

A legal doctrine whereby each individual defendant is responsible for the entire amount of damages awarded against all defendants.

joint underwriting association

A government-administered risk pooling arrangement, commonly referred to as a JUA, established by law in a number of states to provide professional liability insurance to health care providers. A JUA is structured to be financed by assessments against its participants, but typically also has the authority to assess property and casualty insurers licensed to do business in the state in the event of a deficit.

JUA

See *Joint Underwriting Association*.

judgment

The final entry in the record of a case, which is binding upon the parties unless it is overturned or modified on appeal. A judgment typically consists of a finding in favor of one or more of the parties and an assessment of damages and costs.

jury

Certain number of persons selected according to law, sworn to inquire of certain matters of fact and declared the truth upon evidence to be laid before them. In trying issues of fact, they function under supervision of a judge who is empowered to instruct them on the law. Their verdict may be set aside if, in the judge's opinion, it is contrary to law or evidence.

jury trial

A trial in which six to 12 registered voters are impaneled to hear the evidence, determine the facts, and render a verdict. In most states, the verdict must be unanimous.

law

Documented guide to conduct, based on the expression of how society views the responsibility of each individual to other individuals. It includes an amalgam of principles that provide a basis for dispute resolution, in addition to the ultimate resolution itself, if necessary.

lawsuit

Civil legal action or adversarial proceeding by which a plaintiff seeks enforcement of his or her rights or redress for the transgression of them by a defendant.

liability

Obligation that a person has incurred or might incur through any act or omission. In civil matters, liability for damages is for a definite amount, ascertained by a final judgment based on the preponderance of the evidence that demonstrates that the defendant was responsible for the plaintiff's injury and, therefore, is obligated to provide compensation to the plaintiff.

license

Permit from an appropriate governmental agency, allowing certain acts to be performed, usually for a specific period of time.

limits of coverage

The maximum amount an insured or a claimant can collect under the terms of a policy. Professional liability policies typically specify limits per claim and a cumulative limit for all claims incurred during the term of a contract, for example, $1 million (per claim)/$3 million (per term).

litigation

Trial of a dispute in a court of law to determine factual and legal issues, rights, and duties between the parties to the controversy.

locality rule

The test historically used by courts to determine the standard of care owed by health care providers to patients. The rule holds that health care providers have the duty to render care consistent with the care of other competent or prudent practitioners under the same or similar circumstances in the same or similar community. Most states have displaced the locality rule with the requirement that care must be consistent with national standards. See *Standard of Care*.

loss of consortium

A claim for damages by the spouse of an injured party for the loss of care, comfort, society, and interference with sexual relations. See also *Damages, General Damages (Noneconomic)*.

malpractice

Professional negligence. In medical terms, it is the failure to exercise that degree of care as is used by reasonably careful physicians, in the same or similar circumstances, of like qualifications. The failure to meet this acceptable standard of care must cause the patient injury.

matter of law

Point that must be decided on the basis of either applicable statute or decisions of case law.

matter of record

Any judicial matter or proceeding entered on the records of a court and to be proved by production of such records.

MCO (managed care organization)

A general term for health care delivery systems that control the use of medical services by participants in various ways. These ways may range from requiring pre-approval for hospital admission or second opinions before surgical procedures in a fee-for-service environment, to delivery systems such as HMO plans.

mediation

The submission of a dispute to an outside facilitator, often with specialized expertise, for assistance in reaching a mutually acceptable settlement. The procedure is private, voluntary, and nonbinding.

minor

Person who has not yet reached the statutorily determined age (in Massachusetts, age 18) of legal transactional capacity. As a result of this presumed legal incompetence, minors ordinarily cannot consent to their own medical treatment unless they are "emancipated," that is, substantially independent from their parents, supporting themselves, married, or otherwise on their own, or unless a statute provides otherwise.

misrepresentation

Manifestation by words or other conduct by one person to another that, under the circumstances, amounts to an assertion not in accordance with the facts. An incorrect or false representation of a condition other and different from that which exists. A "fraudulent misrepresentation" is made by a person with a knowledge of the falsity of the representation, which causes the other party to enter into an arrangement or an agreement. A "negligent misrepresentation" is made by a person who has no reasonable grounds for believing that the representation is true, even though he or she does not know that it is untrue, or even believes it to be true. An "innocent misrepresentation" is made by a person who has reasonable grounds for believing that the representation is true.

monitoring

The systematic and ongoing collection and organization of data related to the indicators of the quality and appropriateness of important aspects of care and the comparison of the level of performance with thresholds for evaluation to determine the need for evaluation.

motion

Written or oral court plea requesting that a judge make an order or ruling affecting the lawsuit.

NCQA (National Committee for Quality Assurance)

An organization providing external review and accreditation surveys to managed care entities.

negligence

Legal cause of action involving the failure to exercise the degree of diligence and care that a reasonably and ordinarily prudent person would exercise under the same or similar circumstances, and the result of which is the breach of a legal duty, which proximately causes an injury that the law recognizes as deserving of compensation. The standard of care of a defendant physician in a medical malpractice case is not that of the reasonable and ordinarily prudent person (such as an automobile operator), but rather, that of the reasonably qualified physician practicing in the same area of specialization or general practice as that of the defendant physician.

comparative negligence

An affirmative defense that compares the negligence of

the defendant to that of the plaintiff. The plaintiff may recover damages from a negligent defendant even if the plaintiff and defendant are equally at fault. The plaintiff's damages are reduced, however, by the percentage that his or her own fault contributed to the overall damage.

contributory negligence
An affirmative defense that prevents recovery against a defendant when the plaintiff's own negligence contributed to his or her own injury, even though the defendant's negligence may also have contributed to the injury.

no-fault compensation
See *Compensation, No-Fault Compensation*.

NPDB (National Practitioner Data Bank)
The NPDB, which began operations on September 1, 1990, maintains records of disciplinary actions taken against health care practitioners and malpractice payments made on their behalf.

occurrence policy
A type of policy in which the policyholder is covered for any incident that occurs during the term of the policy, regardless of when a claim arising from the incident is made. Occurrence policies have been largely supplanted by "claims-made" coverage in the medical liability insurance market. See *Claims-Made Insurance Policy*.

pain and suffering
Element of "compensatory" nonpecuniary damages that allows recovery for the mental anguish and/or physical pain endured by the plaintiff as a result of injury for which the plaintiff seeks redress. See also *Damages, General Damages (Noneconomic)*.

partnership
Contractual state resulting from the agreement of two or more associates (partners) to engage in a commercial enterprise for the benefit of all co-partners, and to share the profits and losses

proportionally. Each person acts as a principal as well as an agent for his co-partners. Thus, when losses occur, each partner is personally responsible for the payment of all partnership debts.

patient compensation fund

A fund established by law in some states that pays benefits to patients injured in the course of medical treatment. Benefits may be awarded on either a fault basis or a no-fault basis, depending on the state program. The fund's benefits may either supplement the payment made by a defendant in a medical malpractice claim or be the primary compensation, again depending on the state program.

period (statute) of repose

A limit on the time within which a suit may be brought, with the limit defined from the date of the defendant's alleged harmful act, as opposed to the date the plaintiff discovered the injury. See also *Discovery Rule* and *Statute of Limitations*.

periodic payments

Damages paid to a plaintiff over a period of time instead of in a lump sum all at once. If a state law permits, periodic payments may be ordered when the damages exceed a certain amount.

perjury

Willful giving of false testimony under oath.

plaintiff

Party who files or initiates a civil lawsuit, seeking relief or compensation for damages or other legal relief.

pleading

Legal documents filed in a lawsuit, which identify and clarify the issues in dispute; includes the plaintiff's complaint and the defendant's answer.

policy

The contractual agreement between an insurance company and

its insured. The policy sets forth the rights and obligations of both parties to the agreement.

POS (point-of-service) plan

A health insurance product that bases its benefits on where (the "point of service") the patient chooses to receive care. It generally combines an HMO option with the freedom to go outside the particular plan by accepting a higher self-pay portion of the care.

possibility

A less-than-probable chance, without excluding the idea of feasibility. A less-than-50% chance that something occurred.

PPO (preferred provider organization)

A contractual arrangement between an insurer and selected health care providers, under which the company's insureds are encouraged to utilize that list of practitioners and institutions for their health care services. The insurer attempts to negotiate better payment rates and/or terms and generally offers its insured patients some financial incentive to use its selected providers, rather than others.

practice parameters

Practice parameters are strategies for patient management that may assist physicians in clinical decision-making. Practice parameters are sometimes referred to as practice options, practice guidelines, practice policies, or practice standards.

premium

The amount of money an insured pays for an insurance policy. The premium is calculated by the insurance company's underwriters to bring in enough money to establish reserves for future losses, pay current losses, cover the company's operating expenses, including the cost of defending claims, and generate a profit if the company is organized as a profit-making business. See *Underwriting*.

pretrial screening panel

A tort reform established in a number of states to require or encourage plaintiffs to participate in a procedure for determining if the claim is unfounded or has merit prior to pursuing litigation in the courts. States differ in the structure of the pretrial screening process, the type of evidence that will be reviewed, and in the rules regarding whether the pretrial screening conclusion is admissible as evidence in subsequent litigation.

probability

Reasonable ground of presumption, because there is more evidence in favor of the existence of a given proposition than there is against it; more likely than not; 50.1%; but not a possibility.

professional review action*

An action or recommendation of a health care entity (a) taken in the course of professional review activity; (b) based on the professional competence or professional conduct of an individual physician, dentist, or other health care practitioner that affects or could adversely affect the health or welfare of a patient or patients; and (c) based on the professional competence or professional conduct of an individual physician, dentist, or other health care practitioner that adversely affects or may adversely affect the clinical privileges of the physician, dentist, or other health care practitioner.

professional review activity*

An activity of a health care entity with respect to an individual physician, dentist, or other health care practitioner to determine whether the physician, dentist, or other health care practitioner (a) may have clinical privileges with respect to, or membership in, the entity; (b) the scope or conditions of such privileges or membership; or (c) whether change or modification of such privileges or membership is required.

professional societies*

A professional society is a membership association of physicians or dentists that engages in professional review activity through a formal peer review process for the purpose of furthering quality health care.

proximate cause

See *Causation*.

publication

Oral or written act that makes defamatory material available to persons other than the person defamed.

punitive/exemplary damages

See *Damages, Punitive/Exemplary Damages*.

qualifications

The credentials or presumed capability of a professional to perform a task.

quality assurance (QA)

Process to ensure appropriateness and adequacy in the care of patients.

rate

An insurance term, reflecting the basis or classification upon which the premium is based; often used as a synonym for premium. See *Premium*.

reasonable

Fit and appropriate to the end in view, not immoderate or excessive.

reasonable degree of medical certainty

As used in personal injury lawsuits, a term implying more than mere conjecture, possibility, consistent with, or speculative; similar to a probability, more likely than not, 50.1%, but an overwhelming likelihood or scientific certainty is not required.

release

Statement signed by a person relinquishing a right or claim against another person or persons, usually for a payment or other valuable consideration. The intent is that the person's alleged injury has been fully satisfied. It is to be distinguished from a covenant not to sue, which is a partial release by the plaintiff, involving the plaintiff's giving up of the plaintiff's claim against one defendant for money damages, but not giving up the plaintiff's claim against other defendants.

reporting requirement

The contractual obligation of the insured to promptly report to the carrier any claim for damages that is or may be asserted against the insured. What constitutes a claim that must be reported varies from company to company, but is always defined in the policy.

res ipsa loquitur

"The thing speaks for itself." A case in which the personal injuries and/or property damage would not have occurred in the absence of negligence. In medical malpractice cases, it allows a patient to prove his or her case without the necessity of an expert witness to testify that the defendant physician violated the standards of care. It is applicable only in those instances in which negligence is clear and obvious, even to a layman, such as foreign object cases in which a surgeon leaves a sponge in the patient following surgical operation.

reserve

Money set aside and invested by insurance companies to pay estimated future losses. A company's claims department typically specifies a reserve amount for every claim that is filed, which may be modified as the claim proceeds in the courts.

respondeat superior

"Let the master answer." The legal principle that makes an employer liable for civil wrongs committed by employees within the course and scope of their employment.

rights

Power or demands, inherent in one person, which that person is entitled to have, or to do, or to receive from others within the prescribed limits of the law.

risk

The chance of loss. The uncertainty that exists as to actual occurrence of loss caused by some event or happening. "Pure risk" is uncertainty as to whether loss will occur. In "speculative risk," there is uncertainty about an event that could produce loss. Pure risk is insurable; speculative risk usually is not.

risk management

A systematic approach to identifying, evaluating, reducing, or eliminating risk due to an undesirable deviation from an anticipated outcome, thereby preventing the loss of financial assets resulting from injury to patients.

risk retention group

A group of similarly situated persons or entities that are permitted under federal law to organize across state lines for the purpose of pooling their liability risk and self-insuring. If the group is licensed in one state, it is permitted to solicit business and sell insurance nationwide, without fulfilling each state's licensure requirements.

settlement

An agreement made between the parties to a lawsuit or a claim, which resolves their legal dispute.

structured settlement

Settlement agreement between the parties to a lawsuit or a claim, in which the damages are paid to the plaintiff over a period of time instead of in a lump sum all at once. These settlements are usually financed through the purchase of an annuity.

severity of claims

Also known as claim magnitude, this is the dollar value of a claim as determined by jury verdict or settlement agreement. Claim frequency and average severity are the principal variables used in determining insurance premiums. See *Frequency of Claims*.

special damages

See *Damages, Special Damages (Economic)*.

standard of care

A term used in the legal definition of medical malpractice. A physician is required to adhere to the standards of practice of reasonably competent physicians, in the same or similar circumstances, with comparable training and experience.

stare decisis

A legal judgment based upon a previous decision.

state licensing board*

A generic term used to refer to state medical and dental boards, as well as those bodies responsible for licensing other health care practitioners.

statute of repose

See *Period (Statute) of Repose*.

statute of limitations

The time period set forth by statute in which a plaintiff may file a lawsuit. Once this period expires, the plaintiff's lawsuit is barred if the defendant asserts the affirmative defense of the statute of limitations.

stipulation

An agreement made by both parties to the litigation regulating any matter related to the case, proceeding, or trial. For instance, litigants can agree to extend the time period for pleadings or to admit certain facts into evidence at trial.

structured settlement

See *Settlement, Structured Settlement*.

subpoena

Court order requiring a witness to appear at a certain proceeding to give testimony or produce documents.

suit

See *Lawsuit*.

summary judgment

Granting of a judgment in favor of either party prior to trial. Summary judgment is only granted when there is no factual dispute, and one of the parties is entitled to judgment as a matter of law.

summons

A legal document that is attached to the complaint or declaration in a lawsuit. It orders the defendant or the defendant's attorney to file an answer within a specified period of time.

tail coverage

Tail coverage, the common term for extended reporting endorsement, is a supplemental policy obtained from a claims-made carrier to provide coverage for any incident that occurred while the claims-made insurance was in effect, but had not been brought as a claim by the time the insurer/policyholder relationship terminated. Tail coverage is generally needed at the time of death or retirement or upon the decision to change claims-made carriers.

testimony

Oral evidence presented under oath during a judicial proceeding by a competent witness in order to prove a fact. Testimony is to be distinguished from nonoral types of proof, such as types of physical evidence (for example, documents).

therapeutic privilege

Withholding of information from a patient by a physician when knowledge of the information might be considered extremely injurious to the patient.

thresholds for evaluation

A preestablished level of performance related to an indicator at which further evaluation of the quality and appropriateness of an important aspect of care is initiated.

tort

A civil wrong, other than a breach of contract, for which the law provides a remedy in the form of monetary damages.

tort reform

A term used to collectively describe a number of legislative and judicial modifications to traditional tort law.

total quality management (TQM)

A philosophy and system of management that can focus an organization on continuous quality improvement (CQI) of its internal processes, services, and products. The system focus is on the customer and incorporates mechanisms for the ongoing assessment of the effects of interventions.

trial

Judicial examination before a proper court having jurisdiction of issues of law or fact between the litigating parties in accordance with the governing law.

trial court

The court of first jurisdiction where the pleadings are filed, the witnesses appear, testimony is taken, and a judgment is entered; also referred to as the lower court.

underwriting

The process by which a company evaluates and classifies risks and measures and calculates the cost of protection, within the framework of the rules, rates, and coverage forms that are permitted by law in a particular state.

unit

A functional division or facility of the hospital.

verdict

The formal decision or finding made by a jury or judge. The verdict is rendered in favor of the plaintiff or defendant, and damages are typically awarded when the verdict is in favor of the plaintiff.

vicarious liability

Civil liability for the torts of others. Physicians may be vicariously liable for the negligent acts of their employees committed within the scope of their employment. See *Respondeat Superior*. In the hospital setting, a surgeon may be vicariously liable for the negligent acts of all members of the surgical team. See *Captain of the Ship*.

witness

Person who is called to give testimony in a court of law.

written consent

Consent given in writing, specifically empowering someone to do something.

wrongful death

A type of lawsuit brought on behalf of a deceased person's estate that alleges that death was attributable to the willful or negligent act of another.

---

* Definition applies to usage in conjunction with the National Practitioner Data Bank (NPDB) and its policies and procedures.

INDEX

Court (bench) trials, 259
Courtroom trials. *See* Trials
Courts
appellate, 254
federal, 263
trial (lower), 282
Covenants not to sue, 278
CQI (continuous quality improvement), 282
Credentialing
in hospitals, 169–171
in managed care organizations, 82–83
and National Practitioner Data Bank reports, 87, 91–93
Credentials of expert witnesses, 115
Credibility
of defendant surgeon, 210, 211, 213
of witnesses, 153
Criminal activity disclosure, 66
Crohn's disease malpractice case, 27–28
Cross-examination during trials, 214, 217, 219

Damages
ad damnum clause involving, 103–104, 253
compensation for. *See* Compensation for damages
compensatory, 39–42
general (noneconomic, intangible), 108, 112, 115, 116, 259, 273
liability for, 269
for loss of consortium, 270
punitive/exemplary, 42–43, 109, 117, 259
special (economic, out-of-pocket), 260
in tort law, 14–15
treble, 81, 82
Danner, D., 155, 206
Data
accuracy of, 90, 92–93
collection of, 105, 172–173
communication of, with medical records, 155
about hospital care, monitoring, 171–175
processing and reporting of, 105
tabulation and study of, 197–199
Davis v. Weiskopf, 11–12
Death
compassion in handling, 166
in hospitals, monitoring, 172
wrongful, lawsuits for, 283

Decedents, 260
Deceit and resident status, 178
Deceptive questions
at depositions, 205–207
at trial, 215
Deep pocket theory, 47, 107, 111
Defamatory material, 277
Defendants, 260
as expert witnesses, 203, 206
expert witnesses for, 199
surgeons as, 203, 206, 209–219, 223, 245, 247, 249–250
Defense (in litigation), 194–195, 199
Defense attorneys, 194, 260. *See also* Attorneys
assessments by, 250
in depositions, 202, 204
versus plaintiff attorneys, 196
selecting, 196–197
in settlements, 222–225
and surgeons, relationship of, 193–200, 212
working with, 197–200
Defenses against malpractice claims, 53–66
patient negligence, 61–63
standard of care adherence, 54–56
statutes of limitations, 56–61
statutory immunity, 63–66
Deferred compensation protection, 231
Delays
in appointments, 141
in care, 77–78, 84, 162
in diagnosis, 20–22
Delinquent accounts, 163
Demeanor, professional, 203–204, 211–213
Denial
of care, 75–77
in litigation coping, 247–248
Dentists in National Practitioner Data Bank, 90
Department of Professional Liability of American College of Obstetricians and Gynecologists, 177
Departments (units) of hospitals, 260, 282
surgery, 169–176
Depositions
admissible evidence from, 201
answering questions at, 204–207, 214
attorneys in, 196, 199, 202, 204
authoritative textbook citation at, 207